Rhoda De Santo

American Historical Society.
Jewish Museum — 212 423-3200
92th Street

2 —

0 operator
4 Stay

Dear David or I should say Hurty — I think you would enjoy the story of Abigail Franks letters to her son. This is a simple story. Happy — Jewish family most for Love & to new age your city travel 1733 are 1748 etc. — I am very long stay of Abigail Franks life to see more special — but you Mestery. The Multiplity is very poor at the point. Hope you read this wants love for her son and family will get the feeling for Paul in letters about the Mestipresified for then the Christmas and other members of the family. So ready

THE LETTERS OF
Abigaill Levy Franks
1733–1748

THE LETTERS OF
Abigaill Levy Franks

1733–1748

Edited and with
an Introduction by
Edith B. Gelles

YALE UNIVERSITY PRESS · NEW HAVEN AND LONDON

Published with assistance from the Annie Burr Lewis Fund.

Copyright © 2004 by Yale University. All rights reserved. This book may not be reproduced, in whole or in part, including illustrations, in any form (beyond that copying permitted by Sections 107 and 108 of the U.S. Copyright Law and except by reviewers for the public press), without written permission from the publishers.

Set in Galliard Oldstyle type by Tseng Information Systems, Inc. Printed in the United States of America by

Library of Congress Cataloging-in-Publication Data
Franks, Abigail, 1696-1756.
The letters of Abigaill Levy Franks, 1733-1748 / edited and with an introduction by Edith B. Gelles.
p. cm.
Rev. ed. of: The Lee Max Friedman collection of American Jewish colonial correspondence. 1968.
Includes bibliographical references and index.
ISBN 0-300-10345-X (alk. paper)
1. Franks, Abigail, 1696-1756 — Correspondence. 2. Frank family. 3. Jews — New York (State) — New York — History — 18th century. 4. Jews — New York (State) — New York — Correspondence. 5. New York (N.Y.) — Biography. I. Gelles, Edith Belle. II. Franks, Abigail, 1696-1756. Lee Max Friedman collection of American Jewish colonial correspondence. III. Title
CT275.F69458A4 2004
974.7′1004924′0092 — dc22   2004042245
[B]

A catalogue record for this book is available from the British Library.

The paper in this book meets the guidelines for permanence and durability of the Committee on Production Guidelines for Book Longevity of the Council on Library Resources.

10 9 8 7 6 5 4 3 2 1

For Michael

Contents

Preface ix

Acknowledgments xiii

Introduction xv

Editorial Method li

List of Abbreviations liii

Franks Genealogy lvi

Levy Genealogy lviii

Illustrations lxi

The Letters of Abigaill Levy Franks, 1733–1748 1

Bibliography 161

Index 181

Preface

Abigaill Levy Franks would be stunned to see her letters in print. She lived in an era when it was considered inappropriate for a woman to have a public persona apart from the men in her life. In that patriarchal world regulated by social prescriptions, men's activities determined women's identities. It was unusual and most often frowned upon for women to write for publication. Letters were one respectable outlet for women's expression, because letters were expected to be privately read. Abigaill Franks did not suspect that I, a historian, or you, readers, would become the beneficiaries of her letters. She did not consider that we would inspect her letters with an agenda that differed from that of the son to whom she wrote. By writing, she was engaging in a personal relationship; we read her letters for pleasure and as a historical source for insights into her world.

When we read Abigaill's printed letters more than two and a half centuries after their composition, they project a different sense of time and continuity. We know the outcome of her stories without the lapses that her immediate correspondents experienced. We evaluate her letters by different standards, knowing or seeking to know her as a historic figure. For us, the privately written letters have become a public document.

Some may read solely for the pleasure of immersing themselves in another person's life or social milieu. Other readers, whose motives are primarily literary, look for stylistic conventions that underpinned the eighteenth-century letter-writing genre. They may compare these letters with those of other epistolary heroes whose works are now collected, Madame Sévigné or Lady Mary Wortley Montague or Abigail

Adams. Historians read letters with a critical and analytic eye for the myriad details that are recorded. Abigaill Franks's letters provide a unique picture of a family, a city, a social world replete with conflict, uncertainty, mirth, pathos, and change.

For many reasons the eighteenth century, when Abigaill wrote, has been called the "golden age" of letter writing. While the roots of this genre go back to the classical period—to Cicero, Pliny, and Seneca—the English postal system had only in the seventeenth century developed fairly reliable, quick, and cheap routes of delivery. The eighteenth century, moreover, was the century of mobility when business, adventure, and opportunity had induced travel far and wide, dispersing families and economic ties that survived distance mostly through correspondence. Language itself had changed from the formal scholasticism of the Renaissance to a more naturalistic style that became the model for letter writing because it was easily adapted from conversation. Letters, indeed, were considered a form of conversation in which a writer and reader carried on a written exchange with all the sociability of informal face-to-face verbal discourse.

Abigaill Franks's letters to her son Naphtali convey the vivid sense of a conversation, though only one side of that conversation, as Naphtali's responses are not extant. Though biased to her viewpoint and her values, her narrative is satisfying; she tells a fascinating and dramatic story. The survival of her letters for well over two centuries, as of all private letters from her era, is serendipitous. In their foreword to a 1968 edition of the letters, Leo Hershkowitz and Isidore S. Meyer explain their history:

> Thirty-seven [now thirty-eight] letters of the Franks correspondence (1733–1748), addressed to Naphtali Franks in London, appear in this work, initiated by Lee Max Friedman and completed by the editors [Hershkowitz and Meyer]. Of these, thirty-four [now thirty-five] were sent to Naphtali by his mother Mrs. Jacob Franks (née Bilhah Abigaill Levy), and one, by his father, Jacob Franks, from New York City; and two others, by his brother, David Franks, from Philadelphia. Thirty-one of these

Preface

letters are located in the Lee Max Friedman Collection and were part of Mr. Friedman's bequest to the [American Jewish Historical] Society. Subsequently, the editors located six others: two were made available through the courtesy of Mr. Bryant Lillywhite of London, England; and four, through the courtesy of Mr. Richard H. Boulind, Frank Staff Collection, National Maritime Museum, Greenwich, England.

The group of thirty-one American Jewish colonial letters were acquired by Mr. Friedman in the fall of 1941. Upon his demise [in 1957], he had left behind him a complete rough transcription of these letters with copious notes, the fruit of his research, which guided the editors and stimulated them into further investigation in preparing this volume for the press.

Among the notes that Mr. Friedman intended for the introduction of this book are two that reveal his motivation in having such a book published. The first reads as follows: "An examination of New York history before 1800 creates an impression of the absence of striking personalities amongst its women. None can read Massachusetts history of this period without a vivid picture of Anne Hutchinson and Anne Bradstreet. . . ." To begin with, these letters by Abigaill Franks fill this void for New York history. They reveal the role and concern of a mother in New York in guiding her son, Naphtali, in far away England and disclose her thoughts about the other members of her family also. The second note indicates that these letters are an invaluable source for the history of provincial New York and other parts of British America. And here, Mr. Friedman quoted the words of Professor Alfred North Whitehead: "I think you get a truer picture of a period from intimate letters written spontaneously and without a thought of publication than you do from its fiction and often better than from its historians."*

Mr. Friedman began working on these letters immediately

**Dialogues with Alfred North Whitehead, As Recorded by Lucien Price* (Boston, 1954), 47.

after acquisition and continued to do so until the very end of his life. He tried to read everything printed that was available to him on American Jewish and Anglo-Jewish history, as well as on British and American Colonial history. He contacted major repositories and historical societies here and in Great Britain in search of published and manuscript material, and corresponded with various scholars in the preparation of this volume. The difficulties entailed by the War prevented him from pursuing his research in greater depth. On his rough transcription of the thirty-one original letters, in addition to his many notes, he indicated that other notations were to be added and further information was to be gathered together to elucidate points in the text and to identify persons, authors, and to locate literary passages quoted by Abigaill Franks.

Professors Hershkowitz and Meyer completed and published a first edition in 1968. Their stories are fully told in the foreword and introduction to their edition, *Letters of the Franks Family (1733–1748)*. I have let stand most of their footnotes, which represent monumental research. I have, further, merged their original bibliography with my own. This book owes a huge debt to their scholarship, industry, perseverance, and sensitivity.

My contribution to this living project has been twofold. I have written a new introduction, informed by my own training and background as an American colonialist and historian of women. And I have punctuated the letters. I did not do this without long consideration of the scholarly, historical, and stylistic implications of tampering with Abigaill's originals. In the end, it seemed to me more important to make the letters accessible to a broad audience by modernizing them than to retain the often ambiguous and always difficult original eighteenth-century format.

Acknowledgments

I am indebted to friends without whom this would not have happened. My husband, Michael Weiss, provided the basic computer expertise by scanning and transcribing the original volume of letters. In addition, Michael's erudition as a historian has informed the entire project.

Several years ago, Professor Jonathan Sarna suggested that I look at these letters. Since that time, he has been the most generous of mentors, the most reliable of colleagues, the most insightful of critics. My deep gratitude to Jonathan. My thanks to Larisa Heimert, Publisher, and others at Yale University Press who have graciously and meticulously supported the publication of these letters: Keith Condon, Margaret Otzel, and Kay Scheuer. It has been a pleasure to work with you.

I thank Dr. Michael Feldberg, Director of the American Jewish Historical Society, for his support of this project over several years. Lyn Slome, Director of Library and Archives, has been welcoming and helpful at the AJHS. Pamela Nadell encouraged this project. I thank Joyce Antler for our several conference presentations. My gratitude to a multitude of friends and colleagues for criticism and encouragement: Doron Ben-Atar, Susan Groag Bell, Bart Bernstein, Patricia Bonomi, Elaine Forman Crane, Arnie Eisen, Pamela Herr, Marty Klein, Phyllis Koestenbaum, Linda Kurtz, Shulamit Magnus, Karen Offen, William Pencak, Elizabeth Roden, David Rosenhan, Holly Snyder, Marilyn Yalom, Bill Youngs, Steven Zipperstein, and as always, the scholars at the Institute for Research on Women and Gender at Stanford. Last, but primary, my children, Adam and Esther and Noah, bring endless joy and interest to my world.

Introduction

No record of her death survives. For that matter, neither is there a record of her birth. The sole extant trace that she lived in New York City in the first half of the eighteenth century is the remarkable legacy of correspondence that descended for a few generations as a family memento, and then among collectors in Great Britain, until at last it found a permanent home by the mid-twentieth century in the archives of the American Jewish Historical Society. Thirty-five letters survive of the correspondence of Abigaill Levy Franks (1696–1756), all written to her son Naphtali in England, dating between 1733, when he initially migrated "home" to the mother country, and 1748, when the letters break off for no apparent reason. This is the earliest-known corpus of letters by a Jewish woman anywhere in Europe's western colonies.[1]

Abigaill Franks's letters are small masterpieces. Standing alone as the sole tribute to the engaging and even surprising life of one woman, they are also representative of women's lives in colonial British America. Few sources, either literary, biographical, or autobiographical, survive to document women's lives in the first half of the eighteenth century in America. Historians have looked to Anne Bradstreet's seventeenth-century poetry or the fragmentary entries in Elizabeth Drinker's mid-eighteenth-century diary. They have used Martha Ballard's late eighteenth-century diary and occasional letters or scraps of secondary information in order to piece together the story of women's lives before the Revolutionary era that produced the highly literate Abigail Adams and Mercy Otis Warren.[2] In this rare trove of thirty-five letters, Abigaill Franks paints a portrait of her early eighteenth-century domestic world—her life within a vast extended family circle—as well as social and political life in colonial New York, when that city was beginning to expand its domain beyond the northern border of Wall Street, populated by (purportedly) hostile Indians. They are, above all, the letters of a mother, and often project a decidedly modern tone: "Good God," she exclaimed to Naphtali in a bad-tempered rebuke to him, "wath an Opinion must you have of your sisters. Sure noe woman of common Sense Can be Soe infatuated As to throw her Self Away upon one who is the most Unaccountable Creature of God Allmightys Creations."[3]

Abigaill's letters are also those of a Jewish woman, unique because they reveal something of the earliest Jewish experience in colonial America, but also an important document of the entire immigrant (most colonials in this period were immigrants or closely descended from immigrants) experience. The letters tell of her successful effort to assimilate, while retaining hyphenated Jewish identity. "It gives me a Secreet pleasure to Observe the faire Character Our Family has in the place by Jews & Christians," she wrote in an early letter.[4] During the first half of the eighteenth century, especially in New York City, people of varieties of religious backgrounds were experimenting at living peacefully with one another. Sensitive to difference, she reminded her son not to flaunt his religion: "Tho' a Person may think freely and Judge for themselves," she warned Naphtali, "Any one Could Take amiss if his Neighbour did not goe the Same Road."[5] Abigaill Franks triumphantly negotiated her hyphenated world—to her own despair in her later years when several of her children married outside the fold.

Abigaill's letters charm as well as inform. She had style. She did not enjoy writing, so she didn't copy or revise. Her correspondence unfolds as a conversation with this son who had left his family at the age of seventeen to pursue a business career among his wealthy uncles in London, where he prospered, married, and remained. Abigaill did not see him again, but in motherly fashion she continued to advise him about his behavior: "I observe You Give me an Acc[oun]t how you Spend you time. I find no fault in it but your not takeing more time for your Studying of books," she wrote several years after his departure.[6] The letters were her lifeline to her beloved eldest son, and they reflect her ongoing friendship in her reports about family life and public life in his erstwhile hometown.

Opinionated and outspoken, Abigaill drew word-pictures for Naphtali, who was not present to see his siblings grow or a park develop on the "Bowling Green" or the governor squirm when the legislature refused to award his salary. She informed her son of the governor's plight: "He has lost Very much of the Peoples good will. the Assembly have done but Very Little yet. . . . I Should Like to heare theire debates."[7] It amused Abigaill to observe the vagaries of human behavior, whether at the level of colonial politics or synagogue politics. As for her taste in literature, it surprises; she read history and poetry and journals. And she read fiction, but only of quality: "Pray, send no more Such Idle Trash," she admonished after committing *The Lady of the Gold Watch* to the flames.[8]

What distinguishes Abigaill's letters from other early American women's writing is her irreverence, her lack of piety as well as literary pretentions. She did not aspire to be a poet; neither does she regularly invoke a holy spirit to guide her behavior. She was neither religious like Esther Edwards Burr nor belletristic like Annis Budinot Stockton.[9] Her letters were written as obligation; she stayed in touch with relatives and sent instructions. What pleasure she derived was in the fantasy conversation that she maintained with the son who aged and matured outside her personal orbit. As result Naphtali received a full dose of her character, and so do readers several centuries later. Abigaill did not have patience for platitudes; her morality was based upon expedience born of experience. She was loyal to the traditions of Judaism and to family even when she criticized or did not like them, and she had a clear-eyed view of people. In tension with her integrity was her consciousness of social status. Perhaps because of her immigrant background, she was careful to maintain good relations within her social world. Privately, however, she skewered fools with her wit. Above all, it is her wit that is endearing, whether it emerges as pun in the case of her "disgracefull" stepmother Grace, or poking fun at the middling folk who ingratiated themselves at Court. The wit is most often subtle; she was not a placid figure; she may have smiled or smirked as she wrote, if not inspired by a higher emotion like anger or contempt. Sometimes her missives were urgent, written in haste before a ship departed or when stealing time from domestic tasks. Abigaill's pen was dipped in the well of her life's passions.

Moreover, there is a social narrative in the arc of Abigaill Franks's life. She had no Jewish grandchildren. In the course of the years that she corresponded with Naphtali, she recorded her reactions to the outmarriages of two of her children, her grief, bewilderment, and outrage at the betrayal by the offspring whom she had trusted would remain in the fold, despite her secular inclinations. She had effectively straddled the bifurcated culture of hyphenation, and she did not understand or accept that her children could not. A familiar story about Jewish assimilation, all of American assimilation, exists in the story of Abigaill Franks's life in the early eighteenth century. It is a conundrum that still resonates and makes her story alive for twenty-first-century readers.

The merchant ship that carried Moses Levy, his wife, Richa Asher Levy, and several of their young children, including their eldest daughter, then called Bilhah Abigaill, docked in the New York harbor around 1703.[10] The long sea voyage—for it took many weeks, perhaps as many as eight, to traverse an ocean—separated them from a numerous clan of Levy relatives in London. By comparison with the metropolis that they had abandoned, New York was a mere provincial village. If no relatives greeted them upon their arrival, a small Jewish community had been long-settled, and there in the midst of familiar tradition, they would establish their new home.[11] What New York did offer to a young merchant was the prospect of good fortune, and Moses Levy settled down in New York to build that fortune.

Bilhah Abigaill, who in New York shed the marked name of Bilhah to become just Abigaill, which she always wrote with two l's, grew to womanhood. Her childhood, for which no reference survives, can only be inferred. As no public education was available in the province, she and her two brothers, Asher and Nathan, were probably tutored. While it is not surprising that middle-class Jewish sons would have been so well taught, Abigaill's learning is atypical for an early eighteenth-century woman. In their surviving correspondence, the three siblings demonstrate unusually cultivated and compatible intellects as adults. However, unlike her brothers, Abigaill never wrote letters in Yiddish or used Yiddish expressions, an indication that while she undoubtedly spoke the language at home, she may not have been taught to write the Hebrew alphabet.[12] Either that or she rejected the Jewish vernacular. Within a few years of their arrival in New York, two more brothers, Isaac and Michael, were born.

Then, when she was eleven, her mother died. As the eldest child and the only female, Abigaill experienced not only the tragedy of maternal bereavement, but increased domestic responsibility, if only in caring for her younger brothers. Typically, her widowed father soon remarried a much younger woman, Grace Mears, who in turn, bore him seven children, half-siblings to Abigaill who retained life-long affectionate relationships with the older children.[13] Typically, as well, there was tension between Moses Levy's children from his first marriage and their stepmother, a tension that later erupted into a court battle for Moses' estate after his death. Abigaill married young, perhaps to escape from this uneasy environment, leaving her father's house before most of the younger Levy children were born.

Jacob Franks had arrived in New York in 1707, also from London, also from a large and successful Jewish merchant family. He, too, came to New York to make his fortune and possibly within the Levy orbit, for he resided in the Levy household. Five years later, Jacob and Abigaill married, she barely of age at sixteen.[14] This pattern of marrying her father's apprentice would be mirrored in the later marriage of her son Naphtali to his cousin Phila, daughter of Uncle Isaac Franks in London, where Naphtali went to stay in 1733.[15]

Jacob's English family, in fact, were distinguished second-generation Ashkenazi residing in London, where they had earned great fortunes. In the large and complex family, there were in addition to Isaac and Aaron Franks, whose names appear most frequently in Abigaill's letters to Naphtali, a third brother Abraham, patriarch to the clan as the eldest and wealthiest. Finally, Jacob's sister, Abigail Solomons, mothered a great brood of children, two of whom eventually arrived at Abigaill's doorstep in New York—Coleman, or Colly, and Moses.[16] An incorrigible wastrel, Colly presented troubles for Abigaill, but however strained family relations might become, it was expected practice, especially among Jews who were widely dispersed, to care for and mentor nieces and nephews. Abigaill loyally looked after Colly.

Abigaill writes always with affection for her husband, mostly with respect, occasionally with deference, though sometimes with irony. She worried that he overworked and noted the benefit of his resting on the Sabbath. She claimed that she did not interfere in his business, trusting his case when disputes arose with relatives on both sides. But she contested his temper. "I offten Tell him I would rather be Accused of Insensibility then have my Passions Under Soe Little command as he has,"[17] she wrote, but she also attributed his outbursts to stress. She added that "in the Family he is the Same good Nature."[18] Jacob was a caring man, who humored his family, and Abigaill's marriage to him was solid. He was also a religious man, who four times served as *parnas,* or president, of his congregation. His own correspondence with his sons, often written in Yiddish, survives, revealing fatherly affection, though later, when they were old enough to be his associates, their business transactions as well. Most evident is his caring for Abigaill, not a typical wife who concentrated exclusively on domestic and social persuits. Jacob's wife read books and had unconventional opinions. Not of an intellectual bent himself, but rather focused on business and synagogue life, Jacob nevertheless provided the environment for Abigaill to thrive.

Marriage meant motherhood, but Abigaill did not give birth to

Naphtali, her eldest surviving son, for almost three years. Thereafter, Abigaill's children arrived at consistent two-year intervals, Moses, David, and finally a girl, Phila, in 1722.[19] Richa's birthdate is unknown, but a long gap exists until the births of Sara and Aaron, both born in the early 1730s and both dead within the decade. Despite the fact that Abigaill was writing to Naphtali in London during this period, no mention is made of the death of either child, perhaps because she didn't write about this too painful event, but more likely because of attrition. Two younger children, Abigail, called Poyer, and Rebecca, are frequent subjects in the later correspondence.

Because Abigaill's family was comfortably affluent, and because she lived in a city instead of on a farm, her role as wife and mother was doubly circumscribed. She had servants, perhaps even a slave, to perform many of the household chores, such as cooking, laundry, and cleaning. Markets existed in colonial New York where she procured fresh produce, brought in from the countryside by farmers or neighboring Indians. Her kosher meats were butchered by the *shohet*, a ritual slaughterer employed by the congregation. She did participate in the preserving of fresh fruits and vegetables for the winter months, and even the "smoking" of fish and fowl, items that she frequently sent to Naphtali as treats from home. Unlike women who were wives of local artisans or small merchants, however, she appears not to have participated in the running of her husband's business, for she never mentions the details of the mercantile trade. This is not to say that Jacob did not discuss business with her, for she did write knowledgably to Naphtali about financial disputes within the family. But, largely, her husband's business was not part of her domestic world.

That world consisted primarily of caring for her children, nurturing them properly, and overseeing their educations. The Franks children received an education that was appropriate to affluent families and preparatory for their future occupations. By this time, the 1730s, the tiny New York Jewish community had built its own synagogue and established a school. Both the Franks sons and daughters attended the Shearith Israel school where they learned, Abigaill reported to Naphtali, "french Spanish hebrew and writing in the morning." In the afternoon the children attended Mr. Brownell's, one of New York's exclusive private schools. Brownell, an itinerant teacher, had advertised in a local newspaper that he taught "Reading Writing Cyphering, Merchant Accoumpts, Latin, Greek, etc."[20] While reading, writing, and ciphering represented a strong curriculum for girls in the early eighteenth century, Abigaill was modern if not radical in sending her daughters to study nondomestic subjects.[21] Nor did she spare her children the artistic training that was obligatory for the leisure hours of affluent urban dwellers, so that music and painting were included as part of their curricula. Abigaill raised her children to enjoy the literary and artistic pleasures that she personally indulged.

When she was not engaged in running her household and overseeing the development of her children or reading, Abigaill spent time with her close women friends, who counted among New York's social elite. They included Fanny Moore, Mary Riggs, and Mary Pearse. She stayed at Morrisiana, the country home of the Lewis Morris family, and was invited to receptions at the governor's mansion. Mrs. Kearny carried her letters to Naphtali as did Mrs. Compton. And although Abigaill reported to Naphtali about their talk of children and gossip about local scandal, the primary attraction among these women was their literacy and concern about public events. Abigaill did not suffer fools as friends. In the New York City of the early eighteenth century, she was freer, as a Jew, to move into a more fluid social scene than anywhere else in the world. And she did.

At the turn of the century, when Moses Levy moved his family to New York, the population numbered a mere five thousand souls, compared with the London they had left, which was approaching one million people. About 15 percent of New York's populace were Africans; some were free, but most were slaves.[22] The Jewish population of New York in 1700 has been estimated at 250 people, one-half of one percent.[23] New York's Dutch origins separated it from other British-American colonies, a feature obvious to the Levy family as they sailed into the harbor, for many of the closely built houses along the waterfront were patterned after Dutch architecture with their unusual stepped and gabled roofs.

Founded exclusively as a trading post, New York possessed the "finest harbor on the continent."[24] Geographically unique, the city was poised at the tip of an island, bounded on one side by the East River and on the other by the mighty Hudson, pathway to the North and its bounteous fur, lumber, and farm produce, all marketed through the merchant community of New York. Moses Levy intended to join that community.

Even then, in 1703, New Yorkers were densely crowded into a small area, for the largest portion of the population lived below Wall Street. To accommodate its burgeoning immigration, the city fathers already in 1687 had begun to offer bargain prices for underwater property along the East River to encourage citizens to fill and reclaim that land for their homes and businesses.[25] In the half-century that Abigaill lived in New York, the city expanded its boundaries northward as well.

More than any other British colony, New York attracted a heterogeneous population. In addition to the Dutch and the English, a sizable group of Huguenots had settled there in the late seventeenth century, followed by Palatine Germans, Swedes, Scots, Irish, and persons of many backgrounds who arrived from the West Indies. It was said that as many as eighteen languages could be heard on the streets of New York.[26] Among the many social problems that resulted from this polyglot population, none was more salient than religion. The Dutch Reformed Church had first struggled to maintain its spiritual monopoly before the British came along to establish the Anglican Church as the official denomination. Such exclusivity could not endure, however, because the need for people exceeded the requirements of the clergy, and grudgingly though pragmatically, the city fathers welcomed other Christian denominations. Within several decades there were Presbyterian, Quaker, Lutheran, Baptist, and even Moravian churches in New York. The constraints on Jewish public worship would endure for a few more years.[27]

New Yorkers did more than work and worship, and taverns had appeared to provide convivial society, especially for men. In that specialized domain—each tavern, functioning most often in a private home, catered to a particular clientele—businessmen could discuss politics and the price of sugar, and sailors could partake of the pleasures of land-leave. In yet others, claimed critics of the institution, including Abigaill Franks years later, sinfulness prevailed, and rebellions were hatched.[28] Most women, like Abigaill, socialized at home.

Architecturally, New York's homes were built of brick in the early eighteenth century, for fire was a terrible hazard in a community that lived by fireplaces and candlelight, and where no fire department, much less a fire truck, would be acquired until the 1730s. Houses were so closely constructed that they appeared to lean one upon the other. In fact, the density was caused by reluctance to populate the northern and outer areas, though the drift toward Greenwich Village and Harlemtown became more pronounced after the century's turn. Streets had developed helterskelter without a plan, at first mere mud pathways but, by the eighteenth century, beginning to be paved with cobblestones.[29]

Neighborhoods[30] also developed in a helterskelter pattern. Immigrants, like the Levys and the Franks, lived near to people of similar background, Jews in their case, so that among the six wards of municipal New York each had its distinct ethnic concentration. Jews, including the Franks family, tended to live in the "Dock Ward," the area where synagogue worship was conducted. Still, they lived among many diverse peoples, for not until the time of the Revolution would neighborhoods reflect social and economic ranking within the population.[31] The community into which Levys moved included prosperous as well as poor families, and in a further merging of interests, businesses and private homes existed in tandem. Most often a building housed a retail or artisan shop at the ground level, while the family dwelled above.[32]

Not all of New York's narrow streets were yet paved in the early eighteenth century, for few private carriages existed. Only the carts

Introduction

that carried merchandise rumbled along, while the polyglot of people—merchants, newly arrived immigrants, sailors, Indians hawking fresh produce—traveled about by foot in the still-small community. However, running through the middle of existing streets were open sewers which, along with the pigs that were allowed free run of the city, suggests that the atmosphere was charged with odor as well as sounds and activity.[33] Abigaill Franks's world changed as paving and lighting appeared, but in the early eighteenth century, New York more closely resembled a medival town in the process of becoming a modern city. There was at first no public schooling, no hospital, no poor house. These institutions developed during Abigaill Franks's lifetime.[34]

The locus of local government was the Fort. Built originally by the Dutch, it changed its name with each reigning British monarch, so what had been Fort Anne during Moses Levy's time was called Fort George by the Franks family. The governor lived within the fortress, the militia trained and was quartered there, the established Dutch, then Anglican Church existed there. But the extent to which Jews, could—or even wished to—participate in local politics was limited. Jacob Franks and his sons trained with the militia, and Jacob paid due social tribute to the governor, but he was conscious that Jewish citizenship was yet dicey. The Fort was the center of social life—and the Frankses, as a prominent merchant family were included on the guest list—but primarily it was a seat of amazing intrigue, as the incredible drama of New York colonial politics unfolded in the course of the next several decades.[35] The Frankses were wary of jeopardizing their community standing by taking sides.

An amazing feature of Abigaill Franks's letters is her ongoing commentary about New York politics. Her letters not only demonstrate her awareness of local politics, but show, as well, that this was a topic of continuing interest and conversation, if not gossip, between herself and her friends. She communicated all of this to Naphtali.

The politics of early eighteenth-century New York, especially of the 1730s when she wrote, were as fractious and vituperative as any in the early American colonies. Abigaill's reports to Naphtali reveal that, although she was informed and involved, she took care not to appear partisan. First, as she repeatedly observed, in the small community that was then New York City, she lived among the warring parties, some of them neighbors, all well known not just by reputation, but socially.[36] The Frankses did not want their social position, upon which their economic well-being rested, to be jeopardized.

As a Jew, moreover, she wished to maintain a low profile in these internecine disputes. While Jews might be considered citizens of New York and sometimes could vote and even hold lower elective and appointive civic positions,[37] as a tiny minority of the population they did not wish to draw attention to themselves in partisan conflicts. Furthermore, because Jews came to America for economic betterment, and nowhere in the world at that time exercised civic rights, they did not yet have expectations for civic participation.[38] Abigaill emphasized this stance to her son: "As to my Own Private Opinion I am inclined to the town Side," she wrote, but she affected impartiality; she wished to "appear neuter."[39]

The contentious situation in New York had developed with the arrival of a new governor, William Cosby, following the death of the previous governor in 1731.[40] Cosby immediately became embroiled in a dispute with local officials over his salary. What began as a narrow issue of salary escalated within the next few years into a conflict over constitutional principles. Since the situation had originated before Naphtali's departure for London, Abigaill was merely keeping him abreast of developments at home. "We have a Perfect war here, and it is dayly increasing, the Court (governor) being Very much disliked," Abigaill informed Naphtali during the same year he sailed for England. The governor had lost the "Esteem of the People," she wrote, and "Young delancy & Fred[erick] Philps have Lost a great deall of good Will by being in the Gov[ernor's] Interest."[41]

The parties to the dispute were, on the one hand, the new governor, supported by the "town party," including the Philipses and

Introduction xxvii

the Delanceys, and the "country party" of the Morrises, Livingstons, and Van Dams, supported by prominent lawyers James Alexander and William Smith of the city.[42] The dispute began with the appointment of an interim governor, Rip Van Dam who served for eighteen months before the arrival of Cosby. When the new governor did appear on the scene, he demanded to be reimbursed for one-half of Van Dam's salary, which, understandably, did not sit well with Van Dam, who refused. Cosby decided to take the issue to court. He did not, however, trust his case with a jury and instead turned to the New York Supreme Court, using (his opponents said usurping) his power as governor to transform that court into a Court of Equity to hear this civil case.

The chief justice of the Supreme Court, Lewis Morris, was outraged both by the governor's mendacious claim and by his unwarranted use of power. In the ensuing conflict, Governor Cosby removed Morris from his high position and in his place appointed thirty-one-year-old James Delancey as chief justice. Morris, after some local maneuvering, decided to "go home" to England to argue his case before the real source of power, the colonial administration in London. He departed in 1734, accompanied by his son Robert Hunter Morris, whom Abigaill recommended to her son as "Very full of himself."[43] In fact, the Franks family were neighbors, if not friends, of most of the figures in this dispute. As complicated and bizarre as the conflict appears nearly three centuries later, it was no less strange and ludicrous to Abigaill.

Contained in this salary dispute, as it escalated over the years, were issues of land tenure in the Hudson Valley, taxation (the town party preferred a land tax, and the country party argued for an excise), as well as freedom of the press. The John Peter Zenger case, testing the principle of freedom of the press, resulted from Zenger's founding of his partisan newspaper, *The Weekly Journal,* as a mouthpiece for the country party. In his zeal to criticize the governor, Zenger found himself jailed for libel, and, in a case that historians now say has been overrated as a milestone in establishing civil rights, he was exonerated.⁴⁴ Finally, when Morris took the political issue to England to be resolved, he was arguing against the unlimited use of power by a royal governor, a constitutional issue, and one that would be settled less than a half-century later by a revolution.

Abigaill not only followed the political machinations as they were reported in newspapers and by her informants; her fascination with the issues took her a step further to learn about the historical background of the current dilemma, and she took pains, in turn, to inform Naphtali. The governor, as a ploy to disarm his opposition, had threatened to overturn the peculiar arrangement of land tenure which enriched many of the country faction. Abigaill accurately explained the history to Naphtali: "When People came first to Settle in this Country," she wrote, "they hardly knew Wath A right Conveyance of Land was, but bought and Settled themselves And Children Opon it without much pains in the form of Titles, soe that According to the Tenour of this Court they may over Look all the records."⁴⁵ If her domestic world was small, she enlarged it with political and historical expertise that was uncanny for a woman in her time, and she was fiercely opinionated. While she was careful to appear unpartisan among her neighbors, she felt free to express herself to Naphtali. She believed that the governor had overstepped his power by suppressing the judiciary and tampering with the system of taxation. Perhaps she was influenced by her husband's stance as a merchant when she complained about the excise tax that would affect imports and exports. She was sufficiently fascinated that she confessed to wanting to observe the debates in the Assembly.

For an entire year, Abigaill's letters reported the dispute to Naphtali, concluding in the end that both sides had overstepped the boundaries of political propriety. "Soe you find," she mused to her son, "its not Soe Eassy to Git friends as to fall Out."⁴⁶ Lewis Morris returned from England, having achieved mixed success on his mission. Then Governor Cosby died. The situation moved on to the next stage, a dispute over his successor. Abigaill's response reflected the general popular disaffection: "Our Politicks is Very much Sunk," and

Introduction xxix

she concluded, "I Shall not be at the Pains to Say any Thing Abouth it."⁴⁷

Remarkably, Abigaill Franks's reports to her son about the Morris-Cosby controversy, as the entire political episode is referred to historically, have become quite useful as a source of information about some of the issues involved. She believed that she was writing friendly letters to her son, keeping him up to date about events at home, writing her side of a conversation just as she would have talked with him had he been in New York, and perhaps exercising her political muscle in a world that excluded women from active participation.⁴⁸ The fortuitous survival and circulation of her letters in print, however, have provided one historian with a unique insight into popular attitudes toward the disputes.⁴⁹ Because of the vagaries of source survival, no other documentation exists, or has yet been discovered, that describes from a more or less neutral perspective some of the factional attitudes among the principal actors of this dispute.

Ironically, Abigaill's letters have been broadly quoted.⁵⁰ They reveal a keen interest in politics from an unlikely source—not just a disenfranchised woman, for whom literacy, much less political literacy, would not be expected, but a Jewish woman, and therefore twice removed from public issues. Poorly spelled and punctuated—it was, after all, before Webster's time, so many men did not do much better—and not eloquently constructed, the letters are lively and accurate in their reporting. Moreover, they illustrate something of the world in which Abigaill lived, the volatile politics of colonial New York, and the careful arrangements that all groups had to consider in their negotiations of everyday life in the city. Most particularly, they shed some light on the world in which a tiny minority of Jews came to make their fortunes.

One known portrait survives of Abigaill Levy Franks, probably painted in 1735 and probably done by Gerardus Duyckinck, a local artist.⁵¹ Abigaill faces the artist, though her head is slightly turned to her right; she smiles a half-smile, and her narrow dark eyes are sharply focused on the viewer. Her oval face is crowned by dark hair, long and pulled behind her ears with one strand of curl cascading over her shoulder onto her breasts, amply exposed above the low neckline of the light teal chemise she wears beneath her dark teal dress. She sits straight on a garnet-colored drapery that covers the chair where her arm is gracefully resting. Her forearms and hands, delicate hands, more accustomed to leisure activities than domestic chores, have been carefully posed to exhibit her gentility.

The portrait's formulaic background resembles those taken of her father and husband, both extant and housed, as is Agaill's, at the American Jewish Historical Society. A dark curtain sets off most of Abigaill's figure, opened enough on the left side to disclose a pastoral setting beyond. Trees, seemingly pine, reach toward the cumulus clouds in an otherwise blue sky. Whereas the men's portraits are poised against a background that indicates status and occupation, Abigail's appears to describe rural America, a country scene. What is fascinating about this picture is that nothing, but nothing in her portrait indicates that Abigaill is Jewish.[52]

Similarly in the correspondence that survives as Abigaill's self-portrait, Judaism gets scant attention. The letters provide pictures of an age and a family as well as some people and events, but rarely do they describe Jewish life in colonial New York. Where, we may wonder, are the depictions of family Sabbath and holiday rituals, synagogue attendance, social activities, or spirituality? Being Jewish must have been salient to Abigaill's identity as well as to her daily activities. If, in fact, Abigaill's Jewish identity was foremost in her consciousness, why doesn't "Jewish" appear more often in the spontaneous letters that she wrote to her son? She wrote about the literature that she read, mostly not Jewish; depictions of people and politics, again not Jewish; family life, without being Jewish. Only on a few occasions does Abigaill mention Jewish life in colonial New York, and sometimes these comments are explicitly derogatory.

In fact, Jewish ritual and Jewish conversation permeated Franks family life. Abigaill's letters aside, her husband's involvement with the building and support of Shearith Israel would argue for a very observant Franks household. Jacob Franks was a founding member, one of the greatest contributors, and an officer many times over, often president, of the congregation.[53] The Franks home on Duke Street was a short walk from the synagogue on Mill Street. It has already been seen that the Franks children attended the Shearith Israel school.

That small synagogue was the earliest dedicated Jewish house of worship in continental North America.[54] Not that Jewish services were absent before its construction in 1730, but they took place in rented spaces. The tiny Jewish community decided to build its own house of worship in 1728, and generous donations to support its construction came not only from the New York Jewish community, but also from congregations in Curaçao, Amsterdam, and London. Jacob Franks was a principal figure in those fund-raising efforts and treasurer of the project. He enlisted his London brothers as subscribers. Later, as a compromise in leadership between the Sephardic and Ashkenazi communities was negotiated, Jacob served as *parnas* for half the year while Moses Gomez, of Sephardic background, served the other half.[55] That level of involvement in the New York Jewish community argues for an intensely Jewish household.

Abigaill, on the other hand, read *Gentleman's Magazine,* a British monthly that was to the eighteenth century what the *New Yorker* is to contemporary readers. Naphtali sent this subscription regularly along with other responses to her persistent requests for books. She read a history of England by Paul Rapin de Thoyras, a French author recently translated into English. She asked for a history of Poland and for Pope's translation of Montesquieu's *Persian Letters.* She particularly enjoyed Addison, and confessed that in general, "I could with Vast Pleasure Imploy three hours of the 24 from my Family Affairs to be diping in a good Author: And relinquish Every other Gaity Commonly Called the pleasure of Life."[56] Her preference in literature, further, ran to Smollett, Dryden, and Fielding. She was modern and secular in thought and taste.

Abigaill was, in fact, a daughter of the emerging Enlightenment, an orientation that valued the individual mind. Its source in her may only be speculated upon. Since she shared her subscriptions with her brother Isaac, it appears that the Levy children were similarly exposed to a secular literature. Beyond that, Abigaill's intellectual versatility, which was extraordinary for any eighteenth-century colonial American woman, much less a Jewish woman, remains a mystery. That she, in turn, arranged for her own children to persue modern and worldly subjects beyond the exclusive religious tradition of the Shearith Israel school, then, is not mysterious.

The Franks children did receive a religious education, and Abigaill maintained strict standards of religious observance. She kept a kosher home. She admonished Naphtali in England to conscientiously follow the *kashroot*. While she advised him not to flaunt his Jewish practice, she did expect him to continue his morning devotions, suggesting that the Franks men, if they did not attend morning services at Shearith Israel, prayed at home, likely wearing the traditional phylacteries.[57] Moreover, Abigaill did not write on the Sabbath; she observed the rituals of preparing special holiday meals, of fasting, of sacrilizing the holy days. Above all, Abigaill was a believer; she asked for holy intervention to bless her son, especially on the occasion of the High Holidays, but also for other occasions and nonoccasions.

Abigaill embraced her Jewish identity, but in character with the rest of her personality, she did so mindfully. She was impatient with ideas that conflicted with her reason. So she condemned "the Many Supersti[ti]ons wee are Clog'd with" and she "heartly wish[ed] a Calvin or Luther would rise amongst Us" to reform the old orthodoxy that she considered "Idle Cerimonies and works of Supperorogations." If such behavior sent people to Heaven, she observed "wee & the papist have the Greatest Title too."[58] Abigaill did not mean to be either irreverent or profane. She lived passionately in a world of books with progressive ideas that shaped her thinking outside of traditional ways. The point is that Abigaill resisted tradition in the best way that she could as a woman and as a Jew; she protested its confining boundaries in rare outbursts of passion. In practice, she mostly conformed.

When she attended services in the little synagogue—it measured thirty-five feet by thirty-five—she would have sat in the balcony reserved for women. Women were, in fact, listed in the roles of the financial contributers, widows especially, as they controlled their own moneys. Otherwise, as *femes couvert,* their pounds and shillings were indirectly represented in their husbands' names.[59] Their direct contributions came in the provision of material objects; they sewed the torah covers, and cloth covers for the *bimah* (the reading table), for instance. Abigaill's participation in the sessions that produced these items is unlikely, for she boycotted that community, dismissing them testily in a letter to Naphtali: "I dont offten See . . . any of our Ladys but at Synagogue for they are a Stupid Set of people," adding the caution, "but Mum for that."[60] Clearly Abigaill Franks's relationship with her religion and its people was complicated, if not unconventional.

Yet, her letters to her son begin with "Dear HertSey." HertSey—she later wrote Hertsey or Heartsey—was his name of endearment, indicating familiarity or in Abigaill's case intimacy. In Yiddish, "herz" means "dear heart."[61] By writing always to her dear heart, her dear one, she expressed affection, but she also did it in Yiddish, the mother tongue of Ashkenazi Jews, even in America. For whatever reason, either because she actually used the Yiddish language, or because she wanted to remind Naphtali of his Jewishness, or, most likely, because she naturally used his childhood name of endearment, Naphtali was permanently "HertSey" to his mother. By her salutation in almost every letter, Abigaill Franks marked herself as Jewish, and the letters as well.

The time came when Abigaill began to consider her children's marriages, especially her daughters'. By the late 1730s, Phila had reached the age of courtship. Richa's age is not known precisely; she may have been a few years older or younger than Phila.[62] In the small Jewish community of New York, prospects for suitable husbands were not great, especially given the Franks family standards. Not only did social class rank high in their consideration, but religion was a given.

And while class may have been negotiable if a man had prospects of advancement, it was taken for granted that no member of the Franks family would marry out of the fold. Possibly, even, a small ethnic prejudice existed; a certain amount of animosity between the late-settling Ashkenazi and the original Sephardic immigrants survived into the mid-eighteenth century, but Abigaill did not consciously express that prejudice. When both groups criticized the marriage of her younger sister, Rachel Levy, to Isaac Mendes Seixas, she belittled the critics, not the match.[63]

Abigaill's vigilance for her daughters' future well-being surfaced when a suitor for Richa appeared on the scene. David Gomez, Abigaill confided in Naphtali, had shown an interest in Richa for years. Gomez, in fact, was a good prospect, both socially and religiously. His father had made a fortune as a merchant and, judging from the family's standing on the tax roles, exceeded the Frankses in wealth. All of the Gomez family, father and several sons, were active in Shearith Israel, both as officers in the congregations and as large contributors. Little is known of David, except for Abigaill's reaction to him: "He is such a Stupid wretch that if his fortune was much more and I a begar, noe child of Mine, Especialy one of Such a good Understanding as Richa Should Never have my Consent. And I am Sure he will never git hers."[64] That took care of David Gomez. He does not appear again in the Franks chronicle.

To Abigaill's great joy, Naphtali announced in late 1742, that he had married his cousin, Phila Franks, daughter of Isaac, in whose household he had long resided. During that near-decade, Phila had grown from child to young woman, and the attachment between them had developed as well. Abgaill wished the young couple well and expressed her approval of Phila, who met and surpassed the Franks standards for matrimony; she inherited a fortune, and she was Jewish. Her pedigree was enhanced by being a family member; in this case, family ensured character. Abigaill continued, mentioning Phila's "good Sence & good Nature," attributes she thought necessary to "Make a Friendship in Marriage."[65] In fact, she described a progressive theory of marriage that was already in existence in the early eighteenth century—the companionate marriage in which partners would be friends as well as sharing the burdens of family life.[66]

Her daughters remained single and at home. Not a good omen, the next letter in the Franks correspondence was written by David, the younger brother of Naphtali. It contains the astonishing news, understated by David, that his sister Phila had married Oliver Delancey, scion of the hugely prosperous and successful merchant family. Not only was Phila married, but she had been secretly married for six months while continuing to live in her parents' house. "Not a Soul Knew of it till Last week when she absented herself & went to his Country house where she has Remain'd Since." David acknowledged, "I was very much Surpris'd when I heard it," and he added, "Am told that (my father) is and my Mother in great greif about [it]."[67]

Indeed, Abigaill did grieve. It was several months before she next wrote to Naphtali, and when she did, her letter was posted from Flatt bush, a resort on Long Island, where the Frankses had a summer home. "I am now retired from Town and would from my Self (if it Where Possiable to have Some peace of mind) from the Severe Affliction I am Under on the Conduct of that Unhappy Girle," she began. "Good God Wath a Shock it was when they Acquainted me She had Left the House and Had bin Married Six months." Even though several months had elapsed since Abigaill learned of the marriage, still she wrote: "I can hardly hold my Pen whilst I am a writting it. Itts wath I Never could have Imagined."[68]

In the ten years that Abigaill had corresponded with Naphtali, she had never revealed such profound emotions. Not when Sara died. Not when Aaron died. Not for the many crises that afflicted large families who lived in the dangerous world of the eighteenth century. To Abigaill, this was a catastrophe of a different dimension. For one thing, her daughter had dissembled: "I heard her Soe often Say that no Consideration in Life should Ever Induce her to Disoblige Such good parents." There had been some rumors, she admitted, but she had discounted them. Phila's conduct "has allways bin Unblemish[e]d," she wrote, adding bitterly, "And is Soe Still in the Eyes of the Christians whoe allow She has DisObliged Us but has in noe way bin Dishonorable being married to a man of worth and Charector."[69] Her Christian friends could not comprehend her distress.

Abigaill wrote that, in her great anguish, it was painful even to speak with people. She understood the concept of depression, and she graphically depicted its symptoms, relating that she had withdrawn from company and suffered in solitude. "My house has bin my prisson Ever Since I had not heart Enough to Goe Near the Street door," she wrote.[70] She appreciated the isolation of Flatt Bush, and wished never to return to the city. So extreme was her resistance to being in New York, she wrote, that she would return to London if it were in her power to decide.

Abigaill's lament is uncharacteristic at many levels. She had never seriously complained to Naphtali. Now she confided in him as a trusted friend; she wrote to him with a freedom that allowed her to unburden the greatest hurt that she had ever experienced. Her world had come undone. She wanted to leave home and live elsewhere. She wanted to escape—from her environment, her friends, and herself. She could conceive of no other relief.

A grief of such magnitude is symptomatic of an upheaval at her very core. Abigaill had lost her sense of who she was. Her daughter's deception reflected on her identity as a mother. Her daughter's outmarriage fractured the family line. From Abigaill's point of view, Phila had violated her mother's identity in two fundamental ways.

The violation to her motherhood is more easily understood. Abigaill had spent all of her married years raising children. That was her occupation, and it defined her. Motherhood was basic to her marriage contract. To carry out that contract, she had developed strong views about her children's upbringing and behavior as well as a vision about how they should come out as adults. She cared for her husband and household; she read; she saw friends. Motherhood was central; her children were her product and her legacy. She thought about them even while she thought about other things. Yet Phila had turned out

Introduction xxxvii

wrongly. She had broken trust with her mother. Her deception symbolized Abigaill's failure.

Given Abigaill's record on the subject of Judaism, however, her reaction appears excessive. She mostly ignores Jewish topics in her letters, preferring to write Naphtali about many other absorbing subjects. The few comments she makes are mostly derisive or critical or sarcastic. She avoided social contact with Jewish women and found her friends among the Christian establishment. She read secular literature. At the same time, she was married to an observant Jewish man, who took a prominent role within the small Jewish community. She cooked according to the Jewish dietary laws. She observed the holidays and the Sabbath. She was pleased with the Frankses' reputation among both the Jews and Christians, which means she was well regarded. Abigaill's relationship with religion was conflicted. But she never would see Phila again. In the Jewish tradition, her daughter was dead.[71]

The apparent magnitude of this offense had to do with Abigaill's identity. Phila had not just misbehaved. She had violated her mother's sense of who she was, and Jewishness, it turns out, was at Abigaill's core. For however she derided the ritual and the people, the way that she knew herself, identified herself, was as a Jew. That can be the only explanation for her unremitting grief and her refusal ever to see her daughter again. Abigaill took religion for granted, like nature, and Phila had transgressed against nature.

Jacob Franks, in contrast to his wife, rationally decided to accommodate the deed, now that it was done. Oliver had called on Jacob to request that Phila's inheritance from her uncle Isaac Franks of London be released to him. "All I can Say ab[ou]t It is & beg t[ha]t If It can be Don so as he may have It," wrote Jacob. He noted that in the small community, it was important to remain friendly with the city's most powerful families. Further he was concerned to ensure Phila's good treatment by the Delanceys. Jacob's mixed message speaks both to his own position among New York's merchants and to his daughter's well-being. He further informed Naphtali that he had heard rumors the "she heartily Repents what she has Don," and that he would invite Phila to visit, "but can Not Bring y[ou]r Mother to it."[72] If Jacob had mellowed, Abigaill remained firm.

Abigaill's matrimonial trials did not end with the ordeal of Phila's marriage. Son David added to his mother's woes. In December 1743, hardly a year after Phila eloped, David married Margaret Evans of Philadelphia, and in another year his first daughter, Abigail, was baptised. The grandmother wrote to Naphtali that she was "in the Midst of my many griefes."[73] Apparently she refused to see David as well, for she later wrote that "if I cant throw him from My heart I Will by my conduct have the Appearance of it," and added "its a Firey Tryall you are Noe parent And therefore Can be Noe Judge."[74] After almost a quarter century of mothering, Abigaill had few romantic illusions about the role.

So it pleased her, several years later, to learn that Moses would go to London to set up in business. Her rationale made sense: His friends all caroused in taverns, getting drunk on weekends, and, despite her missing him, she wanted him out of "this degenerate place."[75] Abigaill's basic concept of mothering involved sacrifice.

Abigaill's correspondence ends with her next letter in 1748. She lived until 1756, but no more letters survived. The reason for her death is not known; the final eight years of her life fall into obscurity. Her health in 1748 was still good, though she had begun to consider herself old.[76] Still, her youngest children lived in her house and she cared for them, as she had her older offspring. Jacob Franks outlived his wife by more than a decade. Presumably he continued in business, and records of Shearith Israel show his continued great involvement with the affairs of the synagogue.[77]

Despite the frustration of not knowing the end of the story, the portion that exists is satisfying and valuable. From Abigaill's extant letters, we become acquainted with a woman of great spirit and intelligence. She has told us about her life in the second quarter of the eighteenth century in a British colony in America. She has shared her prejudices and her pleasures—her judgments about books and people, her take on politics and the role of mothering. She has presented an intimate view of family life at a time when all life was fragile for many reasons. Abigaill Franks changed in the course of a decade and a half; she struggled, she suffered, and she recovered.

Mostly, her struggles and her suffering derived from her work of mothering. She had early discovered the principles that governed her approach to mothering; she was no less demanding of her children than she was of herself. She expected to shape her children in a model that repeated her own life and that of her husband. The violation of that expectation when her daughter and son married outside her religion created a wound that would not heal. She, nevertheless, covered the bitter wound and persisted with her own life. She had long been a skeptical person, and so the great disappointment, while its source in her children's outmarriages surprised her, did not destroy her gusto for the challenge of life.

In many respects, Abigaill Franks represented the ideal immigrant to colonial New York City, a city that she gave mixed reviews. She was tolerant of difference; she was intolerant of corruption, whether it occurred at the personal level or in public matters. Against the backdrop of New York's polyglot people and fractious politics, she functioned with social equanimity, sometimes amused, other times appalled by people's behavior. She negotiated well in a fragmented environment; she adapted well. In fact, it was her ability to adapt that in the end compromised her sanguine nature.

The same qualities of rationality, acceptance, and adaptability became the source of her greatest jolt in life. So confident was she about her own Jewish identity, enough so that she felt free to criticize the religion and the people, that she was stunned to discover that her children did not experience the same fundamental loyalty to their lineage. To her, being a Jew and being a British-American New Yorker seemed compatible—the one formed identity and character, the other formed social behavior. She lived at ease with both. That was why she was pleased to observe the good reputation of her family among both

Jews and Christians. She believed that the Frankses had successfully negotiated a cultural chasm.

Yet, rational as she was, Abigaill did not calculate for the unknown. The cultural bifurcation that she managed could not be long sustained, and its equilibrium collapsed with a new generation. Perhaps her children chose the easier path of undivided loyalties. Perhaps the pragmatic circumstances of minority life in New York no longer appeared viable. Perhaps they discovered they had a choice about issues that provided no choice to their parents.

Abigaill and Jacob Franks had no known Jewish grandchildren. In two generations, the Jewish identity of the entire Franks family had disappeared.[78] Among the English Frankses, Naphtali and Phila's children married out, as did the daughter of Moses, who had married another cousin Phila. The Oliver Delanceys moved to England as loyalist émigrés after the Revolution, where they entered the ranks of the gentry. The David Frankses of Philadelphia became members of the Christian establishment. Richa never married. Nothing is known about the youngest girls, Poyer and Rebecca.[79]

Some scholars have suggested that Abigaill was the cause of her children's disaffection, because she courted secular and enlightened thought. That is too facile an explanation, and also one tainted by the "blame the mother" syndrome.[80] Rather, the explanation lies in the powerful realm of social and cultural forces. At the social level, in the small universe of Jews in New York City, there simply were not enough suitable mates to go around, especially when class and background were considered. More to the point, very little overt prejudice existed against Jews in the colonies during the early eighteenth century; they were welcomed into New York society, American society, in a manner that did not exist elsewhere in the world. Jews were not forced to be clannish; they were quite free to move out into the broader society. Social class, in many respects, counted more than religion as a mechanism for group identification.

The question may be asked, then, why was it that Abigaill remained so fiercely identified as Jewish in the face of these social and cultural forces? Was her generation of immigrants merely a bridge to assimilation? The answers to these question are less obvious. Clearly some immigrants did deny their Judaism and slip into the mainstream; it would have been easy in the colonial environment. Most did not, and, against great odds, they persisted in forming communities, retaining their demanding religious practices, supporting synagogues and leaders. The best explanation seems to lie in what historians call a collective memory, a connection with people from the past that continues into the present. The bond may exist with history, with ancient ritual, with one's parents and family. It is a difficult bond to maintain in a world that looks to tomorrow, that promises a bright future to its working immigrants.[81]

Abigaill Levy Franks sensed that bond strongly, and she did it in her own, deeply personal way. Most intensely, she believed that her children would live better lives if they stayed within the fold and practiced the tradition. She acknowledged that the ancient ritual needed to be modernized, and said that she would follow the reformer, but she did not conceive of stepping outside Judaism. With all its failings for her, her religion served her as the gyroscope for negotiating her identity. For a time, she had the capacity to straddle two great cultural streams and find the merit of both without sensing the tension between them.

Abigaill Franks's world of provincial New York has disappeared, but her story resonates more than two and a half centuries later, because many of the challenges she faced are familiar. As a mother, she thought and behaved from sound standards that she believed would form her children into good family members, good Jews, and good citizens. She weathered separations and disappointment from some of her children, while holding fast to her values. She herself lived by those values, and she expected no less of them. In the end, she maintained her integrity, and that afforded her peace and also some humor.

The letter that concludes this correspondence, written some eight years before her death, reflects the major themes that occupied Abigaill's thoughts during her decade and a half of letter-writing: family, books, the little world of New York, the big world of war and politics. Her character shines as she wittily chides her brother Isaac for "the Noise" he made because she claimed seniority of age; as she expresses affection for this son whom she had not seen for fifteen years, admitting that "her constant thought And wish is all Your Welfare"; as she describes her pleasure in the "views and prospects" of her summer house in "harlemtown" and as she reviews books that she had recently read. Most typically the admonition in her postscript speaks volumes for her loving relationship with HertSey: "Must take the Peaches from amongst the peper and put fresh Vinegar to em and Some Spice."[82]

NOTES

1 For Abigaill's dates, I have used Leo Hershkowitz and Isidore S. Meyer, eds., *Letters of the Franks Family (1733-1748)* (Waltham, Mass., 1968), xvi (hereafter Hershkowitz). I spell Abigaill with two lls because that is the way she signed her name.

2 Elaine Forman Crane, ed., *The Diary of Elizabeth Drinker: The Life Cycle of an Eighteenth-Century Woman* (Boston, 1994); Laurel Thatcher Ulrich, *A Midwife's Tale: The Life of Martha Ballard, Based on Her Diary, 1785-1812* (New York, 1990).

3 Letter XXVIII, Dec. 5, 1742.

4 Letter I, May 7, 1733.

5 Letter II, July 9, 1733.

6 Letter VI, June 9, 1734.

7 Ibid.

8 Letter XXXVII, Oct. 30, 1748.

9 Carol F. Karlsen and Laurie Crumpacker, eds., *The Journal of Esther Edwards Burr, 1754-1757* (New Haven, 1984); Carla Mulford, ed., *Only for the Eye of a Friend: The Poems of Annis Boudinot Stockton*, (Charlottesville, 1995).

10 The actual date of Moses Levy's arrival is ambiguous. Cathy Matson notes that Levy became a freeman in New York as early as 1695, but by all reports, Bilhah Abigaill was born in London in 1696. Moses may have left his wife behind in London when he emigrated and later returned to England to bring his family to America. Hershkowitz, xvi; Cathy Matson, *Merchants and Empire:*

Introduction xliii

Trading in Colonial New York (Baltimore, 1998), 188. See also N. Taylor Phillips, "The Levy and Seixas Families of Newport and New York," *PAJHS* 4 (1896), 189–213; David de Sola Pool, *Portraits Etched in Stone: Early Jewish Settlers, 1682–1831* (New York, 1952), 198 (hereafter *Portraits*).

11 Eli Faber, *A Time for Planting: The First Migration, 1654–1820* (Baltimore, 1992), 4; Jonathan Sarna, *American Judaism* (New Haven, 2004); Hyman B. Grinstein, *The Rise of the Jewish Community of New York, 1654–1860* (Philadelphia, 1945); Arthur Hertzberg, *The Jews in America* (New York, 1989), 19–20; Jacob R. Marcus, *The Colonial American Jew, 1492–1776*, 3 vols. (Detroit, 1970), I: 215; Jacob R. Marcus, "The Colonial American Jew," in Jonathan D. Sarna et al., eds., *Jews and the Founding of the Republic* (New York, 1985), 4; Jonathan D. Sarna, "The Jews in British America," in Paolo Bernardini and Norman Fiering, eds., *The Jews and the Expansion of Europe to the West, 1450–1800* (New York, 2001); Jonathan D. Sarna, "Colonial Judaism," in David L. Barquist, *Myer Myers: Jewish Silversmith in Colonial New York* (New Haven, 2001); Arnold Wiznitzer, "The Exodus from Brazil and Arrival in New Amsterdam of the Jewish Pilgrim Fathers, 1654," in Abraham J. Karp, ed., *The Jewish Experience in America: Vol. 1, The Colonial Experience* (Waltham, Mass., 1969), 19–36.

12 For women and Yiddish, see Chava Weissler, "Prayers in Yiddish and the Religious World of Ashkenazic Women," in Judith R. Baskin, ed., *Jewish Women in Historical Perspective* (Detroit, 1991), 159–160.

13 For Grace Mears Levy, see *Portraits*, 225–226.

14 Abigaill married young for Jewish women in America; their marriage patterns followed those of New England women during the same period, whose average age was 22.9 years. Jacob Franks was eight years her senior, following the prevailing pattern for men. Doris Groshen Daniels, "Colonial Jewry: Religion, Domestic, and Social Relations," *AJHQ* 66 (1977), 392–395. Also see Laurel Thatcher Ulrich, *Good Wives: Image and Reality in the Lives of Women in Northern New England, 1650–1750* (New York, 1983), 6; Philip Greven, *Four Generations: Population, Land, and Family in Colonial Andover, Massachusetts* (Ithaca, 1970), 117–120, 206–209.

15 Much later, in 1765, Abigaill's son Moses, who by that time had moved to London, married another cousin, also Phila, daughter of his uncle Aaron Franks. In addition to Phila, daughter of Abigaill and Jacob Franks, there are two other Phila Frankses in this story; clearly Phila was a popular family name. See Rachel Daiches-Dubens, "Eighteenth-Century Anglo-Jewry in and around Richmond, Surrey," *TJHSE* 18 (1953–1954), 143–170. Hershkowitz 71–72. For intermarriage within Jewish families, see Virginia D. Harrington, *The New York Merchant on the Eve of the American Revolution* (New York, 1935), 18.

16 The family name of Jacob Franks's sister Abigail is variously written as

Solomons, Salomons, and several other variations by Abigaill. See Daiches-Dubin, "Eighteenth-Century Anglo-Jewry," 150. Also Hershkowitz, passim.

17 Letter XX, Apr. 26, 1741.

18 Letter XXI, June 21, 1741.

19 For birth patterns, see Mary Beth Norton, *Liberty's Daughters: The Revolutionary Experience of American Women, 1750-1800* (Boston, 1980), 72.

20 Letter III, Oct. 7, 1733.

21 On women's education in colonial America, see Thomas Woody, *A History of Women's Education in the United States*, 2 vols. (New York, 1929); Lyle Koehler, *A Search for Power* (Urbana, Ill. 1980), 42; Norton, *Liberty's Daughters*, 262-63; Ulrich, *Good Wives*, 43-44.

22 Carl Bridenbaugh, *Cities in the Wilderness: The First Century of Urban Life in America 1625-1742* (New York, 1955), 143; Joyce D. Goodfriend, *Before the Melting Pot: Society and Culture in Colonial New York City, 1664-1730* (Princeton, 1992), 112, 134; Matson, *Merchants*, 128; Gary B. Nash, *The Urban Crucible: Social Change, Political Consciousness, and the Origins of the American Revolution* (Cambridge, Mass., 1979), 19. Bridenbaugh (49) notes that the nucleus of the free African community was formed in 1644, when the governor freed 11 slaves and their wives after 19 years of service. After a 1712 insurrection, manumission of slaves was discontinued by British law, and slave property was forfeited to the British Crown. Elizabeth Blackmar, *Manhattan for Rent, 1785-1850* (Ithaca, 1989), 20-21.

23 Marcus, *Colonial American Jew*, 1: 308. In contrast to most Jewish estimates, which follow Marcus, Goodfriend estimates the Jews as 1 percent of New York City's population in 1695, in *Before the Melting Pot*, 67. After 1790, when the first national census was taken, it was possible to measure the Jewish population more reliably, and it appears that about 250 Jews lived in New York City in a population of 33,130, or about .73 percent. Ira Rosenwaike, "An Estimate and Analysis of the Jewish population of the United States in 1790," in Karp, *The Jewish Experience in America*, 1: 391-413, especially 395-396.

24 Bridenbaugh, *Cities in the Wilderness*, 3; Nan A. Rothschild, *New York City Neighborhoods: The 18th Century* (New York, 1990), 11. For a contemporary (1704) description of New York City, see Sarah Kemble Knight, *The Journal of Madam Knight* (Boston, 1972), 28-31.

25 Rothschild, *New York City Neighborhoods*, 16.

26 Bridenbaugh, *Cities in the Wilderness*, 95. Patricia U. Bonomi, *A Factious People: Politics and Society in Colonial New York* (New York, 1971), 22-26. For the significant Huguenot population in New York, see Jon Butler, *The Huguenots in America: A Refugee People in New World Society* (Cambridge, Mass., 1983), 144-198.

27 A measure passed by the Common Council of New York in 1685 prohibited the exercise of religion by those who did not profess faith in Christ. Nevertheless, Jews worshiped in private homes and after the mid-1690s in rented space, while officials overlooked the practice. Bridenbaugh, *Cities in the Wilderness*, 102; Edwin G. Burrows and Mike Wallace, *Gotham: A History of New York City to 1898* (New York, 1999), 133; Marcus, *The Colonial American Jew*, 1: 404–411, 483–489; David and Tamara de Sola Pool, *An Old Faith in the New World: Portrait of Shearith Israel, 1654-1954* (New York, 1955), 39; Faber, *A Time for Planting*, 55; Sarna, *American Judaism*. It should be noted that into the mid-eighteenth century there were political squabbles among Anglicans, Presbyterians, and Lutherans over the establishment of new congregations in New York. See Cynthia A. Kierner, *Traders and Gentlefolk: The Livingstons of New York, 1675–1790* (Ithaca, 1992), 176–178.

28 Bridenbaugh, *Cities in the Wilderness*, 114–15; Rothschild, *New York City Neighborhoods*, 43.

29 Bridenbaugh, *Cities in the Wilderness*, 11–17, 55; Burrows and Wallace, *Gotham*, 110; Rothschild, *New York City Neighborhoods*, 11. A famous drawing of the New York harbor, known as the "Burgis View," done by an otherwise unknown engraver, William Burgis, shows the density of buildings along the Manhattan shore line as it appeared from Brooklyn in 1717 (Collection of the New-York Historical Society).

30 Rothschild uses "neighborhood" to mean a group of people who interact in a particular spacial unit. Each neighborhood has an image, and the people share some social characteristics. Rothschild, *New York City Neighborhoods*, 18–20.

31 Ibid., 91–92, 182–183. I thank Holly Snyder for pointing out that some historians dispute the clustering of Jews in one New York City neighborhood in this early period. See also Doris Groshen Daniels, "Colonial Jewry: Religion, Domestic and Social Relations," *AJHQ* 66 (1977), 375–400, especially 382. For the clustering of Jews into "neighborhoods" two centuries later, see Moses Rischin, *The Promised City: New York's Jews, 1870–1914* (Cambridge, Mass., 1962).

32 Bridenbaugh, *Cities in the Wilderness*, 191.

33 Ibid., 17–18, 152–170, especially 160; Rothschild, *New York City Neighborhoods*, 11–12. See also Graham Hodges, *New York City Cartmen, 1667-1850* (New York, 1985).

34 Bridenbaugh, *Cities in the Wilderness*, 370–371, 287, 448, 236–237, 397; Rothschild, *New York City Neighborhoods*, 21.

35 Harrington, *New York Merchant*, 22; Rothschild, *New York City Neighborhoods*, 15. See Michael Pye, *The Drowning Room* (New York, 1995) for a historical

novel set in seventeenth-century New Amsterdam and New York that especially captures the conditions of colonial life.

36 The Frankses' neighbors were Philipses, Livingstons, Van Cortlandts, Bayards. See Letter VI, June 9, 1734.

37 The position of Jews as citizens in New York was ambiguous. There was the law, and then there was practice. By law, Jews could not become citizens or hold public office. The so-called Donegan Constitution of 1683 confirmed earlier British law, affirming religious liberty to Christians. In essence, this was not changed until 1740, when the British Naturalization Law opened citizenship to all residents who had been in the colonies for seven years. The laws were enforced idiosyncratically, however. Early in the eighteenth century, Jews could become endenizened, that is they were allowed to conduct businesses in the colony. Some were even elected "constable," a nondesirable position which in effect served a policing function, but a public office nonetheless. Jews may even have voted in some local elections. The religious restrictions were not directed at Jews alone; earlier, Presbyterians were not welcomed, nor Quakers, nor especially Catholics. See Burrows and Wallace, *Gotham*, 91, 114–115, 133–135; Faber, *A Time for Planting*, 101; Richard B. Morris, "Civil Liberties and the Jewish Tradition in Early America," in Karp, *The Jewish Experience in America*, 1: 404–423, especially 408–410; Sarna, *American Judaism*.

38 Marcus, *The Colonial American Jew*, 3: 1198; Marcus, "The American Colonial Jew," 7. Todd Endelman describes the shifting political consciousness of Jews in eighteenth-century England, where during the early part of the century they primarily identified themselves as Jewish. Later, as they became more affluent and socially accepted, many considered themselves first as English. At the same time the most acculturated among the Jews began to seek political rights. Endelman, *The Jews of Georgian England 1714–1830, Tradition and Change in a Liberal Society*, 2nd ed. (Ann Arbor, 1999), 272–276.

39 Letter VI, June 9, 1734. It is not clear what Abigaill meant by "town Side." It seems to imply the governor's faction, including the Delanceys and the Philipses. Abigaill's closest friends, however, appear to be among the opposition, the Morrises (Mrs. Kearny, mentioned in the previous letter, was a Morris daughter) and Livingstons. Yet, while the "town" folk tended to be royalist, they also numbered among them many merchants, which would indicate Franks sympathy. For the ambiguity of parties, or factions, see Bonomi, *A Factious People*, 56–102, and passim.

40 New York was a royal colony, meaning that it had a Crown-appointed governor, who in turn selected a Council, as well as a popularly elected Assembly. Bonomi, *A Factious People*, 32, 158.

41 Letter V, Dec. 16, 1733.

42 The story of the Cosby-Morris dispute has been told in many places, especially in Bonomi, *A Factious People,* 103–139. Also see Burrows and Wallace, *Gotham,* 151–157; Michael Kammen, *Colonial New York: A History* (New York, 1975), 202–210; Stanley Nider Katz, *Newcastle's New York: Anglo-American Politics, 1732–1753* (Cambridge, Mass., 1968), 63–68; Nash, *The Urban Crucible,* 140–148.

43 Letter VII, Dec. 25, 1734.

44 For Zenger, see Bonomi, *A Factious People,* 115–118; Katz, *Newcastle's New York,* 44–47; Leonard W. Levy, "Did the Zenger Case Really Matter? Freedom of the Press in Colonial New York," *William and Mary Quarterly,* 3rd. Ser., 18 (Jan. 1960), 35–50. See also Leonard W. Levy, *Freedom of the Press from Zenger to Jefferson* (Durham, N.C., 1996); and Leonard W. Levy, *The Emergence of a Free Press* (New York, 1985), 38–45.

45 Letter VI, June 9, 1734. For the pioneering study of conflicts over land grants in colonial New York, see Irving Mark, *Agrarian Conflicts in Colonial New York, 1711–1775* (New York, 1940).

46 Letter IX, June 15, 1735.

47 Letter XII, Dec. 3, 1736.

48 For a survey of women's constitutional rights and obligations from the 1770s to the 1990s, see Linda K. Kerber, *No Constitutional Right to Be Ladies: Women and Obligations of Citizenship* (New York, 1998).

49 Bonomi, *A Factious People,* 107 n. 5 and 121 n. 26.

50 Abigaill's letters are frequently cited by historians, though strangely, there has been no full-scale study of her life. See, for instance, Burrows and Wallace, *Gotham,* 134, 175; Goodfriend, *Before the Melting Pot,* 268 n. 146; and Kammen, *Colonial New York,* 232, 270. Within the Jewish-American historic literature, especially of the colonial period, citations to Abigaill are ubiquitous.

51 Gerardus Duyckinck came from a family of eighteenth-century craftsmen-limners, who also "decorated glass and painted fire buckets." See Mary Black and Jean Lipman, *American Folk Painting* (New York, 1987), 2; also Letter VI, June 9, 1734 n. 17. The attribution of Abigaill's portrait, as well as of the companion portrait of her husband, Jacob Franks, and other paintings of the Levy-Franks family, is now contested. See Richard Brilliant, *Facing the New World: Jewish Portraits in Colonial and Federal America* (New York, 1997), 30; Ellen Smith, "Portraits of a Community: The Image and Experience of Early American Jews," in ibid., 9–21, especially 20 n. 10; and Erica E. Hirshler, "The Levy-Franks Family Portraits," *The Magazine Antiques,* Nov. 1990, 1025–27.

52 This point is clearly made by the accompanying essays to the catalog of the 1998 exhibit at the Jewish Museum in New York City. See Richard Brilliant, "Portraits as Silent Claimants: Jewish Class Aspirations and Representational

Strategies in Colonial and Federal America," in Brilliant, *Facing the New World,* 1; and Smith, "Portraits of a Community," 12–13, 20. Ellen Smith also notes that the Levy-Franks portrait series "are the earliest surviving portraits of colonial American Jews, and the oldest family series portraits to survive in all of American painting." Ibid., 11.

53 David de Sola Pool, *The Mill Street Synagogue (1730–1787) of the Congregation Shearith Israel* (New York, 1930), 23, 71–72; Pool and Pool, *Old Faith in a New World,* 266, 460.

54 The "Mill Street Synagogue," as the original building is often called, has long since moved uptown, where it is still known as Shearith Israel. Services are still conducted in the Sephardic form. The small original building survives and has been reconstructed at Shearith Israel, where services take place regularly. Pool, *The Mill Street Synagogue.*

55 Ibid., 50.

56 Letter IV, Oct. 10, 1733.

57 *Tefilin,* in Hebrew, are small leather cubes, containing Scriptures, that orthodox men wear during weekday morning prayers, one bound to the left arm and the other to the forehead.

58 Letter XV, Oct. 17, 1739. Of all immigrants to New York in the colonial period, Catholics, along with Quakers, were the most persecuted.

59 *Femes couvert* refers to a wife becoming one with her husband after marriage, so that most of her rights, including children and property, revert to her husband. See Norton, *Liberty's Daughters,* 45–50.

60 Letter XXV, Dec. 20, 1741.

61 Another interpretation of Hertsey is suggested by Hershkowitz. The stag or hart was the symbol of the tribe of Naphtali and hence the derivation. Further, "Hirz" or "Herz" probably comes from the older Judeo-German "Hirsch," which means hart or deer. Hershkowitz, Letter I, n. 1. Todd Endelman notes that Yiddish continued to be the language of Jews in eastern Europe. Jews who settled in England, however, learned to speak in the vernacular, though some continued to use Yiddish among themselves. It appears that Jews who settled in British America followed a similar pattern. See Endelman, *The Jews of Georgian England,* 123–24. Though we use it to denote the Judeo-German language, the OED indicates that the term "Yiddish" did not come into use until the end of the nineteenth century.

62 The Franks genealogy (see infra) has no dates for Richa. She must have been close in age to Phila, for they were best friends. Also, Richa had admirers by the late 1730s. See below.

63 "I fancy Mr. Pecheco's quarle is her being a Tudesco," Abigaill wrote,

Introduction xlix

using the Sephardic term for Ashkenazic Jews. "The Portugueze where in a Violent Uproar abouth it." Letter XVII, Aug. 3, 1740.

64 Letter XXVIII, Dec. 5, 1742. Gomez may have been unattractive to the Franks women, but it turns out he was a very successful businessman. David Gomez, as profiled by David de Sola Pool, was close to Abigaill in age, born in 1697, which may account for her objection to him. See *Portraits,* 474–475, 217–223. See also references to David in a sketch of his brother in Leon Huhner, "Daniel Gomez, a Pioneer Merchant of Early New York" in Karp, ed., *The Jewish Experience in America,* 1: 175–193.

65 Letter XXV, Dec. 20, 1741.

66 For a description of the "companionate marriage," see Lawrence Stone, *The Family, Sex, and Marriage in England, 1500–1800* (New York, 1977), 324–404. But see Alan Macfarlane, *Marriage and Love in England: Modes of Reproduction, 1300–1840* (Oxford, 1986) for a corrective view.

67 Letter XXX, Apr. 1, 1743.

68 Letter XXXI, June 7, 1743.

69 Ibid. Indeed, the Delanceys had social pedigree and political clout as a Huguenot family that early left the French Church to become Anglicans. Jon Butler suggests that given Oliver's secrecy about his marriage to Phila, he too may have been concerned about his family's reaction to it. See Butler, *Huguenots,* 189, 193.

70 Letter XXXI, June 7, 1743.

71 By Jewish folk custom, a child who married out of the religion was considered dead, and the parents sat *shiva,* a period of mourning. While it is not mentioned that Abigaill sat *shiva,* she acknowledged that she remained indoors at home.

72 Letter XXXII, Nov. 22, 1743.

73 Letter XXXIII, Nov. 25, 1745.

74 Ibid. David Franks became a wealthy and prominent citizen of Philadelphia. He also was a loyalist during the Revolutionary War and lost his fortune. He went to England for several years and then returned to Philadelphia. Although his wife and children were Christians, David never renounced Judaism. See Cecil Roth, "Some Jewish Loyalists in the War of American Independence," in Karp, *The Jewish Experience in America,* 1: 292–318, especially 307–309.

75 Letter XXXV, Jan. 4, 1747. Abigaill was not alone in her appraisal of New York's social life. John Watts, a prosperous merchant, condemned his native city. "Ignorance, Vanity, Dress, and Dissipation [were] the reigning Characteristics of their insipid Lives," he wrote of its people in the mid-eighteenth century. Quoted in Kierner, *Traders and Gentlefolk,* 143.

76 Letter XVI, July 6, 1740.

77 David de Sola Pool, "The Earliest Extant Minute Book of Shearith Israel," *PAJHS* 21 (1913), 68, 87, 97, 99.

78 Hershkowitz, xviii. Her known Jewish grandchildren either converted or married out.

79 Marcus, *The Colonial American Jew*, 3: 1151–1152. Daiches-Dubin suggests that a Rebecca Franks moved to England and lived with her brother Naphtali's family. "Eighteenth-Century Anglo-Jewry," 159. The third edition of Malcolm H. Stern, *First American Jewish Families* (Baltimore, 1991), 75, notes that Richa married in England "sometime after 1789." Since she was courted by David Gomez in 1740, that would mean she was quite advanced in age by 1789, which makes that marriage questionable.

80 The term comes from David Spiegel, "Mothering, Fathering, and Mental Illness," in Barrie Thorne with Marilyn Yalom, eds., *Rethinking the Family* (New York, 1982), 95–110. For the concept in Judaism, see Marion A. Kaplan, *The Making of the Jewish Middle Class* (New York, 1991), 64.

81 In a recent article, several historians have noted the importance of this concept. See Peter Seixas, Peter Sterns, and Sam Wineburg, "History, Memory, Research, and the Schools," *American Historical Association Perspectives* 37 (Mar. 1999), 1 ff. The classic modern statement of this concept is Yosef Hayim Yerushalmi, *Zakhor: Jewish History and Jewish Memory* (Seattle, 1982). The point is made for all religions by Jack Miles, *God: A Biography* (New York, 1995), 3–4. See also Peter Novick, *The Holocaust in American Life* (Boston, 1999), 3–6, 170–91; and Steven J. Zipperstein, *Imagining Russian Jewry: Memory, History, Identity* (Seattle, 1999).

82 Letter XXXVII, Oct. 30, 1748.

Editorial Method

The editors have attempted to present these letters as literally as possible. For the sake of accuracy and to retain the form and spirit in which Abigaill wrote to her son, we have basically not changed the spelling with all its errors, the dating, or the sentence and paragraph structure. In the interest of clarity and ease of reproduction, however, a number of changes have been made. Punctuation has been judiciously added in order to modernize and clarify Abigaill's early eighteenth-century style. She used dashes to denote periods, commas, and semicolons, but since they were used indiscriminately, they have been omitted in print. The rules which the editors followed in the transcription of the material are as follows:

Superior letters as in the abbreviations Capt, rec^{ed}, Sep^t have been lowered. In addition, all abbreviations have been expanded, and the missing letters placed within square brackets. Hence, Capt[ain], rec[eiv]ed. Sept[ember]. Abbreviated names such as I^s have become Is[aac] and Napt^y, Napht[al]i. In the case of the latter name, when it was spelled out in the letter, the original spelling has been retained, but where it has been abbreviated, a corrected spelling has been used.

Other eighteenth-century abbreviations used by Abigaill have also been expanded. The thorn [y] is written as th, thus y^n, y^t, y^m become respectively then, that, them. The word "ye," however, has been retained, since we believe it will present no problem in understanding.

The tilde is replaced by the letter or letters represented in brackets. The ampersand is retained.

Typical of the time, Abigaill Franks used i and j interchangeably enjoy or enioy, jest or iest. The editors have changed such uses of "i" to "j" to conform with modern spelling.

The form of the letters has been preserved except that the names of the correspondents and the date are always placed at the top of the letter in brackets. The day of the week has been inserted within brackets. The address and endorsement, if any, are labeled as such and placed at the foot of the letter in the center. Where a missing or unintelligible word or words are conjecturable they have been supplied in brackets.

One of the major problems in editing these letters was Abigaill Franks's consistent omission of first names. Her Lindsays, Malcolms, Williamses, Needhams, Livingstons, etc., are thus very difficult to identify properly. Added to this is the confusion created by many contemporaries with the same names, for example, Isaac Levy or Simson Levy. These confusions are not cleared up in the letters, since Abigaill obviously felt that her references would be understandable to her son. We have attempted to present various possibilities, and to indicate which person in our opinion was referred to.

All dates in the letters are Old Style and have been printed as found. England and the colonies did not accept the New or Gregorian calendar until September 1752. New Year's or Lady Day was March 25th, although January 1st was by the eighteenth century considered by many as the beginning of the New Year. To translate dates used here to New Style, add eleven days.

Abbreviations

AJHQ *American Jewish Historical Quarterly.*
AJHS   American Jewish Historical Society.
AJHSL American Jewish Historical Society Library.
AJQ *American Jewish Quarterly.*
Burghers *Burghers and Freemen of New York, New-York Historical Society Collections, 1885* (New York, 1886).
Calendar Edmund B. O'Callaghan, *Calendar of New York Colonial Commissions, 1680–1770* (New York, 1929).
Colden Papers *Cadwallader Colden Letters and Papers, 1711–1775, New-York Historical Society Collections,* 9 vols (New York, 1918–1937).
Colonial Laws *Colonial Laws of New York from the Year 1664 to the Revolution,* 5 vols. (Albany, 1894–1896).
Con. Lib. Conveyance Liber, New York City Register's Office, 31 Chambers Street, New York City.
Dictionary Joseph R. Rosenbloom, *A Biographical Dictionary of Early American Jews* (Lexington, Ky., 1960).
DNB Sir Leslie Stephen and Sir Sidney Lee, eds., *Dictionary of National Biography,* 23 vols. (London, 1921–1922).
Doc. Rel. Edmund B. O'Callaghan and Berthold Fernow, *Documents Relative to the Colonial History of the State of New York,* 15 vols. (Albany, 1856–1887).
Entry Books Entry Books, 1728–1766, New York State Library, Albany.
Gentleman's Magazine *Gentleman's Magazine: Or Monthly Intelligencer* (London, 1731–1800).

Hershkowitz   Leo Hershkowitz and Isidore Meyer, eds. *Letters of the Franks Family (1733–1748)* (Waltham, Mass., 1968).

HDC   Historical Documents Collections, Queens College of the City University of New York, Flushing, New York City.

HSP   Historical Society of Pennsylvania.

Iconography   Isaac N. P. Stokes, *Iconography of Manhattan Island*, 6 vols. (New York, 1895–1928).

Jay Day Book   Peter Jay Day Book, New-York Historical Society Library.

Jay Ledger   Peter Jay Ledger, New-York Historical Society Library.

Jewish Obituaries   Albert M. Hyamson, "Jewish Obituaries in the *Gentleman's Magazine*," *MJHSE* 4 (1942), 33–60.

MCC   *Minutes of the Common Council of the City of New York, 1675–1776*, 8 vols. (New York, 1905).

MCM   Mayor's Court Minutes, New York County Clerk's Office, 31 Chambers Street, New York City.

MCNY   Museum of the City of New York.

MCP   Mayor's Court Papers, New York County Clerk's Office.

Minute Book   "Minute Book of the Congregation Shearith Israel," *PAJHS* 21 (1913), 1–171.

MJHSE   *Miscellanies of the Jewish Historical Society of England*.

Morris Papers   Robert Hunter Morris Papers, Rutgers University Library, New Brunswick, N.J.

NOL   Naval Office Lists, Public Record Office, London, CO 5/1222–1229.

NYAL   New York Assessment Lists, Vols. 1699–1702, 1702–1709, 1722–1734, New York City Comptroller's Office, Rhinelander Building, 238 William Street, New York City.

NYCCO   New York County Clerk's Office, 31 Chambers Street, New York City.

NYHSC   *Abstracts of Wills. New-York Historical Society Collections*, 14 vols. (New York, 1893–1906).

NYHSL   New-York Historical Society Library.

NYPL New York Public Library.
PAJHS *Publications of the American Jewish Historical Society.*
PCC Prerogative Court of Canterbury, Somerset House, London.
Portraits David de Sola Pool, *Portraits Etched in Stone. Early Jewish Settlers, 1682–1831* (New York, 1952).
State Papers Calendar of State Papers. Colonial Series. America and West Indies, Vols. 42 and 43 (London, 1953, 1963).
TVR Trinity Vault Records, Library of the Trinity Corporation, 32 Trinity Place, New York City.
TJHSE *Transactions of the Jewish Historical Society of England.*
Valentine's Manual David T. Valentine, ed., *Manual of the Corporate of the City of New York* (New York, 1842–1865).
Wills Leo Hershkowitz, ed., *Wills of Early New York Jews (1704–1799)* (New York, 1967).

FRANKS GENEALOGY

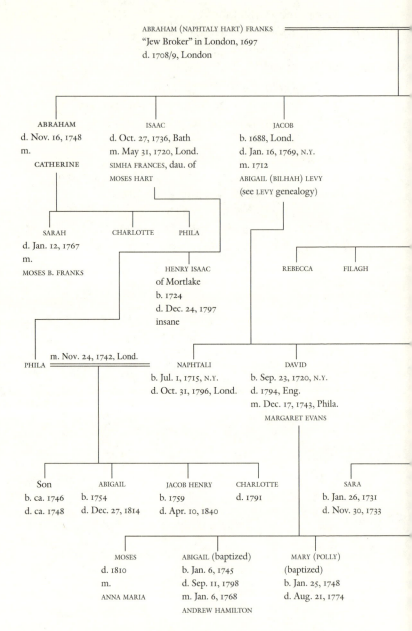

Franks Genealogy. Compiled by Malcolm H. Stern. F.A.S.G. from his *Americans of Jewish Descent*. Copyright 1960. Hebrew Union College Press, Cincinnati, Ohio. Used by permission.

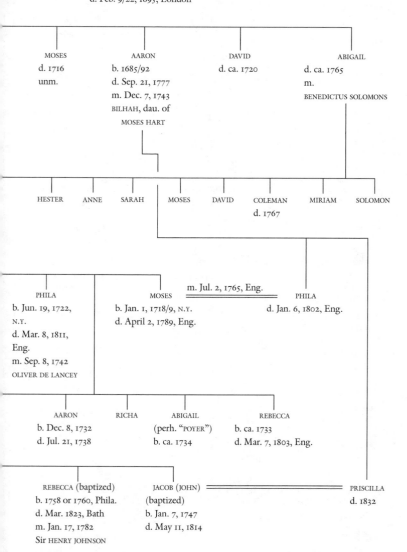

LEVY GENEALOGY

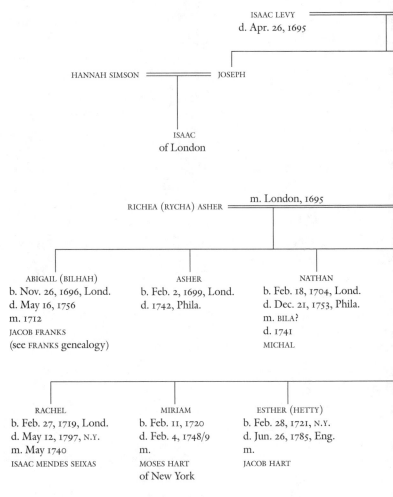

Levy Genealogy. Compiled by Malcolm H. Stern, F.A.S.G. from his *Americans of Jewish Descent.* Copyright 1960. Hebrew Union College Press, Cincinnati, Ohio. Used by permission.

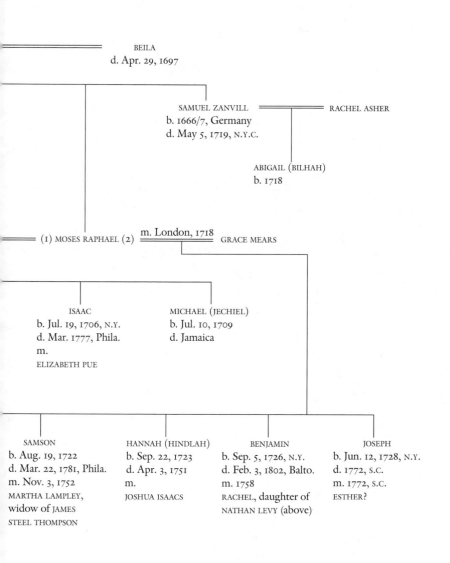

Illustrations

Abigaill Levy Franks [Bilhah Abigail Levy] (1696–1756).
Attributed to Gerardus Duyckinck (1695–1746). c. 1735.
Courtesy of the American Jewish Historical Society.

Dear Hertley

My Last by this Vessle was friday Just Sabath Since wich by the Post
I have received two of yours by Via boston bearing Date yͤ 26 Janʳʸ & 4ᵗʰ Febʳʸ
and allso Some from your father of Severall date's they all Confirm the then
injoying a happy State of Health In Company of all friends my wishes will be Compleat
If this finds you Still in the Same Agreeable Situation

you will find Some Postage to pay by this Every one being writing
to Assure you themselves of theire good Will Could I have my Other two Letters back
again I would put all the Contents in this One not that I think you will be
uneasy at the Charge but Still its to No purpose to have Soe many Letters About
nothing

I Observe yͤ uncommon Article you mention Concerning the mans
Teaching to Write in a fortnight And the Progress Miss franks has made
in it pray my Love to her the Pretty Creeter your inclyna favour of her good Sence
& aptness to Learn has made me beleive a great Vallue for her (as indeed I must
have for Every thing belonging to Mrs: franks) and tell Miss I shall be Very
glad to have her keep a Corispondence with her namesake who will be Very Proud
of the Favour I Shall take Care by the next Oppertunity Let Phila write her
a Letter you would be Amazed to See how she is grown she is much Taller then
david I shall put her next week att Mr Brownalls

your fathers not bringing any goods makes most People
Imagine he intends for London & I cant Convince em to the Contrary every body
Seems Very Much Concerned at it Mrs Moore Sent for your Sister & Look't as
Ever she heard it and Atharbe Concerned that she was glad to get from em
I Confess tho there is nothing in it Stil it Gives me a Secret pleasure to
Observe the faire Character Our familys has in the place by Jews & Christians
who Express a Regreet & I beleive Some are Realy Sincere I think its the
greatest happyness a Person can injoy Next to the having a good Conscience
for As Addison Says a good Conscience is to the Soul wath health is to the body

I have just now Sent for the box from burling pray make my thanks
due for the first Vol: of Addison & Lett me know wat books you have made
Choise of for your Uncle Isack My Respects to all friends Sr Colly is in Raptures
to think of goeing home I wish him Very Well & hope it will be to his advantage
I Salute you with my blessing and Am

Dear Hertley your Affectionate Mother
Abigaill Franks

New York May yͤ 7 1733
to Nap: Franks

Naphtali Franks (1715–1796). Thomas Hudson.
Courtesy of the Jewish Museum, London.

Moses Raphael Levy (c. 1665–1728). Attributed to Gerardus Duyckinck (1695–1746). c. 1720–28. Courtesy of the Museum of the City of New York. Bequest of Alphonse H. Kursheedt.

Grace Mears Levy (1694–1740). Attributed to Gerardus Duyckinck (1695–1746). c. 1720–28. Courtesy of the Museum of the City of New York. Bequest of Alphonse H. Kursheedt.

Jacob Franks (1688–1769). Attributed to Gerardus Duyckinck (1695–1746). c. 1735. Courtesy of the American Jewish Historical Society.

Phila Franks (1722–1811). Attributed to Gerardus Duyckinck (1695–1746). c. 1735. Courtesy of the American Jewish Historical Society.

Children of Abigaill and Jacob Franks.
Attributed to Gerardus Duyckinck (1695–1746). c. 1735.
Courtesy of the American Jewish Historical Society.

THE LETTERS OF
Abigaill Levy Franks
1733–1748

I
[Abigaill Franks to Naphtali Franks, May 7, 1733]

Dear HertSey[1]

My last by this Vessle was friday, Just Sabath Since wich by the Post I have received two of yours by Via boston, bearing Date ye 26th Jan[uar]y & ye 20th Feb[ruar]y and AllSoe Some from your father of Severall date's. They All Comfirm the[e] then Injoying A happy State of Health In Company of all friends. My Wishes Will be Compleat If this finds you Still in the Same Agreeable Situation.

You will find Some Postage to pay by this, Every one being willing to Assure you themselves of theire good Will. Could I have my Other two Letters back Again, I Would put all the Contents in this One. Not that I think you will be Uneassy at the Charge, but Still its to Noe purpose to have Soe many Letters Abouth Nothing.

I observe ye Uncomon Article you mention Concerning the mans Teaching to Write in a fortnight[2] And the Progress Miss franks[3] has

---

1 Hertsey or Heartsey, the opening salutation to most of the letters written by Abigaill Bilhah Franks [=A.F.] to her son Naphtali [=N.F.] was a term of endearment. See above xxxiii.

2 A.F., an avid reader of the *Gentleman's Magazine*, first published in London in 1731, was probably referring to an article which read in part: "I can almost excuse the hyperbolical Style of a Grammarian who had just published a proposal of a new Scheme of Grammar, and Method of Instruction, by which the Grounds of Language may be learned in a few Hours, so as to read an Author and write intellegibly, because his pretences are supported by Probabilities." *Gentleman's Magazine* 2 (1732), 742. The advertisement alluded to was *The Whetstone*, a "proposal of a new Scheme of Grammar . . . by which the Grounds of Language may be learned in a few Hours . . . price 6d. per 5 pages." Ibid., 5.

3 Phila Franks [of England], born in 1715, was the daughter of Isaac and Simha (Hart) Franks. Isaac Franks was a wealthy English merchant and brother

made in it. Pray my Love to her. The Pritty Charecter you [give] her in favour of her good Sence & aptness to Learn has made me have a great Vallue for her (As indeed I must have for Every thing belonging to Mr. Is[aac] Franks), and tell Miss I Shall be Very glad to have her keep a Corispondence with her name Sake, Whoe will be Very Proud of the Favour. I Shall take Care by the Next Oppertunity to Let Phila[4] write her a Letter. You would be Amazed to See how She is Grown. She is much Taller then david.[5] I shall put her her [sic] Next Week Att Mr. Brownalls.[6]

Your fathers not bringing any goods makes most People Imagin he intends for London,[7] & I cant Convince e'm to the Contrary. Every

---

of Jacob Franks (=J.F.). Phila later married N.F. (see Letter XXVIII, Dec. 5, 1742). Samuel Oppenheim gives her year of death as 1765. "Genealogical Notes on Jacob Franks," *PAJHS* 25 (1917), 77.

4 Phila Franks, the daughter of J.F. and A.F., who was born in New York on June 19, 1722, and died in England March 8, 1811, was at the time of this letter almost eleven years old. Simon W. Rosendale, "A Document Concerning the Franks Family," *PAJHS*, 1 (1893), 103–104; *Jewish Obituaries,* 40. Phila, a popular name in the Franks family, was also the name of her cousins Phila Franks (of England) and Phila Salomons, a daughter of Abigail Salomons, J.F.'s sister. Will of Moses Franks, Fox 162, PCC.

5 David Franks, son of J.F. and A.F., was born in New York on or about September 23, 1720, and probably died in England in 1794, and not, as many believe, in Philadelphia in 1793 as a result of yellow fever. Con. Lib. 32, cp. 41; Rosendale, "A Document Concerning the Franks Family"; Hilda F. Finberg, "Jewish Residents in Eighteenth-Century Twickenham," *TJHSE* 16 (1952), 130.

6 George Brownell resided in 1731 near the Customs House where he "Taught Reading Writing Cyperhing, Merchant Accompts, Latin, Greek etc. also Dancing, Plain-Work Flourishing Embroidery and various Sorts of Works. Any Person may be taught as private as they please" *Gazette,* June 14, 1731. He was remembered by Benjamin Franklin, one of his pupils, as a "Skilfull master," who was successful by employing "gentle means only." Between 1736 and 1738, he was in Philadelphia, which may indicate his New York stay was not profitable. Carl Bridenbaugh, *Cities in the Wilderness* (New York, 1938), 277, 282–283, 438, 447, and 449.

7 J.F. probably had been or was in Philadelphia at this time. A.F.'s reference to his "not bringing any goods" and "intends for London" indicates he might

body seems Very Much Concerned at it. Mrs. Moore[8] Sent for your Sister As Soon as Ever She heard it And Where Soe Concerned that She was Glad to get from e'm. I Conffess (tho' their is nothing in it), Still it Gives me a Secreet pleasure to Observe the faire Charecter Our Familys has in the place by Jews & Christians,[9] whoe Express a regreet & I bleive Some are Really Sincire. I think its the greatest happyness a Person Can Injoy Next to the haveing a good Conscience, for As Addison Says, A good Conscience is to the Soul wath health is to the body.[10]

I have Just Now Sent for the box from burling.[11] Pray make my thanks due for the first Vol[ume] of Addison[12] & Lett me know Wath books you have made Choice of for your Uncle's Libr[ary]. My Re-

---

have just returned to New York. J.F., like many merchants, made frequent business trips. See Letters VI, June 7, 1734, and VIII, April 11, 1735, for reference to such occasions.

8 Mrs. Frances Lambert Moore (1692–1782) was the wife of Col. John Moore (1686–1749), one of the more prominent merchants and politicians of the city. At David Franks's marriage in 1743 to Margaret Evans, Mrs. Moore's niece by marriage, she became David's aunt.

9 Jewish-Christian relations in New York were a source of pride to A.F. On the whole these relationships were good, with few instances of overt anti-Semitism. One of these occurred in 1737 when the Assembly voted to disenfranchise Jews after a particularly bitter and violent anti-Semitic tirade by William Smith, a member of the Assembly. This Act of 1737 did not bind further Assemblies, since Jews did vote in subsequent elections. Peter Kalm writing in 1748 found that Jews "enjoy all the privileges common to the other inhabitants of this town and province." Peter Kalm, *Travels into North America* (London, 1772), 1: 191. In 1747, on the other hand, Jacob Franks advertised for the culprits who defaced the Jewish cemetery; *Post-Boy*, July 2, 1747. Acts of this kind, however, were rare.

10 For maxim, see Joseph Addison, *Maxims, Observations, and Reflections, Moral, Political, and Divine* (London, 1719), 1.

11 A.F. probably refers to Samuel Burling, who witnessed the will of Simja De Torres. *Wills*, 81. There was a Burling Slip, fronting on the East River.

12 There were a number of multivolume works of Joseph Addison published prior to this date, including the *Miscellaneous Works of Joseph Addison* (London, 1726), 3 volumes, and a second edition in 1730.

spects to all friends. Coz[i]n Colly [13] is in Raptures to think of goeing home. I wish him Very Well & hope it will be to his advantage. I Salute You with my blessing and Am,

> Dear HertSey, your Afectionate Mother,
> Abigaill Franks

New York [Monday] May ye 7th 1733
to Nap[htali] Franks

II
[Abigaill Franks to Naphtali Franks, July 9, 1733]

Dear HertSey

The Arrivall of the Acceptable bearer of your Letter gave Me Inexpressable Joy. Your Presence would have bin a Vast addition, but As the pres[en]t must give way to the futer and that the hopes of your Stay will in All appearance be Soe much to your advantage, I cant Say but that It in a great Measure Mitigates the Uneassyness I might Else have bin Under. But As I Allways taught my Self that Vallueable Lesson of Rissignation, I have the Consolation to attend this in the hopes of Your Carefull Observence of a due Gratitude and respect to the Admonitions of Your kind Uncles.[1] They have all favoured me

---

13 Colly was the pet name for Coleman Salomons [Solomons], the son of Abigail Solomons, sister of J.F. He was in New York in 1729 and had been living with J.F. and A.F. since 1732 and possibly earlier. He returned to England in 1734, but in December of that year was in Philadelphia, where he appears to have spent some time in jail, probably for debt (see Letter VII, Dec. 25, 1734). Minute Book, p. 21; NYAL, Dock Ward, Feb. 18, 1731/2; Feb. 24, 1732/3; Feb. 23, 1733/4. He died in London early in 1767. Letters of administration were granted to his widow Elizabeth Salomons in June of that year. Letters of Administration, Solomons, PCC. Colly was one of the more troublesome of A.F.'s relations.

1 N.F.'s uncles in England at the time were, on his father's side, Isaac, Aaron, and Abraham Franks and, on his mother's side, Asher and Nathan Levy. Isaac Franks, a wealthy merchant, was reputed at his death in 1736 to have been worth £500,000. *Gentleman's Magazine* 6 (1736), 685. Aaron Franks, almost as affluent

with th[ei]r Letters, wherein they Speak Soe Favourable of you and with Soe much Tenderness that tho' I've all the Gratitude Possiable, my words fall short of wath I think.

Your Uncles, Messrs: Isaac & Aaron, have Assured me of there Endeavours to put you forward, but that they Had not Come to a Determination yet in wath Method. But wathever they Intend, I imagine will be Soe well Considered that the Consequence gives me noe Uneassy thought.

I have Soe Offten recommended You to be Wary in y[ou]r conduct that I will not Again make a Repetion. But this I must recom[men]d to you: not to be Soe free in y[ou]r Discourse on religeon and be more Circumspect in the Observence of some things, Especialy y[ou]r morning Dev[otio]ns. For tho' a Person may think freely and Judge for themselves, they Ought not to be to free of Speach nor to make a Jest of wath ye multitude in A Society think is of the Last Consequence, and As You Observed to me some time agoe, you wondered Any one Could Take amiss if his Neighbour did not goe the Same Road. Pray why are You Soe Intent by your Disputes to think Anyone will follow you? It Shows in one of your Age a Self-Opinion wich Quality I would have you Carfuly avoid, for it will grow opon you with time if not Nipt in the bud. You wrote me Some time agoe you was asked at my brother Ashers[2] to a fish Dinner, but you did not Goe. I Desire you will Never Eat Anything with him Unless it be bread & butter, nor noe where Else where there is the Least doubt of things not done after our Strict Judiacall method. For wathever my thoughts may be Concerning Some Fables, this and Some other foundementalls I Look Open the Observence Conscientioussly, and therefore with my blessing I Strictly injoin it to your care.

---

as his brother Isaac, died September 21, 1777, at Isleworth, England, at the age of ninety-two. *Jewish Obituaries,* 42; Finberg, "Jewish Residents in Eighteenth-Century Twickenham," 129.

2 Asher Levy, A.F.'s brother, returned to the colonies after this letter was written (see Letter XVI, July 6, 1740), and died in Philadelphia in 1742 (see Letter XXVII, Aug. 1742). He appears to have been in New York in 1718. Power of Attorney made by Moses Levy to Asher Levy and Jacob Franks, dated Aug. 8, 1718. Con. Lib. 28, cp. 513–514.

I rec[eiv]ed a Letter by the boston Post Last night, dated ye 19th Apr[il]. I observe your Complaint on Acc[oun]t of my not writting, but for this time I hope you will be Satisfyed that It did not Proceed from from [sic] Negligence, but because there Was Vessles at the Same time goeing from hence. For Since I was ascertained of your Stay, I have wrote you many Letters. I have Justly the Same Complaint, for you have neglected writting by Some boston Ships. However Wee will pass this and take more Care for the futer. Mr. Cope[3] Sailed Last fryday for Antig[u]a with Col[one]l Gilbert[4] with whome he is to Live. It was with Some pains before he Could Gitt Leave of Mr. Hossmendon.[5] He gave his kind Love and Service to you and Desire you would by All Oppertunitys Let him hear from you. Your Sisters thank you for your Pres[en]t and Richa in Perticuler, who Intends you a Letter by Downing. Your brothers Joyn with e'm in theire Love & Service to you. In mine to Mr. Isaac Franks, I forgot to thank him for his Picture, pray Soe you doe it for me. I think it a Very handsome Picture, tho' every one that knows him Tells me it falls Short of the Originall. I have nothing more to add, Soe Shall Conclude this with my Prayers to the Allmighty to have you in his Portection. I am, My Dear Child,

your Loveing mother,

Abigaill Franks

New. York [Monday] July ye 9th 1733
Mr. Nap[hta]ly Franks

---

3 Probably Frederick Cope (1710–1739) who held several administrative jobs in Antigua including clerk of the Assembly and justice of the peace. Vere L. Oliver, *History of the Island of Antigua* (London, 1896), 1: ci, and 3: 98 and 458.

4 Col. Nathaniel Gilbert (d. 1761) was a veteran of the Flanders war and colonel of the militia and member of the Antiguan Assembly in 1734 and from 1750 to his death. Oliver, *History*, 1: xcix and cxix; 2: 12 and 14; 3: 157.

5 Daniel Horsmanden (1694–1778) was a lawyer, merchant, politician, and judge who was appointed chief justice of the Supreme Court in March 1763. *Calendar*, 21, 41, 57 and 59.

[Address]
To

Mr. Napthli Franks
To be left att Tom's Coffee House[6] & behinde
the Royall Exchange
In
London

Via Dover
~~QDG~~[7]

III
[Abigaill Franks to Naphtali Franks, October 7, 1733]*

Dear HeartSey

I am now Seated to write, but after I have told you that I have rece[ive]d three of yours by Oliver[1] and that they rece[ive]d a hearty

---

6 Tom's Coffee House was one of many congregated on Cornhill near the Royal Exchange. It was located at 31 Cornhill. In this area, also, were a number of bookshops, such as Ashley, Walthoe, Strahan, Brotherton, Meadows, and Willock's, where N.F. could have purchased the literature his mother so often requested. Coffee houses were at their height of popularity during the eighteenth century, as centers of trade and lodging. Seventeen of the letters included in this volume were sent to Tom's. It is possible that N.F. lived there at times, prior to his marriage, but more likely he used it, as did many other merchants, as a business and mailing address. Private mail was deposited in the pouches located there, much to the chagrin of the post office.

7 The abbreviations QDG stands for the Spanish *"quo Dies guarde"* and is similar to the English abbreviation WGP [=Whom God protect]. It expresses the prayer of the sender of the letter that the bearer of it should have a safe journey and bids him Godspeed.

* Letters III (Oct. 7, 1733) and IV (Oct. 16, 1733) were sent together as one, the latter having been written on the reverse side of the former.

1 William Oliver was master of the *Dorset of London*, a Pennsylvania-built eighty-ton vessel.

wellcome, I've Very Little more to Say but that this parts with Us in the purfect Injoyment of our wishes in regard to Our State of health. And I must Anex the Ussall Sentence with hopeing this may meet you in the Same, attended with that tranquality of mind wich your Last Seem to intimate, dated from Mr. franks's Country Seat,[2] wich You give a Very agreeable discription of. But If your Letter was dated at the bottom of a hill, It was Read on the Top of a Very high one, for I was at harlam[3] and Mr. Moore[4] brought me my Letters. You'll be Surprised that I have taken a ramble for a day twice this Summer, but I cant Avoid it, it being on y[ou]r Sisters Score, for Mr. Moors Family Are Very pressing and will not Goe without her, and She will not Goe without me. It is only our Selves and Mr. Riggs & his Wife[5] and fanny make up our Company, Soe t[ha]t I Tell you Fanny

---

2 Naphtali was frequently a guest at the home of his uncle Isaac Franks, whose country house was at Mortlake, Surrey, some fifteen to twenty miles from London. Rachel Daiches-Dubens, "Eighteenth Century Anglo-Jewry in and around Richmond, Surrey," *TJHSE* 18 (1953–1954), 148.

3 The hill referred to was probably "Snake Hill," part of the present-day Mount Morris Park in the vicinity of 122nd Street and Fifth Avenue, New York City. A.F. was possibly staying in Harlem during an Indian summer vacation, at the old Ferry House located at the southeastern corner of present-day First Avenue and 126th Street quite close to the Harlem River, as a guest of the Moores who may have rented the premises. The house, owned prior to the Revolution by Peter R. Livingston, was used as a tavern after the war and later became known as the Benjamin S. Judah house. In 1822, it was purchased by John Moore, probably related to the Moores mentioned in the letter, and destroyed in 1867. The Moore-Judah occupancy gives some reason to suspect that the locations are indeed identical. If so, A.F. could enjoy a fine view of the river, stately trees, and country lanes. A Dutch Reformed Church was nearby, just off of what is now 125th Street. Mount Morris could be seen in the distance from this location. James Riker, *History of Harlem* (New York, 1881), 191; Book of Inquiries MSS. Vol. B 23 and folder 3 in Box 12, James Riker Collection, NYPL.

4 Probably Col. John Moore, husband of Frances Lambert Moore, an alderman, merchant, and noted New Yorker. See Letter I, May 7, 1733, note 8.

5 Mr. Riggs is possibly John Riggs, Commissioner of Indian Affairs and commander of a militia company. *Doc. Rel.* 5: 532, 538, and 572. The Fanny men-

rigs and my Self from a Very agreeable Prospect Sat down and read y[ou]r Letters and one I rece[ive]d from Coz[i]n ab[raham] Sallomons,[6] wherein He Took the pains too Oblige me with an Acc[oun]t of the Religeon, Manners, & Custom of the East Indians, Inter mixt with things that had come under his Observation, and I will Assure you, he puts things down in a Very prety method.

Your Sister takes it Unkind you have not answered her Letters. I cant think at Soe great a distance Answering of Letters Ought to be deffered, but I fancy its a Sort of Catching DisTemper on y[ou]r Side of the watter to think a Letter not worth Answering. I pray you to be more punctall henceforth. In the Interim She Sallutes You with her best Love & Soe doe all the Rest of your brothers and Sisters. Moses[7] is a Learning the Mat[hemat]ecks at Mr. Mallcoms,[8] whoe

---

tioned in the letter could have been the daughter of John Riggs's marriage to Frances Colburne.

It is often difficult to identify definitely the persons referred to by A.F., since she rarely uses first names.

6 Abraham Salomons may have been the son of Abigail Salomons, J.F.'s sister, and therefore a cousin to N.F. This interest in East Indian affairs is indicative of the world-wide trade carried on by Jewish merchants.

7 Moses Franks, born in New York on or about January 1, 1719 (Con. Lib. 32, cp. 41), died intestate at Teddington, England, April 2, 1789. Letters of Administration of Moses Franks, PCC. Moses at the time of this letter was fifteen years old and was probably named after a brother of J.F. who died in 1716. Will of Moses Franks, Fox 162, PCC Con. Lib. 26, cp. 411; Samuel Oppenheim, "Supplemental Notes on the Jacob Franks Genealogy," *PAJHS* 26 (1918), 266.

8 Alexander Malcolm, formerly of Aberdeen, Scotland, "Master of the Grammar School in the City of New-York," taught scholars "Latin, Mathematicks, Geometry, Allgebra, Geography, Navigation, and Merchant-Book Keeping after the Most Perfect Manner." His attempts at maintaining a private school brought an income "short of a comfortable support for him and his family," and he was appointed master of the Public School for the "Teaching of Latin Greek and Mathematicks" established by an Act of Assembly dated October 14, 1732. He was to receive £40 annually from funds arising from peddlers' licenses and £40 from an annual tax to support the ministry and the poor, for which

tells me he will Goe thro' it with abundance of Ease and be perfect in a Very Little time. Phila Learns french, Spanish, hebrew, and writting in the morning, and in the Afternoon She goes at Mrs. Brownells. She makes a Quick advance in wathever She Learns. Mr. Lopas[9] Tells

---

he was to teach twenty youths chosen from different counties in the province. New York City Chamberlain's Journal, 1706–1736, 326–340, NYHSL; *Colonial Laws,* 2: 813–817. In 1730, a subscription was established for Alexander and his brother, Quintin, as private schoolmasters. They were given £5 for every boy or youth recommended by a subscriber. *Iconography,* 4: 516. Malcolm, therefore, ran both a private and a public school. In 1736, he announced that "Meer Beginners in Latin" would be accepted only in February and August. *Gazette,* Dec. 30, 1735. By July of the following year, he announced that he would receive at any time such "Scholars as fit any of the Classes." Ibid., July 18, 1736. For another advertisement, see the issue of July 17, 1738.

Moses was apparently sent to Malcolm rather than to Brownell so that he could receive instruction on the violin, as well as in academic and commercial subjects, since he was the most musical of the brothers. Richard Ashfield wrote that his son Lewis "plays pretty Well on the fiddle, but is in want of a good one and goes to Mr. Malcolm which he is well pleased with." Richard Ashfield to Robert H. Morris, June 2, 1735 and Nov. 10, 1735, Morris Papers.

There were a number of other private tutors available in the city including William Thurston who taught "Grammar, Writing, Arithmetick, Vulgar and Decimal . . . dwelling at the Corner-House by Koentis Market, . . . *Gazette,* Sept. 4, 1732. In a letter dated March 15, 1747, John Richard wrote to Henry Van Rensselaer: "The Skoolmaster Lipkins where your sons went to Skool has broke Skool Keeping and is Going for Holland and have put the Children by Van Wagens where I believe they will Learn More then where they were first." Van Rensselaer–Fort Papers, NYPL.

9 Phila also could have studied with a private tutor, some of whom taught girls. Betsey Van Rensselaer, writing to Henry Van Rensselaer on June 2 [1740?], said "I go to school every day . . ." Van Rensselaer–Fort Papers, NYPL. More likely, however, Phila studied languages and writing at a school provided for by the Congregation Shearith Israel. The Lopas referred to in the letter is Moses Lopez da Fonseca (d. 1752), first *hazzan* of the Congregation at its dedication in 1730 (he had been appointed to office in 1728). He was not originally required to teach school, but this task probably developed on him. Some time during

me he is Surprised at her advancement in ye Spanish. I intend to Send for Some patterons for her to work opon next Summer. As for News, you will have Soe much of it from your Father & Colly that I have nothing of that Nature to touch opon. But As I would not Send too Short a Letter, I hope to fill it Up with these triffles, for the most Mateirell is to Come, Wich is to recommend the Same Care on your Conduct wich You have had hitherto. I've wrote soe often to you on that Subject that I Shall at preas[en]t not dwell Any Longer opon it, but Desire you to Dispose of my best regards to your U[n]cles & Aunts, And Love to All Your Coz[i]ns. My Service to Mr. Is[aac] Levy & his Family,[10] to Mrs. Norris & her Capt[ain][11] & all other friends. Desire my brothers to Accept[ance] of my Love, and I Con-

---

1736 he went to Curaçao, and in a letter from there dated January 30, 1737, he indicated that he would not return. Although his name does not appear again in the Minute Book of the Congregation as either an officer or a member, he appears to be in New York in 1743 since his name is listed in an account book for that year. Isaac S. Emmanuel, *Precious Stones of the Jews of Curaçao* (New York, 1957), 315–316; Entry of Sept. 19, 1743, Jay Day Book, 309. See also 337, 341 and 350.

When David Mendez Machado (d. 1747) was appointed *hazzan* in the stead of Lopez da Fonseca on March 3, 1737, he was pledged to "keep a publick School in due form for teaching the hebrew language, either the whole morning or afternoon as he shall think most proper and that any poor that shall be thought unable to pay for their children's Learning they shall be taught gratis." Minute Book, 4 and 35–36; *Portraits*, 52 and 206.

10 This is probably the Isaac Levy who was a London merchant and son of Joseph Levy, A.F's uncle. Thus this Isaac was A.F.'s first cousin. Will of Samuel Levy, *Wills*, 28–29. A.F. also had a brother called Isaac Levy, to whom she usually refers as Uncle Isaac.

11 Capt. Matthew Norris (d. 1738), son of Admiral John Norris, was in command of the *H.M.S. Lowstoffe*, stationed at New York from 1727 until 1733. Around 1734 he married Euphemia Morris, daughter of Lewis Morris (1671–1746), chief justice of the Supreme Court of New York and later governor of New Jersey and an important political figure. *Gazette*, May 29, 1727, and June 20, 1737; Bowery Ward, Feb. 24, 1733, NYAL.

clude with An Indulgent parents wish towards her childs Happyness. My Dear,

Your Affectionate Mother,

Abigaill Franks

New York [Sunday] Octob[er] ye the 7th 1733

IV

[Abigaill Franks to Naphtali Franks,
October 10, 1733]*

On the Other Side I wrote Last week, thinking the Vessle would have gon in a day or two. But According to Custum, haveing Stayed Soe much Longer has Given me an Oppertunity to Look over the Letter, and I find I have made Noe Mention of the receipt of ye Catalogue of books.[1] You may bleive I Like e'm, for Some have heretofore fallen Under My Perusiall and Gave me the Pleassure that good Authors Genrely Infuse to a mind Inclined to books. I could with Vast Pleassure Imploy three hours of the 24 from my Family Affairs to be diping in a good Author And relinquish Every other Gaity Commonly Called the pleasure of Life. But As few Can Arrive to the Summit of theire Wish, I have Learnt to be Content with any thing And think its a Lesson Every one Ought to Endeavour to be perfect in.

I Should be pleased to See the Tryall of the Widow da Costas, with A Jewish Love Letter Especialy wrote by a Portugeuse.[2] If you Can Procure it, pray doe.

* On reverse side of the first page of Letter III.

1 Perhaps A.F. referred to a catalog of a private library, examples of which can be found in the April 16, 24, 25 and May 2, 1733 editions of the London *Daily Advertiser*. The April 16th issue contains a catalog of the library of the Rt. Hon. Richard Hampden which was being offered for sale.

2 This request apparently refers to a book which had been published con-

Coz[i]n Colly has at Lenght got Leave to Come home. I would have you be Very Carefull wath you Say to him or how you Bleive wath he Says to you, for he does not keep Very Close to truth. By noe means Disoblige him, for you know his Temper. Pray Let Noe One See this, for he and I are Very good freinds, And I would not Say Soe much to Any one Else of him, tho' I have often told him his faults And Shall Give him a Great Caution before he Goes, If he will but Mind me, for I wish him Very Well and am Sorry he is soe odly Tempered. This being wath offers, I Conclude as on the other Side.

A Franks

My Service to Mr. Pechco.³

At Night & without Spectacles, soe blots must be allowed.

[Tuesday] October ye 16th [1733] to Mr. Napt[hal]y Franks
    [Docket]

---

cerning the interesting relationship of Catherine Villareal and Jacob Mendes da Costa. Catherine da Costa had married Joseph da Costa Villareal in 1727. After his death in 1730, Catherine, then twenty-one years old, allegedly promised to marry Jacob da Costa, her cousin. Catherine had a change of heart, however, and Jacob brought suit before the Court of the Archbishop of Canterbury in 1733. The court claimed jurisdiction despite the fact that the parties were Jewish, but ruled that Catherine's promise was conditional and dismissed the application. Jacob then brought suit before the King's Bench, where he was also unsuccessful. Catherine subsequently married William Mellish and became a Christian. Alfred Rubens, *Anglo-Jewish Portraits* (London, 1935), p. 116; James Picciotto, *Sketches of Anglo-Jewish History* (London, 1875), 103–104; Cecil Roth, ed., *Anglo-Jewish Letters 1158-1917* (London, 1938), 98–105; *Daily Advertiser,* June 19, 1733. Cf. Cecil Roth, *Magna Bibliotheca Anglo-Judaica* (London, 1937), 249.

3 Rodrigo Pacheco (d. 1749), one of the most prominent and influential of New York and London merchants, was made a freeman of New York City in 1711. *Burghers,* 91. In 1731, the province appointed him an agent in London to represent the colony in Parliament in opposition to the Molasses Act. *Colonial Laws,* 2: 731. It is not clear whether he ever returned to New York City after that date.

                from my Mother
                    [Address]
                       To
                To Mr. Napthli Franks
              at Toms Coffee house Cornhill near
                  the Royall Exchange
            via Bristoll London
                 ~~WGP~~

V
[Abigaill Franks to Naphtali Franks, December 16, 1733]

Dear HeartSey

My Last Was but a Short Letter and Dont find I have a Subject for a Larger at preas[en]t, nor Indeed Soe Large, for After I have repeated wath You hear in all Your Letters, that wee are well &c.,[1] I find I have nothing Else to Say—tho' Something I forgot in My Last Gives room to Lenghten this, wich is that I have not delivered your Letter to Mrs. Kearney[2] for these following reassons: I had Seen the Letter She Sent you wherein She mentions Something Concerning the Gover[nor]s Family,[3] wich I thought you would answer. And As

---

1 It seems strange that A.F. did not comment on the death of her daughter Sara who died November 30, 1733, aged two years, ten months, and four days. *Portraits*, 209–210. Sara may or may not have been born before N.F.'s departure for England. Infant mortality was an accepted part of life in the eighteenth century.

2 Mrs. Kearney (1695–1736) was probably Sarah Morris, daughter of Lewis Morris and the wife of Michael Kearney, a merchant and land speculator of Perth Amboy, New Jersey. For further material relating to the Kearney family see James Alexander Papers, Box 4, NYHSL.

3 Gov. William Cosby (1695?–1736), a former governor of Minorca and colonel of the Royal Irish Regiment and equerry of the queen, arrived in New York

all that Family have a Diference with Our Court,[4] I knew wath Ever you Might Say would Give them a handle to Say more, they, haveing all A Very Extensive faculty that way of Puting Every thing in its best or worst Light as Suits. I chose, theirefore, to keep ye Letter And desire You to write another with an Excuse for your Omission.

Wee have a Perfect war here, and it is dayly increasing, the Court being Very much disliked. I think they are best that have nothing to doe with him. I bleive they are Sorry they have Carrid it with Soe high A hand at first, and now, if he would be more Complying, it would hardly regain the Exteem of the People. Young delancy & Fred[erick] Philps have Lost a great deall of good Will by being in the Gov[ernor]s Interest.

Sam will not have Rach[e]ll[5] Unless he has £200 with her, Soe that is of[f]. I bleive its a mortification to her, but her thinking he would have her proved a benifit to Some Sombody. The Proverb Says its an Ill wind that blows nobody good. My Love to Nat[han].[6] Tell him I

---

on August 1, 1732, aboard the *H.M.S. Seaford.* With him came his wife Grace (d. 1767), sister of George Montague, Earl of Halifax, two daughters. Grace and Elizabeth, two sons, Henry (d. 1753) and William, his brother Maj. Alexander Cosby, and his son-in-law, Thomas Freeman, husband of Grace. *Gazette,* Aug. 7, 1732.

4 A.F.'s reference is to the family of Lewis Morris. The "Court" refers to Cosby's party, arch enemies of Morris.

5 Samuel Myers Cohen (1708?-1743), a prominent merchant, naturalized July 12, 1729, and made freeman on October 6, 1730, was a *shohet* and *bodek,* and later president of Congregation Shearith Israel. In September 1730, he was elected constable of the Dock Ward, but his position was taken by Christopher Nicholson. Minute Book, 6, 13, and 14; *Burghers,* 114; *Colonial Laws,* 2: 513; *Portraits,* 228-230; *MCC,* 4: 27 and 30.

Samuel Myers Cohen finally married Rachel Michaels, referred to in this letter, some time before 1734. See Letter VI, June 9, 1734.

6 Nathan Levy (1704-1753), brother of A.F., was a merchant of London, New York, and Philadelphia. He was in England at the time of this letter, probably having left New York in 1732. Like his sister A.F., he had a great interest in literature and music. At his death, his library was varied and extensive

Expected a half Sheet of Paper Some times, but find he has got into the fashion. I think the Poets have a fable of being Dipt in a river to Cause Oblivion.[7] I bleive its the river of thames. Methinks you have A Little Sprinkling Some times; pray take Care how you Come to nigh.

Wee have had a fine winter hither to, for its not Cold nor noe Snow. My humble respects to your Uncles & Aunts, My Compliments to all your Coz[i]ns. Your Sister Phila Shall work you a Purse against the Next Ships Goe in the Spring. Wee are Just goeing to diner, wich makes mee Conclude this. With my Prayers for your happyness, I am

> Dear Child,
>
> Your Affectionate mother,
>
> Abigaill Franks

I am reading Rapin.[8]
New York [Sunday] Decemb[er] ye 16th, 1733
> Nap[htali] Franks
> *[Address]*
> To
> Mr. Napthly Franks
> att London

---

and included twenty-two Hebrew volumes and twenty-five books on music as well as the works of John Locke and Paul Rapin. Jacob R. Marcus, ed., *American Jewry—Documents Eighteenth Century* (Cincinnati, 1959), 8–9. He may have been the Levy referred to by Dr. Alexander Hamilton as playing a "very good violine." Carl Bridenbaugh, ed., *Gentleman's Progress* (Chapel Hill, 1948), 191.

7 The reference is to the River Lethe of Greek mythology.

8 Paul Rapin de Thoyras (1661–1725) was a French author who wrote the popular *History of England*. It was translated into English with additional notes by Nicholas Tindal and published in London in 1732 in two volumes. Later continued by Tindal to the time of George II, the *History* was described in the *Gentleman's Magazine,* 2: (1732), 1023 as furnishing the "best material against the two worst Evils, Superstition and Tyranny; and 'tis a pleasure to see such vast Numbers of them sold every week."

VI
[Abigaill Franks to Naphtali Franks, June 9, 1734]

[Sunday] June ye 9th [1734][1]

Dear HeartSey

 I have Severall of yours bearing Variety of Dates as well as Subiect, In Wich I have had Vast deall of Delight relating to Some matters, Especialy that wich Concerns Your Self. Nothing in Life can be more gratefull then to hear that you Discharge your duty to y[ou]r Relations and your Self in soe Agreeable And Aproved of a manner, in wich I hope you May be Soe happy as to allways Acquit Your Self. I shall not dwell on the Subject of advice on that Score, haveing heretofore in Severall of Mine bin Very Copious and with Success, even to my wish [that] the Excuses you Make in not writing to me Soe often as to your father meets with an Eassy forgiveness. I will allways Compound for one Letter in three, Provided you Make it Up in Lenght when you doe write and not Send me a Letter writt upon a "Scrap of Gilt paper noe biger than a Supeana."

 As I Observed, your Letters contain Variety of Subject, Soe as they where in Some parts Agreeable, they had an Allay boath of Greife & Surprize in the Affair relating to Coz[i]n Colly. It's Curell [cruel] to Charge your father and My Self with any Cause of his Ill Conduct in hideing his faults or giveing him a good Charector. As for Any Perticuler Vice, Wee never knew him Guilty of Anny, Unless they call not Complaining Constantly of his Violent Temper be a fault, I Own my Self guilty. You are Senciable your Father knew Very Little of it, being Colly had Some awe before him, And As for his Carriage towards me and the Family, I Should Never have Complained

---

 1 The year in which this letter was written is not mentioned at this point and is torn out in the original at the end of the letter. The year 1734 is ascribed for a number of reasons: one, the date of sailing of Capt. Thomas Smith, the bearer of the letter, and two, the news discussed such as the Fitzroys' departure for England, the Cosby-Morris dispute, and the Smith-Murray debates in the Assembly, give ample evidence as to the date.

had his humour bin Possiable to have bin Ten times Worse. I Allways hid it As Much As I could, for as He was Not my relation, I would not for the world [have] made any Difference between Him and his Uncle. I was Surprised when he made Up his Acc[oun]t to find Soe much of his money Spent. Wich Way he Spent it, he best can Tell. As for Gameing and Drinking,[2] he never did; the first he knew nothing of & the Latter he could not be Often guilty of, being he allways kept Very good hours and was not Often abroad. As to his Saying that Rach[e]ll[3] run him in debt is Very false. She has noe fine things and as for wath She has, you are Sensiable I had the buying of Every thing for all that Family, Even to there Very Shooes. I have inquired of Mrs. Stillwell[4] & She Protest Solemnly he Never had for the Vallue of three pence for Rach[e]ll at her Shop. I know he gave her once a foolish ring, wich I made her give him again. But he has the Unhappy faculty of Saying any thing & Swearing to it. Its wath I have often reproved him for, but to Little purpose. He has Said Cruell things of Rach[e]ll and Whenever I Taxe'd him therewith, he Denyed it. But in Short As I Wrote you before, there is noe bleiveing Any thing he

---

2 Many New Yorkers feared the "Multiplicity of Gaming Houses within the City and the evil consequences attending the same by Debauching the Youth and others." Petition dated March 31, 1736, *MCC,* 4: 311–312; *Colonial Laws,* 3: 194–195. A.F. shared the concern of her contemporaries as is evident from the comments in a few of her letters. It was one of the aspects of New York society that she found appalling.

3 It is not clear to which Rachel A.F. refers. It may have been her halfsister, but this is doubtful since she usually calls her "Aunt Rachel" and the latter did not have any need for A.F.'s support. It may also have been Rachel Michaels, who at this time had not yet married Samuel Myers Cohcn and who as indicated in Letter V, Dec. 16, 1733, did not have £200 as a dowry. A.F. might have reference to the other daughters of Moses Michaels who also were not yet married when she says she bought goods for that family.

4 She may have been Mrs. Mercy Stillwell, wife of Richard Stillwell, shopkeeper (d. about 1743), or she may have been Elizabeth Stillwell, who bought goods from the executors of Samuel Levy. Con. Lib. 32, cp. 480; Inventory of Samuel Levy, HDC.

Says, for he is neither Ruled in his Passions by right nor reason. I bleive he Spent Mrs. Barberie's[5] money here, for Just Opon his departure Judahs[6] maid Swore her Self with child by him, & I bleive he Made Up the matter with that money, for his Uncle quarled with him, and he went from home for two days, and I Sent for him again. I Am Satisfyed I have don nothing to reproach my Self on his Score, but have taken all the pains in the world to reclaim that Violent Ungovernable Temper, And he Promised Very fair when he went from hence of an intire amendment, And I am Extreemly Concerned to find a Disapoint[ment]. I Must Own I would Very Willingly take Him with all his Ill Humours in My house again rather than Lett him be abouth in Soe Distitute a Condition. I am Sorry Mrs. Salomons did not Endeavour to make Up that Unhappy Affaire. I know him Soe well, that with Lenity She might have brought him to a due Concern for his faults. God knows wath will become of him, for he is but a help Less Unhappy Creature And Noe ways Capable of thinking right for himself. I Question Very much wether he will write a Letter to Us at his Arrivall, for I bleive Shame will deter him. I confess If It Lay in My Power to Serve him, I would gladly doe it, but Your Uncle's Commands to your father are Soe Strong that I am Positive all I can plead for him will availe nothing. Therefor must Leave him to Providence and his Own Conscience for a Conviction of his folly, wich I hope may be to his futer amendment.

I find You Seem not Soe Well pleased with your Commission[7] re-

---

5 Possibly a reference to Catharine Barbaric, widow of John Barbaric (d. about 1727), a member of the provincial Council, who in 1734 lived in the East Ward. NYAL, Feb. 18, 1734.

6 This is probably a reference to Judah Hays (d. 1764), a merchant who was naturalized July 12, 1729, and elected constable of Montgomerie Ward in September 1746. *Colonial Laws,* 2: 513; *Portraits,* 471–474. There was also a Judah Mears, brother of Grace Mears, A.F.'s stepmother, but A.F. usually refers to him by his last name, and not as Judah. Hays married Rebecca Michaels, one of Moses Michaels's daughters, and Mears married Michaels's daughter Jochebed.

7 Gov. Cosby had apparently asked N.F. by private letter to serve as his busi-

lating to ye Governor. Since You have no buissness yet but your Divers[io]ns, I would Make noe Excuse for you to him. I cant See any matter of trouble it Can be to you at Preas[en]t. Its time enough when you are in an Imploy to Send him a Letter to be Excused. Lord Augustus & his Lady are Goeing home this Summer. They would have gone with these Vessles but She Looks to Lay in dayly.[8] As Soon as She is Up, they will begon. My Lord has bespoke a Letter to Carry to you allready. He is young & Extreemly Good Nature'd I bleive. As for his Lady, She is a Perfect Agreea[bl]e Person And Endowed with her mother's Penetration tho' not Experience. Most of the Ladys that Visit the fort[9] Are Concerned at her goeing away, for she gives a Zest to ye Conversation wich the Other daughter[10] wants. As to the Gov-

---

ness agent in London. N.F., aware of the political situation in New York and being acquainted with the Morris family, may have thought it tactful to decline such an offer.

8 Lord Augustus Fitzroy (1716–1741), son of Charles Fitzroy, Duke of Grafton, and lord chamberlain to George II, arrived in New York shortly after Gov. Cosby, "to pay a visit to his Excellency the Governor his Lady and family." *Gentleman's Magazine* 3 (1735), 156.

Despite social differences, Augustus married Elizabeth (d. 1788), daughter of Gov. and Mrs. Cosby. According to accepted social views, the marriage was beneath Fitzroy, and the governor and his wife could not give their consent. Nevertheless, by the intrigues of Mrs. Cosby, the couple arranged the matter themselves. Fearful of the consequences however, Cosby instituted a mock prosecution against the Rev. Alexander Campbell, who had solemnized the marriage. Martha J. Lamb, and Mrs. Burton Harrison, *History of the City of New York* (New York, 1896), 1: 543–544; Richard B. Morris, ed., *Select Cases of the Mayors Court of New York City, 1674-1784* (Washington, 1935), 407. Their haste in returning to England was due, in part, to the necessity of presenting Elizabeth to the Court properly.

9 Fort George at the southern tip of Manhattan, the present-day Battery, first built at that location in 1626 by the Dutch (then called Fort Amsterdam), was the official residence of the governors. The name of this fort was changed to the name of the reigning English king upon his accession to the throne (Fort James, Fort William, Fort George). It contained not only the governor's house, but also military, administrative, and legislative buildings.

10 Elizabeth's sister, "the vertuous and Honorable" Grace Cosby, married

ernors Affairs, wee know not yet Wath turn it will take. That that [sic] must have its Desission from your Side of the watter. In his affair relating to Col[one]l Morris and Mr. Van dam, there was a publick debate before the Assembly by the Lawyers, Concerning this new Court of Equity.[11] Against it was Mr. Smith and for it Mr. Murry; the former held forth from Elleven in the morning Untill two in the after [noo]n with Abundance of Eloquence. When Mr. Murry made answer, he was Not prepared & theirefore desired a Longer time. People are Very Much Against this Court in the manner it is Purposed, for, Say they, when People came first to Settle in this Country, they hardly knew Wath A right Conveyance of Land was, but bought and Settled themselves And Children Opon it without much pains in the form of Titles, Soe that According to the Tenour of this Court they may over Look all the records. As it will be in the Judges breast to give wath Sentence he pleases, As there will be noe Jury, Soe that its as Much Caviled at as the Excise Scheme[12] with you. I bleive F[r]ed[erick] Philps finds himself in an Intricate peice of work and, it's thought, wishes he never had Undertaken the Affair. He has Lost Very much of the Peoples good will. The Assembly have don but Very Little, yet Col[one]l Morris gives them Pusleing [puzzling] work. I Should Like to heare theire debates, Expecialy Some of our Igno-

---

Thomas Freeman, who on August 24, 1733, was made freeman of New York City. *Burghers,* 490–492. After his death. Grace married Joseph Murray, a noted New York attorney. E. B. O'Callaghan, *New York Marriages* (Albany, 1860), 276.

11 Cosby's attempt to have the Supreme Court made a court of equity was interpreted by his enemies as a usurpation of political power and a threat to courts of law which, unlike courts of equity, required trial by jury. A.F.'s description of colonial process and procedure underlies this concern. Zenger's *Weekly Journal* took a similar position with respect to the courts of equity. See issues of Feb. 11 and March 18, 1734. Interestingly, A.F.'s report of the proceedings coincides closely with the Assembly's account of this debate.

12 The Excise scheme introduced in 1732 by Sir Robert Walpole, prime minister, was an attempt to abolish the land tax by levying additional import duties. It led to many months of acrimonious debate both in and out of Parliament. Archibald S. Foord, *His Majesty's Opposition, 1714–1830* (Oxford, 1964), 177–182.

rant du[t]ch members.¹³ The governor has altered his Conduct Very much Since his Comeing & Tries, by being Affable & Courteous, to regain the Peoples Exteem. He invites 'em frequently to dinner. Our Neighbour brincroft,¹⁴ Van Wyck,¹⁵ Ten eyck,¹⁶ duyken,¹⁷ and Severall more of these Sort of Gentry are frequently in theire turns invited to dine at Court. As You will observe, the Jounalls Are Very merry opon These feasts¹⁸ And, I think, Some times have bin to[o]

13 The Twentieth Assembly, which met from July 1728 to May 1737, had among its members from Westchester Lewis Morris, Sr. and Jr., as well as Frederick Philipse. Lewis Morris Jr. became Speaker at the next Assembly. The Morrises, especially the elder, were political gadflys and kept the Assembly members busy discussing procedure and content. Stephen C. Hutchins, *The New York Civil List* (Albany, 1880), 275; *Journal of the General Assembly*, passim. The statement about "ignorant du[t]ch members" reflected A.F.'s dislike of the many Dutch inhabitants of New York who still spoke and wrote in Dutch. This probably was true for the Albany members, such as Myndert Schuyler, Derick Ten Broeck, and perhaps Philip Schuyler, as well as the other persons named by A.F. in the letter.

14 Contemporary records do not mention a Brincroft. A.F. probably referred to George Brinckerhoff, a merchant, who lived near Coenties Market close to the Franks residence on Duke Street, and who became an assistant alderman in 1743. *Weekly Journal,* March 1, 1736; *Burghers,* 504.

15 Possibly Abraham Van Wyck, a merchant and resident of New York City and assessor of the Dock Ward. Entry of Nov. 18, 1733, Jay Day Book; *MCC,* 3: 310–311; *Burghers,* 116.

16 Possibly Samuel Ten Eyck listed in *Burghers* as a mariner, p. 135, but more probably either Coenraedt, Jacob, or Anthony Ten Eyck, all of whom conducted business within the city at this time. Jay Day Book, 64; Elizabeth Schuyler Account Book, 44 and 252, NYHSL; Bill of Exchange of Anthony Ten Eyck, dated Dec. 1, 1742, Box 10, James Alexander Papers, NYHSL.

17 Probably Gerardus Duyckinck, a noted limner and merchant. For advertisement for the sale of "Lookin-glasses" and "painting coullers and oyl," see *Weekly Journal,* Jan. 20, 1735.

18 Zenger's *Weekly Journal* was undoubtedly in A.F.'s mind. See particularly the issue of January 21, 1734, which printed an article that read in part: "We the widows of this City . . . find ourselves intirly neglected. While the husbands that live in our neighborhood are daily invited to Dine at Court; we have the vanity to think we can be full as Entertaining."

free with his Excellency & Family. As to my Own Priviate Opinion, I am inclined to the town Side. Soe is Mr. Moores Family and many more, but, however, all appear neuter. Fanny Rigs and my Self often are togather and then Wee Settle the Nation. Our Family are for appearance great Favourits and tho' mad[a]m keeps her Visiting day once a Week, She and the Governor have often desired me to Spend any other afternoon and Eavening there. But I never have, for I desire noe more honour then the rest of my fellow Cit[izen]s, tho' your father has bin there of an Eavening. They have Not many Woman Courtiers. Mrs. Ashfield [19] was One formerly, but the Tables are turned [to] Mrs. dick at Albany,[20] Soe that Pauls wife[21] is the Only Person that Sees em dayly, for the Coach is allways at her house Either Carrying them to her house or fetching her to the fort. She has Allmost forgot to walk a foot. People have an Ill Natured Mirth at Paulls Politeness. The Governor has made a Very Pretty bowlling greens[22] with a handsome Walk of trees, Raild and Painted, Just before the fort in t[ha]t Large Durty place. It Reaches three doers beyound Mr. Nickles[23] and Looks Very Well. I must not forgit to doe

19 Mrs. Isabella Ashfield was the wife of Richard Ashfield (d. 1742) and daughter of Lewis Morris.
20 Mrs. Jean Dick was the wife of William Dick, captain of one of His Majesties Independent Companies stationed at Albany.
21 Probably A.F. refers to the wife of Paul Richard (1667–1756), merchant, appointed mayor of New York City one day after the death of Col. Robert Lurting for the period July 4, 1735, to October 15, 1739. Mrs. Richard was most likely a Van Rensselaer. Paul Richard to Henry Van Rensselaer, July 4, 1735, Van Rensselaer–Fort Papers, NYPL.
22 On March 12, 1732, the Common Council resolved to lease property at the lower end of Broadway, fronting to the Fort, to some inhabitants to "make a Bowling-Green with Walks therein, for the Beauty and ornament of said street, as well as for Recreation," leaving fifty feet on either side. A.F.'s description is one of the few extant contemporary remarks and indicates the date of the fencing of the property. The Green appears on a Maerschack Duyckinck plan of 1754–1755 (original in the NYHSL) as a quadrangle, but today is in the shape of an oval. See also *Iconography*, 1: 34 and 274–276.
23 Possibly A.F. refers to Richard Nicolls, coroner, postmaster, and attorney who resided in the West Ward. *Burghers*, 116.

Justice to Mrs. Cosby on Acc[oun]t of Saying that she liked noebody but Mrs. Dick & Richards. I Never heard She Said any Such thing, and [has], I bleive, to[o] much Sence to think Soe, Especialy of Insipid Mrs. R[ichar]ds. Soe much for Court Affairs. But Mum.

I Observe You Give me an Acc[oun]t how you Spend your time. I find noe fault in it but your not takeing more time for your Studying of books, for If You dont doe it now, you will hardly fallow it when you grow oulder and will have an Excuse that buissness is a hindrence. My advice Should be that two mornings in a Week Should be intirly Untill diner time Dedicated to Some Usefull book, besides an hour Every morning throughout the Year to the Same Purpose. Pray Let me know wether you have forgot Versifying. Now I am Talking of Verses, I must Tell you Some thing Merry. You remmember the Assembly member that made Verses on Inoculation?[24] Some one Acquainted Mrs. Cosby of his fine Genious and One day at dinner amidst abundance of Company, in her Agreeable Courtly Method, beg'd he would favour her with a Coppy. He told her he had em not Abouth him, but would repeat Some to her, wich he did, you may be Sure, in a Very Elegant manner. Mrs. Cosby Seem'd mighty delighted and at Every Period would turn to Lady fits Roy: "dear betty admire the beauty of it. Did you Ever hear any thing Soe fine?" They all humered [humored] the thing, and ye poor Creature was in [such] a Extacy at the admiration of his fine Tallent that As Soon as he could, he procured her Ladyship a Coppy.

I am mightly pleased with all the things you Sent, Especialy the books and Pam[phlet]s. Your Care therein deserves my due regard. I shall be Carfull to send you the pepers etc. when in Season. The wine there is noe Need of. [As to] My Plea in your favour to y[ou]r father, He is inclined As much as you can wish to Gratify you in any request

---

24 Smallpox had resulted in the deaths of some 800 New Yorkers in 1731, causing the Assembly to adjourn for almost a year from September 1731 to August 1732. While the merits of inoculation were known, there were many reports that spread through the province to the contrary. *Gazette*, March 15 and Nov. 8, 1731; *Doc. Rel.*, 5: 929; *Iconography*, 4: 521 and 524.

You can Make him that is in his power to Comply with. I Shall now Send you the Smoakt fish you wrote for Some time agoe, but they was then Out of Season. You Say you are Concern'd at my disagreeing with My mother.[25] Wee have Never Quarled, Are As good friends as Ever. I dont Goe to her house Often. You know I never did, because I never bleived her Pretended friendship Sincere, Especialy to your Father. And As I hate a Crafty Carriage, I chuse to Shew good manners but Noe Overfondness, for as Puff^{or}

"to Death I hate the man whose tongue revealls a Different tale from wath his heart Concealls."[26]

Mears[27] And Your Father have had a Quarle; they dont speak to Each other. I cant say but I think Your Father Something to hasty Sometimes. It relates to the Affair of the Brig[antine] that was Lost. However I Never Interfere in these matters. I was Very Sorry when they had this quarle, for I Sate by a Silent Lisener. He is now at Phil[adelphia], where I Suppose he will meet with Poor Colly. I wish your Uncle may relent. I cant think of him but with Some Sampthy of his Unhappyness.

Mrs. beckford['s][28] Charector has run the Gantlet. Some Said her

---

25 Grace Mears Levy (c. 1694–1740), widow of Moses Levy, was A.F.'s stepmother. She lived with her sons in the Dock Ward. NYAL, Feb. 23, 1734. As subsequent letters reveal, A.F. did not get along too well with her stepmother. For additional information, see Letter IX, June 15, 1735, note 9, and Letter X, Dec. 12, 1735.

26 These lines have not been identified.

27 Judah Mears (d. 1762), brother of Grace Levy, was a merchant of New York City and Princeton, New Jersey, and husband of Jochebcd Michaels. Elizabeth Schuyler's Account Book, 79, NYHSL. Stephen Delancey, Oliver Delancey, and William Montagne were indicted for assaulting Judah Mears in 1742. Minutes of the Court of General Sessions, Vol. 1722–1743, p. 320, NYCCO.

That Mears was related to Grace Levy did not endear him to J.F. There is no information concerning the quarrel between the two as to a lost brig.

28 Mrs. Molly Beckford, daughter of George Clarke, died in July 1743. *Weekly Post-Boy,* Aug. 15, 1743. She married Ballard Beckford of Jamaica. It is interest-

husband had Left her on Acc[oun]t of her Ill Conduct; others Said She had Left him. But now I think its Confirm'd that he Lived to far beyond his Ability and was Obliged to make his Exit in order for a Repreive. But all agree in this, that She would be glad to be Molly Clark again, they Liveing a Very Disagre[eable] life, wich, If true, I bleive is Owing to her Implacable Temper. He has Never Wrote to Mr. Clark[29] a Letter from Jamiaca, tho' he has bin there this 6 months. I shall be Very Glad to See Mrs. Norris here again, but Capt[ain] Long[30] has Noe orders to come home, wich Makes me fancy Capt[ain] norris[31] will not be here as Soon as they wish. Col[one]l Morris's family are mightly Pleassed at his come[in]g, being Mrs. Cosby Said they had Such Intrest that would hinder his being Stationed here.

Your Sister Rich[a] has bin out of town this three weeks at huntington & Oyster bay.[32] She will Not be at home this fortnight. She has

---

ing, in view of A.F.'s reference to the Beckfords' marital difficulties, to note that in 1739 Edward Manning sued his wife Elizabeth for divorce and named Ballard Beckford, member of the Jamaican Assembly from the district of St. Mary, as co-respondent. His bill was granted and Beckford expelled. Frank Cundall, *The Governors of Jamaica in the First Half of the Eighteenth Century* (London, 1937), 174; E. B. O'Callaghan, *Voyage of George Clarke* (Albany, 1867), lxiii.

29 Probably George Clarke (1676–1760), a native of England, who arrived in New York in 1703 and was lieutenant-governor from 1736 to 1743. He was married to Ann Hyde (d. 1740), daughter of Edward Hyde, Lord Cornbury, a former governor of the province.

30 Robert Long (d. 1771) was commissioned captain in 1726 and in 1729 was in command of the station ship *H.M.S. Shonham*. As captain of the *Seaforth [Seaford]* he had carried Gov. Cosby and his family to the city and had later entertained them in his house in the South Ward.

31 Capt. Norris, husband of Euphemia Morris, had been in New York prior to the arrival of Long as his relief. A.F.'s remarks relate to the fact that Norris could not return to take command of the station ship until Long was recalled. Norris's coming to the province would be a sign of the strength of the Morris faction. He did return to New York on July 26, 1734, on the *H.M.S. Tartar. Weekly Journal,* July 29, 1734. See Letter III, note 11; *Pennsylvania Gazette,* July 25, 1734.

32 Possibly Richa (also known as Rachel or Ritze), went to visit the Franks

Learned to ride a horseback and Intends to come down in that Manner, but I hardly bleive She rides well enough to take a Jurney of fourty Mile. Mr. Simson & his Wife[33] Come down with her. Your brother Moses Picture[34] is don to be Sent Mrs. Salomons. As for mine and richa's, its to[o] chargable. Therfore, you must Content Your Self without. I dont doubt but you may have mine at your Uncle Ashers Lodgeings, As he is not in England. I had rather you Should have it then to be where I bleive it is. Apply to Uncle nath[an] & I question not but he can git it. You have heard of Sams marriage[35] before this, but I bleive it will be news to Acquaint you that Judah hays is[36] Makeing all the hast Imaginable towards that State & has writ to Mos[es] Mich[e]lls[37] for His Consent to Compleat his happyness in

---

property in Oyster Bay. In 1743, J.F. sold more than sixty acres in Oyster Bay plus a large dwelling house two stories high, adjoining the property of Samuel Townsend. *Journal,* May 23, 1743. In 1745, J.F. and A.F. sold to Richard Harcutt a house and ten acres of land in Oyster Bay for £100. There is no record to show whether and when the Frankses ever lived on any of the Long Island property.

33 Joseph Simson (d. 1792), a noted merchant made freeman on February 1, 1743, owned considerable land in Oyster Bay with his wife Rebecca Isaacs Simson. Since Richa returned with the Simsons, she may have been visiting them. The Frankses and Simsons seem to be the first Jews owning property in the Oyster Bay area.

34 Moses', Richa's, and A.F.'s portraits could have been done by one of several limners in New York including Gerardus Duyckinck. No early portrait of Moses alone is known, but there is one of Abigaill alone. See Albert Ten Eyck Gardner, "An Old New York Family," *Art in America,* 5: no. 3 (June 1963), 58–61. In 1761, a portrait of Moses Franks was made by Joshua Reynolds, and in 1766 he painted Phila's. She was also painted by Gainsborough. Alfred Rubens, *Anglo-Jewish Portraits* (London, 1935), 33–34.

35 This is the marriage of Samuel Myers Cohen to Rachel Michaels discussed previously in Letter V, Dec. 16, 1733, note 6.

36 Judah Hays wrote to Moses Michaels, who then resided in Curaçao. The marriage was agreed to and, some time during 1734, he married Rebecca, the sister of Rachel and Jochebed Michaels, both of whom are also referred to in this letter. See Letter VI, June 9, 1734, note 5.

37 Moses Michaels died in Curaçao, but lived in New York as late as 1709.

giveing him his daughter Rebecah. He is Perfectly refined; he often Puts me in Mind of Cymon in Dryden's fables.[38] I bleive they will be Marrid within this four Months. There is Something in Agitation with Mears & his mate. You Certainly Will be Surprised to hear [of] my mother & Josey friendship. The Latter Lives in huntington. She came to town the week after her Sister was marrid, when my Mother Went to See her And Saluted her with as much kind[ness] as the dearest friends could doe. They was frequently togather, And I have of a night Seen em walk with mears between, that I have Actuly blushed for it to think wath has bin Said amongst 'em, tho' all this friendship is but Outwardly, for I am told My Mother Spares Jose as Little as Ever. If you Say any thing to Uncle Nat[han] abouth this, desire him not to write it back Again as from me, tho' Tell him in Conformity [that] I hope he will recant all the Cruell things he has Said. I think he Showed A Vast deall of Weakness If it be true, as Mrs. Levy Tells me, He has Sat whole Eavenings at Is[aac] Levy's, Railling at Josey.[39]

I beg the <the> the next Spectecles[40] you Send may be good. The

---

He was married to Catherine Hacher and had four daughters, Rebecca, Rachel, Jochebed, and Bloeme. *Wills,* 59–61; NYAL, Dock Ward, Aug. 1709.

38 John Dryden, *Fables Ancient and Modern* (London, 1700), is a translation into verse from Homer, Ovid, Boccaccio and Chaucer. The fifth edition, which appeared in 1745, contained the following last fable from Boccaccio, "Cymon and Iphigenia." Cymon

Exeell'd the rest in Shape, and outward Shew;
Fair, Tall, his Limbs with due Proportion join'd
But of a heavy, dull, degenerate Mind, . . .
The People from *Galesus* chang'd his name
And *Cymon* call'd, which signifies a Brute;
So well his Name did with his Nature sute.

39 This is probably the Isaac Levy referred to in Letter III, Oct. 7, 1733, note 10, not A.F.'s brother Isaac Levy. Josey is probably Jochebed Michaels Mears.

40 A.F., who used glasses regularly, could have purchased them in New York. Rita S. Gottesman, *Arts and Crafts in New York, 1726–1776: New-York Historical Society Collection* (New York, 1937), 77, 82, and 96–97.

Person you bought the Last of Imposed opon you, for they are the Very Worst and Dear, for they Sell the Same here for 15 & 18 pence & you gave a Shilling. Send me a Couple that Magnifie, being I doe Most fine Work & reading. Phila's Earings are Very dear. You gave ten Shill[in]g & 6 d., and I realy bleive you Might have had 'em for five. As You are not Well acquainted with these things, you Ought Never to buy 'em Upon your Own Judgement. I have Exhausted all my Store and therefore Shall write you noe Letters by any of the Other Ships that Goe now. Pray give My humb[le] Service to your Uncle & Aunt with my Love to all y[oulr Coz[i]ns. My Service to Mrs. Norris Warren[41] & beckford. I Shall goe this Week With fanny riggs to Morrisania. All that Family Salute You And Soe doe all the rest of your Acquaintance with our Whole Congregation & Mr. Lopas at the head of 'em. He, poor Man, is made for Esther Lucena,[42] but she has the Sence to refuse him. I begin to be tired with Writting, Especialy Now I've Lookt over this Long Epistil and find not[hin]g worth Notice in it. Its the first Such a Long Letter I've Ever wrote, and I bleive I shall hardly Perswade my Self to write Such another. In haste, Soe Conclude in recommending you to the Peculier Care of Providence. I Am

My dear child,

Your Affectionate Parent,

Abigaill Franks

41 Mrs. Peter Warren, *née* Susanna Delancey, was the daughter of Stephen Delancey and sister of Oliver Delancey, later Phila's husband. Her husband, Peter Warren (1703–1752), was Captain of the Royal Navy in 1727 and rose rapidly through the ranks until he became "Admiral of the Red" in 1748. The couple were married in 1731. See notes, Peter Warren Papers, NYHSL; G/AM, nos. 1–66 and 95–112, Peter Warren Papers, Sussex Archaeological Society, Lewes, England.

42 Esther Lucena was the daughter of Abraham Haim de Lucena (d. 1725), a rich and noted merchant of New York. Very little is known of her. She did have an account with Elizabeth Schuyler. Will of Abraham de Lucena, *Wills,* 33–34; Elizabeth Schuyler Account Book, 88, NYHSL.

Your brothers & Sister Send you
there kind Love. Moses' Picture
Capt[ain] Smith[43] will deliver. I must
Tell you Its not flatered. My mother
would Not have me Send it, being She does
Not think it well don, but I would not goe
to the charge of a Nother. Thomey Moore[44]
goes with this Opertunity. Pray dont faill to goe
and See him. I would have you take a good deall
of notice of him being wee are Very intimate
here.

[Friday]
New York June ye 14th 1[734]
    Napthly Franks

        [Address]
        To
        Mr. Nap[tha]ly Franks
        att
        London

VII
[Abigaill Franks to Naphtali Franks, December 25, 1734]

Dear HeartSey

    Its Some time Since I have wrote to You, and Still I dont find I have any Subject to Inlarge upon further then Acquainting you t[ha]t Wee

---

43 Capt. Thomas Smith was in command of the *Beaver*, which was registered to leave for London from New York on June 13, 1734. NOL, CO 5/1225; *Gazette*, June 10, 1734.

44 Thomas Moore (d. 1768), son of Col. and Mrs. John Moore, close friends of A.F.

Are Well and Wishing You the Same happyness. You have bin Very remiss All this Last Summer in writing, And Your Excuse is hurry & Out of town. As You have noe buissness to write Upon, Your Letters might have bin Equaly As Well wrote in the Country as in town, And I doubt not If You would Give'n Your Self the time, you Could have found many agreea[b]le Subjects to have Inlarged Upon. Pray dont Give me Cause to Complain again on that Score, for tho' I am Very Glad to hear of your being in health by your Short Letters, It would Ad Very Much to My Satisfaction to See the Improvements of Y[ou]r Mind in Some Ingenious Observations of your Own.

Your Uncle Nath[a]n is here at pr[e]s[en]t, but intends to Sett Out Again in a few days. You may be Sure I've asked Many Questions Concer[nin]g your Conduct & how you behave towards y[ou]r relations, wich has bin agreeable to my Wish in all Respects but in that relating to y[ou]r Aunt, Who, he Says, wathever Appearance of friendship there may be on Each Side, is not Very Cordiall. She takes Much Amiss your Intimacy with her daughter[1] (And I have heard your father blame you Very much for it). It gives me Some Uneasyness. I hope you Will not be Soe forgitfull of yours Self to give your relations any Cause to Complain by any Unworthy Action. Your discreet behaviour has hitherto bin a Subject that has recommended you to Every one. Pray dont Veryfie the Proverb that the Still Sow drinks all the draught.[2] I Desire y[ou]r Aunt May be Used with All the duty due to a parent, And if any thing you doe She takes aMiss, I intreat You would not Presist in doeing of it. Let it be wath It will, but by a Very Obsequious Resignation to her Will, give her noe Cause to Complain, And you will Very much Oblige y[ou]r father & my Self. I desire You would Not take Any notice to her that I write You this, for your Uncle Nath[a]n beg'd I would not.

---

1 A.F. may be referring to N.F.'s intimacy with Isaac Franks's daughter Phila, whom N.F. later married. J.F.'s concern would seem to rule out the Levy family.

2 This proverb appears in John Ray, *A Compleat Collection of English Proverbs* (London, 1737), 159, as "the still sow eats all the draught." This is an example of A.F.'s. malapropism.

As for news, y[ou]r father is Soe large on that Subject that Wathever I Say would be only Tireing you with repetitions. I hope you have bin to pay your respects to the Gentry t[ha]t [are] gone from hence. If you Should Meet With Col[one]l Morris before you hear of his Arrivall, you will Certainly be Very Much Surprised. Pray pay him the regard due to his Age and Charector.[3] As for his Son, Mr. Robert,[4] whoes age will make him y[ou]r Companion, I desire you would Make your Company as Agreeable to him as you Can. He does not want for Sence, but I will not dwell on his Charector but Leave you to find it, tho' I'll give you this Item: he is Very full of himself. Mrs. Norris Is the Same Agreeable Person. Wee often See Each Other. She gives her Love to you

I am Under a Vast Concern for Colly. I am Surprised his mother & brother are Soe Indiferent Abouth him. He is Certainly Very blamable & nothing Can be Said in his Justifycation, but Still he must Live, and they would be Sorry if he Should doe worse then he has don in order to Procure himself a Liveing. I have don Something for him in Perswading y[ou]r father to Assist him, but he Says now he [neither] can nor will doe noe more for Him. I wrote my brother Is[aa]c[5] a Letter to Git him Out of Jayl, for I was quite Sick at the

---

3 Lewis Morris and his son Robert Hunter had left for England on November 23, 1734, to solve their problems with Gov. Cosby. See Letter VIII, April 11, 1735, note 2. Shortly after, on January 21, 1735, the Pennsylvania House of Representatives appointed Lewis Morris their agent in England. *Pennsylvania Gazette,* Jan. 28, 1735. Lewis Morris was at this time sixty-three years old.

4 Robert Hunter Morris (c. 1700–1764) was about thirty-four years old at this time, while N.F. was only nineteen. There is no record of their meeting in extant correspondence, despite A.F.'s hopes. The correspondence from his mother, Isabella Morris, which is in the Morris Papers, reveals a personality somewhat akin to A.F.'s, particularly in regard to giving advice on behavior. See especially her letter to Robert dated April 8, 1735.

5 Isaac Levy (1706–1777), A.F.'s brother and a resident of Philadelphia, New York and London was an affluent merchant who had a long career. At the time of this letter, he seems to have been in Philadelphia. Edwin Wolf and Maxwell Whiteman, *The History of the Jews of Philadelphia from Colonial Times to the Age of Jackson* (Philadelphia, 1957), 23–26.

thought of his being there. And After I Sent the Letter I Acquainted your Father with it, for wich I had ye reprimend I Expected. However I was not Uneasy at It. I Expect y[ou]r Uncles will be Very Angry with me for it, but Give my Service to e'm and Tell them Alltho' I Saw the Strict Orders they gave Not to Assist him, I was resolved to break thro' if Such a Misfortune Should befall him. In Short, wath the Consequence will be God Only knows. It was a wrong Step to Send Him Away in that Manner in Soe distant a place, for Unless he is Under Some Care, he Never will keep within bounds, for you See as Soon as y[ou]r father was gon from here, he fell into these Extraveganceys, which generly Is attended by Such I'lls As requires A Vast deall of trouble, charge & Shame before a Person Can Extricate themselves out of e'm.

All friends Pres[en]t there Service to you. You are not to Expect A Letter from y[ou]r brother & Sister Untill the Spring. They recommend theire Love to you. My Love to all friends. Fanny Riggs returns your comp[limen]ts and to Coz[i]n david[6] with regard. I've Said All I can think of at Pres[en]t and Shall Only ad my hearty Adieu And blessing. I am, my Dear child,

Your Affectionate mother,

Abigaill Franks

New York [Wednesday] Decem[ber] ye 25th 1734
to Nap[hta]ly Franks

[Docket]
From my mother[7]
[Address]
To
Mr. Napthly Franks to be Left at

---

6 David Salomons, son of Abigail Salomons, J.F.'s nephew and N.F.'s cousin, was licensed as a broker in 1745 in England. Dudley Abrahams, "Jew Brokers of the City of London," *MJHSE* 3 (1937), 90.

7 In Naphtali's hand.

Toms Coffee house Corn Hill near the
Royall Exchange
London
by Capt. Wingfield
~~QDG~~

VIII
[Abigaill Franks to Naphtali Franks, April 11, 1735]

Dear HertSey

I have Deffered writing to this Very Last moment In hopes to have had Some Letters from You to have Answered (Stephens being hourly Expected),[1] for realy I have nothing to Say but that wee are Well, and I hope you are Soe Likewise, Wich happyness I wish wee may Long injoy. I could Some times find Subject to write, Was Noe one in the Family to write but myself, but y[ou]r father Sends Letters Soe often that he gathers all thats worth Communeicating, With Wich I fancy You may be Sattisfyed. Our party affairs Subsists Still with a Vast deall of heath on Each Side. People are Impatient to Learn the result from Col[one]l Morris's Goeing home[2] And in the Mean

---

1 The sixty-ton brigantine *Thomas,* John Stephens, master, was registered as arriving from London on May 10, 1735. NOL, CO 5/1225. A.F.'s "hourly" expectation was a little longer than anticipated, a good illustration of the delays and vagaries of colonial trade and transportation. Also A.F.'s reference to this "very last moment" is strange since there were no commercial ships sailing directly to London at this time; the first to leave after the date of this letter was the brigantine *Joanna,* Samuel Payton, master, early in May 1735. *Weekly Journal,* May 5, 1735.

2 Lewis Morris, who had been removed from his office as chief justice in 1733, was still in the center of political opposition to Cosby. As a member of the Assembly from Westchester he obtained leave of the House in November 1734, "to go Home," pleading a sore leg which often proved a hardy expedient and was called by some his "Politick Skin." "Home" to the Assembly meant his Morri-

time pleas themselves with theire Own Speculations, wich is Regulated According as a Person Stand Affected. I bleive when Capt[ain] Norris first Arrived,[3] he did not intend to Interfer Soe much As he has don Since, for he Waited on the Governor Severall times And had A Visit returned. But After the New Choice of Our Corporation, In wich I think he was Something to buissy and Showd Some folly in Puting out Candles by way of rejoyceing,[4] Wich broak of all Show of Civillity, I bleive Norris wishes he had not gon Soe far in that matter. Wee have had Severall reports of a New Governor comeing Over, but it Never meets with Much Cr[edit]. Most People bleived it was made here with a design to mortyfye Mr. Cosby.[5]

By your Next I hope to hear wath resolution is taken in regard to

---

sania estate, but to Morris it meant England, where he could present his case on the transgressions of Cosby to the Crown. Accompanied by his son, Robert Hunter Morris, the ex-justice went to Shrewsbury, New Jersey, where on Saturday, November 23, 1734, he sailed for England, probably on board the *Joanna*, Samuel Peyton, master. This account, found in William Bradford's *Gazette*, a pro-Cosby newspaper, was protested by Zenger, who claimed Morris did not leave in secret but as ambassador of the northern colonies. *Gazette*, Nov. 25, 1734; *Weekly Journal*, Nov. 25, 1734, and Dec. 9, 1734. A.F.'s reference to Morris "Goeing home" is obviously intended in a satirical sense.

3 Capt. Matthew Norris, son-in-law of Lewis Morris, who arrived in New York in July 1734, was obviously in favor of the Morris faction. *Weekly Journal*, July 29, 1734. He seems to have provided a pinnace from his ship *H.M.S. Tartar* to carry Morris to Shrewsbury, New Jersey, from whence the latter departed for England. Ibid., Dec. 9, 1734.

4 The "new Choice of our Corporation" refers to the election of John Moore to the Common Council from the Dock Ward by one vote on September 30, 1734. Moore, Zenger's *Weekly Journal* explained, was not selected by Cosby's opponents, but he did receive their support.

5 Many rumors circulated concerning the Morris-Cosby dispute. Rumors had it that Morris would return either as governor of New York, or as governor of New Jersey, which heretofore had been governed by New York's executive. His power in England, while nor great enough to accomplish the former, succeeded with the aid of his friend Sir Charles Wager in obtaining the latter. Beverley McAnear, "An American in London, 1735–1736," *Pennsylvania Magazine of History and Biography* 64 (1940), passim.

your Goe ing Abroad. I am & have allways bin Very Eassy on that Score because I Am Assure'd your Uncle's will Act with care, and I hope your Conduct will Answer theire Good intentions. Pray Give my humble Service to them all and Allsoe to your Aunts. Docter Ramsey[6] Will Dliver you a Virginia Nightingale, wich pray present with my Love to Mr. Is[aac] Franks's Dau[gh]t[e]r. She Must take Care and feed him with Rice, but it must be broak and Once or twice a Week with ye Yolk of an Egg boiled hard. I must beg of you to be Acquainted with Dr. Ramsey, for he Seems Very much to desire it. Capt[ain] Long intends to goe to y[ou]r Uncles As Soon As he comes Up to London but desires you would Send him a penny post Letter at wills Coffee[7] house Near the admirallty Office. Fanney Riggs Gives her Service to you and thanks You for all Your Letters. Uncle Ashers[8] Gives his Love to You And Soe does all friends you can remmember. Your father desires you would Pray your Uncles to Give Capt[ain] Long An invitation, for it was his Own Motion to goe to Your Uncles, for Wee told him you Should Wait opon him but he insisted opon the Other. He is Very Sorry to Leave this place. Lady fitz Roy writt her mother you had bin to see her. I wonder you never mention Mr. Williams.[9] I expect a Vast deall of News by him. I think

---

6 Probably Dr. Archibald Ramsey, who was in England at least during 1738–1739. Entries of Nov. 17, 1738, and Jan. 6, Feb. 28 and March 21, 1739, Sir Peter Warren's Account with Mr. Edward Jasper, Peter Warren Papers, Sussex Archaeological Society, Lewes, England.

7 In 1772, Will's Coffee House was located at 17 Cornhill by the Royal Exchange. Bryant Lillywhite, *London Coffee Houses* (London, 1963), 398 and 651–652.

8 Asher Levy, A.F.'s brother, may recently have arrived in the colonies. In 1733, he was in England. See Letter II, July 9, 1733. In A.F.'s letter dated June 9, 1734 (Letter VI), she indicates he is no longer there. He, therefore, must have left England some time between 1733 and the date of this letter. There is a reference in Letter XII (Dec. 3, 1736) and Letter XIII (June 5, 1737), which indicates he is back in England and another reference in Letter XVI, July 6, 1740, to his being in the colonies again.

9 Williams is a very common name in England and New York, and without a first name it is impossible to know to whom A.F. referred.

I Shall Conclude this Medly with Presenting your brothers & Sister Love to You, Accompanyed with my blessings And Affections. I am, Dear child,

Your affectionate Mother,
Abigaill Franks

Dear HertSey

Pray accept of my Love

R.F.[10]

My service to Mrs. Salomons. Tell her my Little Poyer[11] take's affter [her], for Every body that Sees her Says She is a beauty. The Governor's Youngest Son[12] is on board the man of war. He came here for a Letter to You, but I told him I had wrote but would take care you Should see him.

New York [Friday] Aprill ye llth 1735

To Mr. Nap[htal]y Franks

[Docket]
From my mother[13]
[Address][14]

10 In another hand, probably Richa's.

11 Poyer, a favorite daughter of A.F., is virtually unknown outside of these letters. She is not mentioned in the wills of any of the relatives including the will of Aaron Franks, proved in 1777. She probably died some time after 1748, the date of the last of A.F.'s known letters. She may have been named Abigail, for in an entry under Nov. 7, 1739–Jan. 1743, Ledger D, Account Book of Elizabeth Schuyler, NYHSL, J.F. is charged £2.12. 3 for various items including one-half yard of brocade "deliver'd to ye daughter Abigail."

12 Henry Cosby (d. 1753), the youngest son of the governor, returned to England to become captain in the Royal Navy. Oliver, *History* 1: 243.

13 In Naphtali's hand.

14 The address, it may be assumed, was written by Richa Franks since the handwriting is similar to that of the statement made by R.F. above.

To
Mr. Naphtaly Franks
at Tom's Coffee house
Cornhill near the Royal
Exchange
p[e]r Doct[o]r Ramsey London

IX
[Abigaill Franks to Napthali Franks, June 15, 1735]

Dear HeartSey

You have bin Very Carefull of Late to Remove all my Complaints of Omission, and it gives me a Vast Deall of Pleassure to Assure you of the receipt of Severall of yours & two in Perticuler of the Largest Size. I note All the Contents And your Intelligence has bin as agreeable As it [is] Various. I dont Supose You Expect I Shall Answer Every Perticuler Paragraph further then wath Justly relates to your Self. In the first place then, I thank god to hear You was Well And in the favour of your Friends, wich blessings I hope may Long attend you, & tho' the first is not In y[ou]r Power to Preserve, the Latter is, wich I am Perswaded you will not Neglect in gratitude to theire Goodness & your Own Intrest. I dont Expect this will find You at London,[1] and, therefore, as You Are Now Launcht out Amongst Strangers, You must be Exceeding Circumspect In Your Conduct. Be Affable to All men but not Credlous, Nor to Soon be Led Away by fair Speeches of friendship. Be Likewise a Very Just Observer of Your word in all Respects, Even in ye most triviall matters, for Ill Habits to too [*sic*] Soon is grown into Customs. I am not at All Uneassy on the Score of your Conduct, and I allsoe bleive you have hade Caution and advice Enough, but Still I Look Opon it As a discharge of

---

1 In the previous letter of April 11, 1735, A.F. mentions that N.F. is "goeing abroad." It is not clear where he went.

The Letters of Abigaill Levy Franks 41

my duty to put in My Mite, for I Shall Say noe more at Preas[en]t on that Subject but pray ye good God to take you Under his Peculiar Gaurd.

I expect to have your Lett[e]r by Mr. houseman this week, a Slo[o]p being Expected. Col[one]l morris writes but Very Seldom to his Family, wich makes it bleived here things dont goe much to his Likeing, for t[ha]t Party have Exulted in Every Small matter they could Lay hold on to Excess, And their Silence now makes it thought they have noe great Success. Party rage has bin Carryed on with Such Violence that for my part, I hate to hear it mentioned. If the Governor has had his fault, the other Side have not bin without theire failings. Capt[ain] Norris, I fancy by y[ou]r discourse, Could wish he had not medled Soe far and heartly wishes a reconcilation, and I dont think the Governor would not be backward If a medium Could be fixt Apon to make it bear without theire Seeming to Seek for it. Soe you find its not Soe Eassy to Git friends as to fall Out.

Your Sister Richa has begun to Learn on the harpsicord and plays three Very good tunes in a months Teaching. Her Master is one Mr. Pachiball,[2] [who] went Over With the Late duke of Portland[3] to Ja-

---

2 Charles Theodore Pachelbel (1690–1750), a noted harpsichordist and musician, was very much a part of New York's musical scene. For an example of a public performance, see the advertisement in the *Gazette,* Jan. 6, 1736, advising that on "Wednesday the 21 of January instant there will be a Consert of Musick vocal and Instrumental, for the Benefit of Mr. Pachebell, the Harpsicord Part performed by himself . . . Consert will begin precisely at 6 o" clock. In the House of Robert Todd Vintner. Tickets 4s." Todd's Tavern was at Broad Street between Pearl and Water Streets. *Iconography,* 4: 544. See also *Weekly Journal,* Jan. 12, 1736.

Pachelbel obviously taught to supplement his income. This reference is one of the few to music instruction in the colony. Malcolm's opinion was respected since he also taught music to Moses, as well as to others. He and Pachelbel were among the few and the earliest music teachers in New York. See Richard Ashfield to Robert H. Morris, June 2, 1735, Morris Papers. See also Letter III, Oct. 7, 1733, note 8.

3 Henry Bentinck (1682–1726), first Duke of Portland and governor of Ja-

miaca. He is allowed to Understand Mussick. Mr. Malcolm Says he is Excellent in his kind. Moses has a great Mind to Learn but the Charge Is to much. He Proffits Very much in his drawing and has begun to Learn to paint opon Glass[4] wich he does Very well. He has don half doz[e]n Pictures for Miss Fanny Moore. Her friendship with Richa Subsist with a Vast deall of Sincerity & Indeed Richa is Like'd by all ~~her Acquaints~~ that know her, And I hope She will Allways have that happyness. Your brother Moses begins to Make a figure. He is a Lad of Very good Sence and Very Ingageing & allways merry.

Your friend Mr. Liveingston[5] was Soe Civill to bring me the Letter You Sent by him the Very Eavening he came. I have not Seen him Since, being he went to Allbany allmost as Soon as he came and Is but Just returned. I shall tomorrow pay his brothers[6] wife a Visit with whome he Lodges, they being Our Neighbours for they dwell in the house next to t[ha]t wich was young Tellers.

I bleive you think wee have abounded in wonderfull Marriages, but Especialy david Hays[7] and Mrs. Grace Levy Must be Something Surprising. For my part I Shall hereafter think nothing Imposiable.

---

maica from 1721 to 1726, died in office on July 4, 1726. Cundall, *Governors of Jamaica*, 104.

4 Perhaps Moses took lessons from Gerardus Duyckinck, a noted New York limner active in this period. See Letter VI, June 9, 1734, note 17.

5 A.F. refers to Peter Van Brugh Livingston (1710–1792), who arrived early in May 1735, after a "Tedious Passage" from London. Peter V. B. Livingston to Henry Van Rensselaer, May 1735, Van Rensselaer–Fort Papers, NYPL. This letter was sent from Albany, for, as A.F. indicated, Livingston went directly to that city.

6 Maria Thong (1711–1765) married Robert Livingston, brother of Peter Van Brugh Livingston, in 1731. The couple lived in the East Ward in a house owned by Peter. NYAL, East Ward, Feb. 24, 1733. Robert was the only brother married at the time. See George Dangerfield, *Chancellor Robert R. Livingston of New York, 1746–1813* (New York, 1960), 517 [genealogical chart].

7 David Hays (d. 1778), a merchant made freeman of New York City on September 16, 1735, married Grace Mears Levy, A.F.'s stepmother, later in that month. It was a second marriage for both. Oppenheim Collection, Case D,

The Letters of Abigaill Levy Franks 43

If Anny thing Occurs in the part of the World You Are an Inhabitant in At pres[en]t, I hope you will Communicate it. I forgot to Tell you Mr. Liveingston Gave me an acc[oun]t of the Masqu[era]d[e] before I Opened my Letter. Mr. Polack And his Wife[8] Goe home by this Oppertunity. I dont know how Collys being Sent to holland will be Approved of, but in short he Would have bin a Continueall plague to Us. It was my Perswasions to his Uncle and himself that got him off. I bleive he will allways be Misserable, and I am Sorry for it. Bryant Talks of Sailling tomorrow. If he Tarrys any Longer & I receive y[ou]rs by Via bost[o]n, I Shall write You Another. Mr. Clark & Family is come to live in Town.[9] Mrs. Beckford bears a Terrible Charector. I hope You will take Care and Lett Uss hear from you as Oft as Possiable. You Charge y[ou]r Fathers Acc[oun]t with Rapine's History & write you Send it, but it has bin forgot to be put Up. I have wrote to y[ou]r Coz[i]n david Salomons abouth it. Pray Lett him know Where he may Git it in order to Send it. This being wath offers, I take my Leave with a Tender parents blessing. I am, my dear Child,

Your Affectionate Mother,

Abigaill Franks

Box 5, Row 4, AJHSL; *Hays vs. Cazelet* (1735), MCP, file 1730–1740, July, 12, 1735; *Portraits*, 225–226. He was elected constable of the Dock Ward the following year. *MCC,* 4: 346 and 353.

8 Probably A.F. refers to Zachariah Polock and his wife, who in 1734 lived in the South Ward. NYAL, South Ward, Feb. 18, 1734.

9 Probably A.F. refers to George Clarke, whose daughter was Mrs. Molly Beckford. See Letter VI, June 9, 1734, notes 28 and 29. Clarke, seemingly upset over the "war" between Cosby and his adversaries, left New York City for his Long Island home early in 1735, implying that he would return to England. It had been rumored that William Smith and James Alexander, pro-Morris adherents, were to be jailed, and he might have felt himself threatened. His return at this time may have been an indication that his political situation was improved. James Graham to Robert H. Morris, Feb. 4, 1735, Morris Papers; *DNB,* 4: 151–152.

Ive made soe Manny blots that you will
be pussled to read this.
New York [Sunday] June ye 15th 1735
    To HeartSey Franks

X
[Abigaill Franks to Naphtali Franks,
December 12, 1735]

Dear Child

All Our Vessle's are Safe Arrived,[1] by Every one of wich I have bin Most Agreeably Delighted in hearing from you And t[ha]t you Was blesst with a happy Tranquility boath in body & mind, the Continnuance of wich may, I hope, Attend you many & many Years to Come. Yours Perticuler to me by Payton[2] mett the Wellcome it merited (Not that I have Less pleassure when I hear from you in Your fathers Letters, for its Still the Same, Lett my Inteligence come from wath Corner it will, its Still ye wish'd for Sattisfaction), but the Wellcome I mean is in regard of the Pleassing Variety it Contains. I have before told you I am Very Well contented to Compound with one Long Letter for many Small ones, but you Observe I dont Answer all Your Paragraphs. I Never thought there was anny Necessity for that as it treats but of things en passant, And I am Pleassed your Opinion agrees with mine on that head. You Tell me you bleive I shall be dis[appointe]d in not finding you Abroad. I conffes it to be Soe, but my disappoint[men]t gave me noe Concern, being I am Very well Assured you are in Such Good hands that wathever they Determin on y[ou]r Score, I am Possitive will be Intended for y[ou]r Advan-

   1 A number of ships arrived in November and early December 1735 from Europe and other ports. NOL CO 5/1225; *Weekly Journal,* Nov. 17, 1735.
   2 Samuel Payton, the captain of the *Joanna,* and his wife, Charity Lawrence Payton, purchased land in the East Ward in July 1733. They lived "on the Dock" fronting the East River. Con. Lib. 31, cp. 488; NYAL, Feb. 24, 1733.

tage. I Should be Very Glad to have You as near home as Possiable, but when my desire can not be Compassed, I have allways bin Soe happy as to make my Self Contented with wath can be don. All my Wishes are Centered in the honourable & Gratefull discharge of your duty in all Respects, and Even in that I have noe fears, being you have made Soe happy a begining in haveing y[ou]r Conduct Approved of by all y[ou]r Friends, and as the Coppy Says, a good begining Makes A good End.[3] I hope it may allways be y[ou]r Fortune in wathever Station of Life you may be Throw'n into.

I am Mightly Pleased to find you have a right way of thinking in Regard to ye many Snares wich Open from One degree of Vice to Another. To[o] much Credulity has Very Often proved the ruin of youth, and one must be Very Cautious in bleiveing those Exteriour marks of friendship & Virtue. Too too Offten the Subterfuge of the Wicked & Crafty minds, the dayly Examples that's heard & Seen in all those great Cittys, must be Very Shocking to A Steady & Virtuous man, from wich all I Joyn with you in y[ou]r Prayers. May the good God Deliver you. Wee have ~~some time agoe~~ had an Acc[oun]t of poor Mr. Everts misfortune Some time agoe. How many years Toill (with a Veiw of happyness to a Parent) one Viccous minute Overthrows. As I Always Sampthyize in the Sufferings of My fellow Creatures, this gave me Some Concern, tho' An Utter Stranger, for as Macduff Says, "none but a parent Can know a parents Greiff."[4]

We have a Vast deall of Polliticall Dissentions, Especially at Preas-

---

3 This maxim appears in Oswald Dykes, *English Proverbs with Moral Reflexions* (London, 1709), 2 and 4, as "A good beginning is a great sign of a good end" and "A good beginning is a fair step to a great as well as good end." Just what A.F. means by *Coppy* is uncertain.

4 In *Macbeth*, Act 4, Scene 3, Macduff on hearing of the murder of his wife and children queries, "He has no children—All my pretty ones? Did you say all?" A.F. was either paraphrasing or possibly had in mind some acting version like *The Historical Tragedy of Macbeth With Alterations As Performed At The Theatre In Edinburgh*, published in Edinburgh, 1753. Macduff says there, "He has no children, nor can he feel a father's grief."

[en]t, our Gover[no]r being Very Ill[5] And has Displaced Mr. Vandam.[6] The Perticuler of all these Broiles Moses will give you an Acc[oun]t of, to wich I reffer. I hope that Gent[lema]n may recover for his Familys Sake. His Death will Prehaps Cause Some Contention in the Place At Least. Vandams Adherents Say they will Not Yeild to Mr. Clark's being Our chieff,[7] tho' my Priviate Opinion is they will Sitt Still, for wathever they doe must be don by Violence, wich they

---

5 The *Gazette* and *Weekly Journal* kept a running account of Gov. Cosby's health, Zenger cheering news of his illness and Bradford attempting to minimize these reports. On December 15, 1735, Bradford wrote that the governor "has for some time past, been very ill, but this Morning he has had a fine breathing Sweat, is something better, and is like to Recover." On December 22, Bradford stated that Cosby, who had been ill with "Pleurisie" for the last twenty-five days, was now out of danger. Zenger on December 29, 1735, noted Bradford's elation and cautioned he should wait until a certificate of health was issued. *Gazette,* Dec. 15 and 29, 1735; *Weekly Journal,* Dec. 29, 1735. See also letter of John Richard to Henry Van Rensselaer, Jan. 22, 1736, Van Rensselaer–Fort Papers, NYPL, in which Richard wrote: "the Governor is Sick and Verry weeck. Yett but there is hopes of his Recoverie."

6 Approximately two weeks after the date of this letter, the *Gazette* on Dec. 23, 1735, reported that the governor had received letters from the Lords of Trade and Plantations dated September 5 in which "they recommend Mr. John Moore and Mr. Paul Richards to be his Majesty's Council, in the room of Mr. Rip Van Dam and James Alexander, Esqs." It was also recommended that Lewis Morris be removed from the Council for New Jersey. The *Gazette* further reported that the letter stated that the Court of Chancery "as now established is approved to be a lawful court, and ought to be continued." Possibly on this advice Cosby dismissed Van Dam. A.F.'s mention of the event predates the newspaper account as well as that given in general histories. It also indicates that the dismissal was not done in secret as is often mentioned, for at least A.F. and her son Moses were quite aware of the occurrence. Lamb, *History,* 1: 561.

7 Cosby's dismissal of Van Dam left Clarke as heir apparent, since he was next to Van Dam as senior member of the Council. As A.F. predicted, the Van Dam–Morris forces refused to recognize their dismissal or to accept Clarke even after he was officially appointed lieutenant-governor after the death of Cosby in March 1736, but they were finally forced to do so. Lamb, *History,* 1: 561; James Alexander to Cadwallader Colden, April 30, 1736, *Colden Papers,* 1 (1919), 148–149.

will have more witt in their anger to Venture at. For As Soon as the Gover[no]r Should dye, Mr. Clark will be Sworn & then noe Power but from y[ou]r Side of the watter can Make it Void, If he Lives & Continues in the Goverment. I Must desire you by a peny Post Letter (Since you will not take the pains to goe) to Acquaint Lady August FitsRoy whenever a Vessle comes to boston or Phil[ade]l[phia], And You will Very much Oblige me, for She writt it was wath you had Promised her but Never had bin Soe kind but once, tho' She Says She bleives you thought Mr. Williams would take care to Lett her know When there was Oppertunitys while he was in England. I am Sure this way Cant be A Vast deall of trouble to you & therefore, I Allmost Insist Opon it. Col[one]l Morris's party are in High Spirits.[8] They Say All Will be Terminated As they would have it, but the Less Violent have there doubts & fears. For my part, If I May fling My Mite Amongst the Mulltitude, I wish it may end in wath will be most Advantageous to Our Country, for Patriots Generly act Opon a Priviate Peek but allways bland theire intrest with the Weall of Commonwealth. Soe Much for Polliticks. Now for the Next part

---

8 There were several reasons for the "High Spirits" of the Morris faction, despite Van Dam's dismissal. The Common Council had on September 29, 1735, made Andrew Hamilton, Zenger's counsel in his famous trial, freeman of the city. *MCC*, 4: 277-278. The fall elections in the city saw a further witness of the popularity of their cause. Finally it was expected that "old Morris" would be successful in London. *Weekly Journal*, Oct. 20, 1735; Feb. 9, April 5, May 3, May 24, and June 7, 1736. As a testimony of their elation a ball was given on January 19, 1736, at John De Honour's Black Horse Tavern on William Street, in honor of the Prince of Wales's birthday. After participating in French dances, the company proceeded to country dances which were led by Mrs. Norris and "On Conclusion Rip Van Dam President of His Majesties Council began the Royal Healths, which were all drank in Bumpers." Ibid., Jan. 26, 1736. A few months previously on October 11, 1735, a similar affair was held at the same hall celebrating the anniversary of their Majesties' coronation. On hand were the newly elected magistrates, merchants, and gentlemen including Rip Van Dam, Matthew Norris of the *H.M.S. Tartar* and Capt. James Compton of the *H.M.S. Seahorse*. Toasts were drunk to the success of Col. Lewis Morris. Ibid., Oct. 20, 1735.

of y[ou]r Letter thats to be answered: You Seem Surprized at the Sway Hymen[9] has had for Some time in our Congregation. I bleive he happen'd to Loose his Torch, for Some Seem to be made in the dark. I wish they may "find these words misplace'd: marrid att Leissure they doe repent in haste,"[10] but Laying Rallery aside, I doe think my grace full mothers marriage disgracefull.[11] I could Allmost Bring in another Verse and Say "frailty thou art Called Woman,"[12] but wath Gave me at first A Concern I now dispise. I think he is the worst of[f], for *[tear]* notheing but a madman would Marry a Woman with Seven child[ren].[13] But Lett them Look Out that have the Watch.[14] As for

9 Hymen, the Greek god of marriage, is usually depicted as carrying a torch.

10 Apparently a reference to Shakespeare's *The Taming of the Shrew,* Act 3, Scene 2, wherein is found "Who woo'd in haste and means to wed at leisure."

11 "My grace full mothers marriage disgraceful" is a play by A.F. on her stepmother's name Grace. This letter reveals A.F. in a jestful mood, in keeping with its literary references.

12 Shakespeare, *Hamlet,* Act 1, Scene 2: "Frailty, thy name is woman!"

13 Grace Levy Hays had seven children as the second wife of Moses Levy—Samson, Benjamin, Joseph, Rachel, Miriam, Hester, and Hannah, all of whom were under the age of twenty-one in 1738. Grace's career as widow and business woman is extremely interesting and argumentative. For her residence in the Dock Ward, see NYAL, Feb. 18, 1733, and Feb. 23, 1734. For litigation, see *Levy v. Hunt* (1733), MCM Vol. 1731–1736, p. 396; *Levy v. Dycks* (1734), MCP, file 1730–1740, Nov. 19, 1734, MCM, Vol. 1731–1736, p. 452; *David Hays and executors of Moses Levy v. Cazelet et al* (1735), MCM, Vol. 1731–1736, p. 493, MCP, file 1730–1740, July 12, 1735. The case which probably most reinforced A.F.'s poor opinion of her stepmother was that of *Gleaves v. Levy* (1729), MCP, file 1725–1729, Dec. 7, 1729, MCM, Vol. 1728–1731, p. 325. In this case Gleaves, a carpenter, sued Grace for £4.6.11 for work involved in making a coffin for A.F.'s father, Moses Levy. Grace denied the charges and refused to pay, insisting rather that Nathan Levy, A.F.'s brother, had promised to pay for the coffin, and that there was nothing in her marriage contract which required her to pay. The result of this suit is not recorded, but it must have left a strong and unfavorable impression on A.F.

For Grace's business activity, see Entries of Dec. 21, 1733, Jay Day Book, 81–93 and 95–96, and Entry of March 7, 1734, Jay Ledger, 96.

14 Perhaps a variant of "Let them that be a cold blow at the coal." William C. Hazlitt, *English Proverbs and Proverbial Phrases* (London, 1869), 259.

the Other Marriages, they May Pass Muster. Sam Myers Seems to doe Very well. If you can Hinder Anny of his Relations coming to plague him, pray doe, for I think its a Pitty he should be Pestered. He behaves him self Very well and Very often remembers to Send them Something at home. Besides he has a brother here allready to mantain, and married A Sister, wich Cost him noe Small matter. I intend to write noe more but this sheet full, And that You will think is Enough. Therefore, I must dwindle into Shorter answers to Some parts of y[ou]r Letter. First, I like the Acc[oun]t of y[ou]r rakes progress. I have Seen 'em in Print and think the design Very good. I have askt Mr. Leveingston if, as the bear, he had those questions asked him; he Says noe. I did not Tell him the reasson of my question, being as he is a Party man[15] he might Say some thing abouth it, wich I Was Unwilling should take its Rise from me. He is Very Well, but I can See nothing of the Surprizing in him. Fanny Riggs insist that you owe her a Letter and intends to put you in mind of it her Self. Your brother moses Intends to Send Farinelli[16] back Again, done opon Glass, wich Way of Painting he does Very Well, As he allsoe does in Indian Ink. Severall Gen[tleme]n that Understand drawing Say he will doe mighty Well in time. His Master, Mr. burgis,[17] Says he Never mett with any one that took the Out Lines of any Soe true and in Soe Little a time as he will. By his bigness you would take him for the Elder brother, for he is much Taller then y[ou]r Uncle Isaac Levy. Richa does pretty well With her Musick. Moses would fain Learn If he Could. He has Stole Some p[ar]ts of tunes by Seeing

15 Just what question A.F. refers to is not known, but perhaps it had something to do with politics.
16 Farinelli, pseudonym of Carlo Broshi (1705–1782), was a male castrate. His fame reached New York, and Moses, quite interested in music, combined his admiration for Farinelli, or that of others about him, with his painting lessons.
17 This is an interesting remark since it indicates that William Burgis, Moses' teacher, was active in New York as of 1735. A standard reference limits his activity to 1716–1731. Burgis is noted for his views of "New York Harbor," c. 1718, and "New York," c. 1729–1731. George C. Groce and David H. Wallace, eds., *The New-York Historical Society's Dictionary of Artists in America, 1564–1860* (New Haven, 1957), 96.

her taught. I wish it was not Soe chargable; they Should all Learn Every thing they had A Mind to, but as it is, Wee must be Sattisfyed. I have not heard of david this Pretty While. I hope his goeing to boston may be for his Advantage.[18] I bleive you have hade a Letter from him before now with An Acc[oun]t of wath he is adoeing And Wath Progress he makes on the fidle. Uncle Nat is here Since Last Week. He intends You a Letter by some of these Ships. I find you have not forgot my Promise of the Smoakt fish. You may bleive Me, I had two don Up for you & two for y[ou]r brother david, and thro' a mistake boath bundls was Sent to boston. Pepers, Peaches, & Wine you will receive by bryant. Your father will Order you a p[ie]s[e] of holland[19] from thence. Had your Letter come a Little Sooner, I Would have sent you a p[ie]s[e] from here wich I had kept for my self. It was Very good, and as I did not intend to make it Up this winter, I Sold it to Mr. Williams. If it was in Our Power your wishes & wants should be Anticipiated in every thing, for its my Opinion all Parents whoe are happy in theire Child[ren]s Conduct after they are Grown Up Ought to Gratify all theire Reassonable demands, If in theire Power. I am Sattisfyed y[ou]r Indulgent father would with Pleassure Answer all y[ou]rs, And if he dont at one time, he will at Anoth[e]r. Therefore, Never Deny y[ou]r Self to Ask for these Small Trifles or think wee think much of your doeing Soe. Your Sister Phila has begun a New Corrispondence, for by this she Send Coz[i]n Becky Salomons[20] a Letter. I cant Imagin the reason I never hear from your Uncle Mr. Abraham Franks's Family.[21] I've not had a Letter from

---

18 David Franks left New York sometime before this letter. In a deposition recorded on August 5, 1735, giving the dates and places of birth of four of A.F.'s sons, it is stated that "David [is] now or lately living in Boston." Con. Lib. 32, cp. 41.

19 Holland cloth is a bleached linen fabric. When unbleached it is referred to as "brown Holland."

20 Rebecca was a daughter of Abigail Salomons and, therefore, J.F.'s niece and N.F.'s cousin. She was left £1,000 by her uncle. Isaac Franks. Will of Isaac Franks, Derby 243, PCC.

21 Abraham Franks (d. 1748), brother of J.F., was a broker residing in Duke's Place in London. Daiches-Dubens, "Eighteenth-Century Anglo-Jewry," 149.

Any of them this two year. I should be Very Glad to know the reasson. Pray commend my kind Love & Service to 'em and beg to know the Cause of this Long Sillence. I have Read the Pessian Letters[22] and think 'em Prittly don. That as A Pres[en]t deserves my Perticuler thanks togather with your Care in Sending the Others. Popes Letters is charming reading. If Any more are Publish[e]d, pray Lett me have them. Me thinks its Very Odd that in Spight of his Teeth, they will Pilfer & Publish his Works at that Manner, and waths more Surprising, I find by the Advertisements they intend quickly to put forth his Life.[23] I dont wonder he is Unwiling to Own the Letters, for Some are wrote with a Spirit of severity on the Court & Some Noble Persons now Liveing, tho' as you say a Gent[leman] said, Whoever wrote them had noe Cause to be ashamed to Own it.

Pray Give my Service to Mr. Pecheco And Tell him his maid hannah Lives with me. He had Like to have Put me to a Great Nunplus this cold weather in Sending for her Over, being She is my Cook & I find it Very Difficult to git one. She intends to goe to him in the Spring, and then I Shall be at A Very Great Loss, for its wath I dont Love to doe my self. I had a design to have got her bound to me for a Term of years, but this has Over Sett it quite.

I am Sorry you Left Sending the Weekly paper,[24] for I think it

---

22 Charles Louis de Secondat, Baron de Montesquieu (1689–1755), was the author of the *Persian Letters*, which was translated by John Ozell, in a third edition in London, 1731. This popular and satirical work first appeared in 1721. It is regarded as one of the first major works of the *philosophes* in their attempts at criticism of European life. Its style obviously was appreciated by A.F.

23 Alexander Pope (1688–1744) was the author of *Mr. Pope's Literary Correspondence for Thirty Years: from 1704–1734. Being a Collection of Letters, Which Passed Between Him And Several Eminent Persons* (London, 1735). Pope's popular works ran through numerous editions, many of them unauthorized. There were at least nine editions of his *Correspondence* in 1735. For episodes of literary theft involving Pope, see *DNB*, 46: 118–120.

24 There were three weekly newspapers in London in 1735. *The Country Journal: or The Craftsman*, which began publication in 1727, reported foreign and domestic news, as well as carrying advertisements. The *Grub-Street Journal* was first issued in 1730 and was discontinued in 1737 and restarted in 1738. The third

Much better then the dayly adevertiser,[25] being ye former Entertained With Some thing of the Learn'd as Well as the Politicall world & the Latter Contains nothing allmost but Roberys & advertisements. Pray give my Service to Mr. Sim[pso]n Levy[26] & Tell him the Last Green Tea he sent is not worth drinking, but Every thing Else is Very Well and for wich I thank him.

To Mrs. Sallomons & Family, Mr. Ab[raham] Franks & Mr. Is[aac] Franks & Mr. Aaron Franks I beg you to make my Compliments Acceptable. I am sorry Miss Franks Lost her bird. I'll take care to Send her a mocking bird Next Spring, for a Winter Voyage will kill it. I have nothing farther to ad but to remember you to make my Spring Letter Very Long & then I am Certain it Will be Agreeable. Mrs. B[eckfor]d bears but an Indifferent Repute here. By All Acc[oun]ts her mother[27] is Mightly Pleased with the Acc[oun]t She gives of her Self; her Letter is Very full of Farinelli. Her mother told me by Way of Mirth, she fancy'd her in Love with him. Some time agoe She Wrote for good horses to ride a hunting with the Princess.[28] She is Mighty full of her Acquaintance with the Nobility, Especially Lord Chester[fiel]d.[29] You Tell me a Certain Lady, you bleive, Will give

---

was the *Weekly Miscellany,* first issued in December 1732. It included accounts of religion, learning, and foreign and domestic news.

25 The *Daily Advertiser* was first published February 1730. A.F. commented that an inordinate amount of space was devoted to crime and advertisement.

26 Simpson Levy, a merchant of Seething Lane, London, was deeply involved in colonial trade.

27 Probably A.F. refers to Mrs. George Clarke, *née* Ann Hyde, eldest daughter of Edward Hyde, Lord Cornbury, a governor of the Province. *Valentines Manual* (1865), 248–249.

28 There were two royal princesses, daughters of George II and Queen Caroline, to whom A.F.'s reference could apply: Amelia (1710–1786) and Caroline (1712–1757).

29 Philip Dormer Stanhope, Fourth Earl of Chesterfield (1694–1773), was noted not only for a varied political career, but also for his letters. Mrs. Beckford, *née* Molly Clarke, may have known him, but she is not mentioned in his published letters. Bonamy Dobree, ed., *The Letters of Philip Dormer Stanhope, Fourth Earl of Chesterfield,* 6 volumes (London, 1932).

you a Pritty good Acc[oun]t of her, wich Verifys the Proverb: Set a theif to Catch a Theif. But Silence is the Word. I find I have said More than I intend[ed] on this Subject, wich I think wrong, being I should have ended my Letter with Some thing better. For I have nothing more to Say but wath I hope will be heard & fulfild by the Power it is adressed to, and that is: May the Allmighty God Guard & keep You to a Long happy & Virtues Life. I remain, My Dear child,

Your Most Affectionate Mother,
Abigaill Franks

I hope Colly is not come to Phil[adelphia] again, for if he Plagues me as he did before, I shall endeavour his return, for these Continuall Complaints gives me to much Uneasyness—

My Pen is Very bad & soe is my Spectacles
and Late at Night, for I never write none
of my Letters but at Night, for thats the Only time I have to be alone.

To Mr. Napt[ha]ly Franks [Friday] Dec[e]m[be]r ye 12th 1735

XI
[Abigaill Franks to Naphtali Franks, October 25, 1736]

Dear HeartSey

As I have not Yet Rec[eiv]ed my Epistile, I Shall not Inlarge, but Just Tell You that the Continued Confirmation of your Good State of health and Good Will & favours of your kind Relations to you Gives me a Vast pleassure. Pray make my best Regards Acceptable to them. I have Sent You two Caggs of Pickles: One is a 15 Gallon filed with peper and the Other Ten with Mangoes, Peaches, And a few peper to fill Up the Cask. When you Receive them, take the Peaches & Mangoes from the peper and put fresh Vinegaer to em, And that will take of[f] the Strenght of the peper. Take care and git your Own Mark, being Mr. Levy has put them in his Receipt.¹ For News And Every thing Else, I refer to y[ou]r Other Letters, tho' If I had never Soe Much to Say, I Could not Digest my thoughts in any method, My Spirits being Soe Low with the Concern I am Under for poor Mrs. Mary Riggs, whoe I Saw a few minutes Agoe dead.² I have nothing Else but Conclude with My prayers for y[ou]r Long Life and happyness, Dear child.

Your Affectionate Mother,
Abigaill Franks

I forgot to tell you in mine that
when Col[one]l Morris, ask'd leave of
the Assembly to go home, Judge Philips
ask'd him if he meant London again.
The old Gen[tleman] did not say a word.
Your Pickles are marked IF no 1.2.
26 Octo[be]r
New York [Monday] Octob[e]r ye 25th 1736
To Mr. Nap[h]t[a]ly Franks.³

---

1 Bills of lading, used as receipts, were made out in the consignee's name. They contained a list of goods being shipped, together with identifying monograms or marks that were also found on the freight, indicating to whom the goods were being sent. The bill and cargo were carefully checked at the port of entry, where appropriate duty was paid. For a discussion of shipping procedures, see Lawrence A. Harper, *English Navigation Law* (New York, 1939), 89–91. A.F. sent the pickles as she indicates at the end of her letter under the mark of IF [=Isaac Franks].

2 The death of Mary Riggs, a close friend of A.F., seems to have been overlooked by history. The event is not reported in the newspapers of the day, or in genealogical references.

3 This note seems to have been written by Richa Franks. The handwriting of both the address and the enclosed note, is the same as that in Letter VIII. She seems also to have written both the note and the address of Letter XXIV.

The Letters of Abigaill Levy Franks 55

[*Address*]

To

Mr. Naphtaly Franks
at Tom's Coffee house, Cornhill
near the Royal Exchange
p[e]r Capt[ain] Gill   London
~~QDG~~

XII
[Abigaill Franks to Naphtali Franks, December 3, 1736]

Dear Child

In my last I Promised to be more at Large wich I Shall hardly be able to make good, being I Deffered writting Untill next Sunday, but Capt[ain] bryant has all att once Determined to Saill Saturday morning, Soe that I am at Preas[en]t in Some haste to finish, it being Fryday afternoon. However, you will not want for Intelligence, being y[ou]r father Sat Late Last Night to write wathever Occured. The most I've to Say is the receipt of y[ou]r Agreeable Letters, And that I was Very much Pleased with the Acc[oun]t you give of A happy State of health. I hope this may have the good fortune to find you in the Same In Company of all y[ou]r kind Relations, whome pray Salute on my Score with my best Affections. Your Father is Under Some concern Still on acc[oun]t of y[ou]r Uncle Mr. Is[aac] Franks's Illness And bleives you dont give him the reall Information in Relation to his health. However, I hope his Fears may Decive him And that this may find him Perfectly recovered, wich Wee Very much Long to hear. I think if England Affords Diverssions, you have your Share, (for att Preas[en]t the Seassons at Bath is the resort of the beau mond.[1] If you

---

[1] Isaac Franks went to Bath, the fashionable resort of eighteenth-century Englishmen, to regain his health at the healing springs.

have made any Perticuler remarks, pray Lett me have them. As for the common Diverssions, I dont Ask a Detaill, being I bleive I Am As Well Acquainted with e'm as its Possible to be in Theory), but pray take A Word of Caution in the Midst of Pleassure: remmember y[ou]r duty to y[ou]r Self. I've Sent a Case for Pickles. Send Noe Wallnuts, for them wee can make our selves. Anchovies, mangoes, & Capers is wath I would have. In the Case is Some Watter mellon Seeds and Some Corn. If you plant them, it must be in Febr[uar]y. The mellons must have ye same Care as muss mell[o]n; the Soill must be Sandy. Dont Laugh at me For Sending Such things, for I think e'm worth the Pains of Planting, tho' if y[ou]r Uncle had not a Garden, I would [not] be So buissy. I have Acquainted My brother Nat[han] wath you Wrote concerning broth[e]r Asher; he justifys himself I think. Nath[an] would be Very Glad if he would come over to Phil[adelphia]. Pray give my Love to him And Tell him his conduct in regard to his not Letting me hear from himself gives me a Vast Concern, besides wath I Suffer in relation to his Unfourtunate Affairs.[2] I did intend by this to have wrote him a Letter, but I did not know if he made Anny Stay in London. Pray Tell him Soe, if with you & Lett me know, if Possible, wath he does or wath he Can doe. Its Suprizing to me he will not be Perswaded to Leave Europe.

Your brother Moses is in great want of a German flute.[3] That wich he brought from Phil[ade]l[phia] he was Obliged to return to the

---

2 The financial affairs of Asher Levy of Throgmorton Street, London, were often fraught with peril. In 1728, Moses and Nathan Levy advertised that the "Scandalous Report . . . that Asher Levy of London, Merchant, is greatly indebted to Sundry Persons in this City . . . [was] entirely Groundless, however, if any Person has any just demand on the said Asher Levy, the same shall be duely paid by Moses or Nathan Levy." *Gazette,* June 3, June 17, June 24, and Oct. 14, 1728. Asher Levy was declared a bankrupt in 1732. *Gentleman's Magazine,* 2 (1732), 1032. A.F.'s appeal finally bore fruit, for Asher came to Philadelphia some time in 1740 and died there in the summer of 1742. See Letters XVI, July 6, 1740, and XXVI, Aug. 29, 1742.

3 The German transverse or modern flute is blown through an opening on the side of the instrument near the upper end. In the middle of the eighteenth century it replaced one which was blown through a mouthpiece at the end.

Owner. Theirefore, he begs you Would Aply to his Uncle, Mr. Aaron Franks, to Lett him have the Pleassure to play on one of his, for he hears he plays on that Instrument. If Moses does not Git A German flute, wee Shall be at a Stand in Our Concern Viz. Richa, moses, & David, And tho' Moses has had noe mast[e]r, he is the best & first hand. Allsoe, he Acts in two Capacitys, for he is chief Singer.

Our Politicks is Very much Sunk, and wath Little theire is you will have from Other hands. Theirefore, I Shall not be at the Pains to Say any Thing Abouth it.[4] You have bin Very remiss in Sending of Some of the Late Ingenious Productions. Pray if Any thing Occurs, Letts have e'm by all Opper[tunitie]s, and Lett me know wath the Magazins will Cost bound, for I have not got them from the beginning. And If they are not to[o] Dear, I would have all I want & Send those I have home to be bound, &, theirefore, dont forgit Letting me know in y[ou]r next. If bryant Tarrys Untill Sunday, I am in hopes wee shall have the Pleasure to have Something to Answer you, for theire is Some Ships Expected at Boston, but, however, I'll finish Att Pres[en]t, praying the Allmighty to be your Gaurd is the Constant Wish of [me], dear Child.

         Your Affectionate Mother,

         Abigaill Franks

My Service to Mr. Simson Levy, and
Tell him the fruit was Very bad & p[l]eas[e]
pray Lett him Retreive my Opinion in Send[in]g
the best Green Tea.

N.B. If I've time will Answer Couzin Davy Salomons Letter. Tell him so.[5]

---

 4 A.F. was probably referring to a vociferous contest between Rip Van Dam and George Clarke for the position of lieutenant-governor to replace Cosby, who had died, until a successor was appointed. Clarke finally received the commission, much to the delight of the "court party." *Gazette,* Oct. 11, 1736.
 5 This N.B. seems to be in the handwriting of Richa Franks.

New York [Friday] December ye 3d 1736
Nap[hta]ly Franks

[Address]

To

Mr. Napthly Franks To be
Left Att Toms Coffee House Cornhill
near the Royall Exchange
London

XIII
[Abigaill Franks to Naphtali Franks, June 5, 1737]

Dear HeartSey

I have three of your Letters answered. The first of them brought Us the Melancholly Acc[oun]t of the death of that worthy and Good man, Mr. Is[aac] Franks,[1] wich truly was a Very great Shock, Especialy to your father, who for a Long while had bin very uneasy on acc[oun]t of His indisposision, and, as he Very justly feard, you had not Given him a true Information How Ill he was. Sam[uel] Myers brought a Letter wich Uncle Ashers had inclosed to him and befor he Opened it, tould him the Sorrowfull Contents. Y[ou]r father Seemed Imoveable for Some time. At Last he broake out in a flood of Tears. He was Very Melancholly for a Long time but now begins

---

1 Isaac Franks died on October 27, 1736. His death was reported in the New York *Weekly Journal* on Feb. 14, 1737, in a notice taken from the *London Evening Post* of Oct. 30, 1736, that stated: "On Wednesday last died at Bath, where he had been for some time for the recovery of his Health, Mr. Isaac Franks, A Jew merchant, reputed worth 300,000£. He was a Gentleman of the most humaine Disposition . . . he annually gave to the Poor for several years past upwards of 5,000 £." See also *Gentleman's Magazine* 6 (1736), 685. Samuel Myers Cohen probably brought the news of Isaac's death prior to its public announcement in February.

to be more setled. For my part, When I find a Person has Soe great a Cause for greife, I can say but Little by way of Releife, knowing nature has its call opon these Occasions, and Nothing but time and Reasson to Aswage the dolor. You Tell me I may Geuss the Concern you Laboured Under At the Loss of Soe Tender a parent & friend. I truly Sampathized with You, but Under that Great misfourtune, you had the Satisfaction of imploying y[ou]r Indefatigable Endeavours in discharg[in]g Your Last dutys to him in Such a manner As procoured you ye commendations of all his friends, & I hope You Still make it your Endeavour in a Strickt preseverance of regard and duty to his remains, for that is all wee have Left to Show our Gratitude to the Memory of Soe kind a benefactor.[2] He was but a Very Young Man, "but in the Grave there is noe Inquisition wether a man be ten twenty or a hundred years Ould."[3] All the difference after deaths is a man's works here on Earth, for that never dyes, and one that has Left soe Great and Good a name may be Said to have Lived full of days and dyed in a Good Ould Age. I hope Soe Great an Example of worth may be an Emulation to All those that have the happyness to be his relations, to fallow his Steps in dischargeing theire duty to God an[d] man in the Severall Stages of Life it Shall Please the Allmighty to Set them in. I hope this may find you in Company of all freinds in A happy State of health, And that happyness And Long Life may allways Attend them. My best respects to Mr. Aaron franks & Mrs. Franks, her Son, and daughter. I Sallute with my Love.

 2 Isaac Franks bequeathed a legacy to all of the Frankses, though the bulk of his estate went to his wife Frances and his children Henry and Phila. J.F.'s debts to Isaac were forgiven, and he was given an annuity of £200 for life. At J.F.'s death, A.F. was to receive £100 per annum while she remained his widow. Each of J.F.'s children was left £1,000—the boys to receive their legacy when they reached twenty-one years of age, the girls at their marriage provided they married with the consent of J.F. and Aaron Franks, the executor of Isaac's will. Will of Isaac Franks, Derby 243, PCC.
 3 This is a variant of a common conception of death as a leveler. See Shakespeare's *Measure for Measure*, Act 3, Scene 1: "Death makes these odds all even," and *Cymbeline*, Act 4, Scene 2.

Your Letter by Farmer was a Sort of Disapointment, for you write me that you had Given Sim: Levy the 6 Voll[umes] of the Magazines to Send me, opon the Strenght of wich I gave all my Loose ones to Uncle Isaac Levy—but I have since reassumed my Gift, finding they Are not Sent by Either of ye Ships. Uncle Isaac has bin here Some time to make Up his Affairs with Mrs. Hays,[4] the Perticulers of wich I refer You to Moses's Letter. Only this I must Say: She is a base Vile woman and her Actions has Allways bin of a Peice, tho' I think in this Last Affaire She has Outdon her Ussall Outdoeings of Malice and Craft. If you See Uncle Asher, pray Give my Love to him and Tell him if, As he thinks, he has bin Ill Used an[d] wishes revenge on his brothers, he has a Sufficient one in the plague My father has Intailed opon Us here in New York by that woman.

By Via boston Last Night, Wee had the pleassure to heare from you and allso that Mr. Aaron franks was returned from bath in good health. Your first Letter that Makes mention of his being out of town

---

[4] Isaac Levy apparently did not "make Up his Affairs with Mrs. Hays," for in December 1738 she and her second husband presented a bill in the Chancery Court which delineates the controversy. The couple maintained that as part of her marriage contract, signed March 24, 1717, with Moses Levy, her first husband, she was to receive at his death £300, in addition to 150 ounces of wrought silver plate and the "best" Negro slave. If Moses failed to live up to this agreement, his executors were obliged to pay her £400. Moses, who died in 1728, left an estate valued at almost £8,500. Grace alleged further that after Moses' death she agreed with his sons Nathan and Isaac, who along with her were the executors of Moses' estate (J.F. was also named, but refused to serve), that they would use her legacy to invest in trade with the understanding that she could have her money whenever she asked for it. Nathan and Isaac also agreed to assist her in opening a retail shop. After she married David Hays in April 1735, she agreed to permit Isaac to take the goods out of her shop at Philadelphia, with the understanding that he would account to her for its value. She alleged further that Nathan and Isaac refused to pay her any money, stating that they had expended all the moneys due her in supporting her and her family. Chancery Papers, File H-No. 19, HDC. See also Inventory of Estates, Vol. 1730–1752, part II, p. 126, New York Surrogate's Court. There is no record of an answer or decision, so the "affair" may finally have been settled out of court.

Allarmed y[ou]r father Very much, for you dont directly tell him he was gon to bath but down to Somersetshir in wich part of the Country bath Lyes, wich he, knowing and allsoe that It was not a proper Season to travell, Made him Very Uneassy. But y[our]s Last night Made all things well again. I was Pleass[e]d with the trust your Uncle reposed in you dureing his Absence, being it Confirms my wishes & Opinion of your good Conduct.

I am Sensibly Concern[ed] at Wath happened in y[ou]r Uncle Abraham Family with regard to his daughter,[5] but its wath I allways Expected, for they will not Consent to Let them have husbands, because the Jews with best fourtunes will not have them, Soe they cant blame e'm if they Chuse for themselves. I Am really concerned for y[ou]r Uncle And wish him better Luck with his Other daughters. Pray give my humble Service to him and Family. I Answered his wifes Letter by Via bristoll, wich I hope She has rec[eiv]ed before now. Att the Same time I wrote to Mrs. franks & Mrs. Sallomons. I cant Tell wath Should be the reasson the pickoles Should be Spoilt, Unless the Vinegar Runs of[f] while they are on board or Else they are to[o] Long in the Cold & Soe freeze. For I keep of the Very Same for my Own Use, and they allways keep Good Untill the return of the Season, Except this year & then it was a Generall Callamity, for the Weather Was Soe Cold that Every thing frooze[6] & Soe of Consequence Spoilt. However, I Shall Send you Some again this year wich hope may prove better. The Silks you Sent are Very dear, but give My Service to Sim Levy and Tell him the Tea Was Very good.

You'll Observe I Sit down to write in a hurry by the Incorectness

---

5 Abraham Franks and his wife Catherine had three daughters, Sarah, Sharlott, and Phila, each of whom received £50 per annum as a legacy from their uncle Isaac while they were unmarried. Seemingly Isaac had some mistrust of their marital plans. Will of Isaac Franks, Derby 243, PCC.

6 The winter of 1736–1737 received considerable comment in the journals. For a period in January no ships arrived or left the port since the ice, which was reported to be four feet thick at Albany, choked the Hudson and New York harbor. *Weekly Journal,* Jan. 17, Feb. 14, and March 14, 1737.

of my Letter, for I put things down Just As they Occur to my memory. I have Very often designed to answer A Letter As Soon As received In order to have Some method, but As I hate write[in]g, I Cant Perswade my Self to take Soe much time. However I would have you bleive You have all the Share in my thoughts that a Constant Series of thinking can Infuse in [a] Mind that is allways Anxious for your happyness, and [I] Should think it a blessing, if it was in my Power by any thing Else but wishes, to Let you know the place you Deserve'dly have in the heart of a Tender parent. Our Little Congregation affords Variety of News & Tatle, but As I Never am Concerned, I dont Care to trouble my Self nor you with it, but refer you to Moses's who will acq[uain]t you with Some. You Complain of Capt[ain] Clark[7] and he makes the Same of you, that you never came near him. I Shall be Very glad of Some of y[ou]r Long Epistles And Allsoe that you would Send Us Some Little Amusements wich You have bin Very remiss of off Late. I sent for the honest yorkshireman[8] & Some other things wich You have not Sent. Pray Send me ye 2^d Voll[ume] of the revolution of Poland;[9] ye first you Sent Some time agoe. Allsoe 2 bottles of the best Scoth Snuf[10] for my Own Use, and 2 p[ai]r Specticles of the Very best. I have endeavoured by a sort of Medly to make a Long Letter, for wich I'll make Noe Excuse, but would have you take it As a Testimony of the pleassure I take in Saying Something to you, and Lett this Assure you that I am, dear Child,

Your most Affectionate Mother,
Abigaill Franks

7 Probably Capt. Thomas Clark who in 1733 resided in the East Ward. NYAL, Feb. 24, 1733.

8 *Honest Yorkshireman*, a ballad farce in one act, was written by Henry Cary (d. 1743) and published in London in the 1730s.

9 A.F. refers to Pierre Massuet's *Histoire des Rois de Pologne et des Revolutions arrivees dans ce royaume*, 5 vols. (Amsterdam, 1734).

10 Scotch snuff is of a dry, fine, powderlike variety.

Pray Give my Love to Mrs. Salomons & Coz[i]n david and Tell them If I should miss writting to them by this, I shall certainly give my Self the pleassure of doeing it by bryant.

New York [Sunday] June ye 5th 1737
    To Napthaly Franks

XIV
[Abigaill Franks to Naphtali Franks, November 20, 1738]

Dear HeartSey

Your Severall gave a pleassure I could wish for more frequently, & tho' you constantly Complain for want of Subject, Still the most Matierall is Confirmed, that is Your being Well, a Subject the most agreeable to me, and wath I wish Long to have Continued.

You Say the Favourable reception your brother meets[1] with gives you pleassure. I Make noe doubt of that, nor your Endeavours to make his Abode there Eassy & agreeable, & I would have him On his part be Gratefull to his friends & himself, that is regulate his Conduct in Such Sort As to Deserve and keep wath is Soe well begun. I have Desire'd moses to make my Compliments to all his relations for theire Favours, wich I Likewise beg you would Discharge.

I have rec[eiv]ed ye Pamphlets by farmer. They are Very Entertaing, Especialy Mr. Pope[2] whoe its Impossiable to be Otherways.

---

1 This was Moses' first visit to England and marked the beginning of a long relationship with that country. He was about twenty years old at this time and had embarked upon his eventful mercantile career. The visit was short, and he returned to New York the following year. See Letter XV, Oct. 17, 1739.

2 These pamphlets probably included the *First, Fourth, or Sixth Epistles of Horace's First Book Imitated by Mr. [Alexander] Pope.* See Register of Books in *Gentleman's Magazine* 8 (1738), 56, 168, and 680.

In Short, if I may Soe Express my Self, I read him with Some Sort of adoration. Wit is Like Wealth: A Very Uneaqull Distribution & Offten bestowed on the most Unworthy. However our Author is not in that Class.

As for news in our Small Spot of the Universe, [it] is hardly worth Communicating and wath there is I reffer you to Moses, whoe, I imagine, will have Epistles in Abundance. I wonder As Much As you can, wath Mrs. B[eckford] Can find to Say to him Soe Constantly, & he, in return, is Very Punctall. I Would rather there was not Soe Strickt a Corispondance Neither At your side of ye Watter Nor in my Family, for alltho' She cannot Commit Soe many Errors & Follys as at St. James's, Still her Vanity is an Example I Should not Chuse Young People should have Soe much of. But its out of my Power to make B[eckford] run in any Other Channell Unless I could be Very rude. I wish her husband Would Come & Fetch her home. You may give moses a Caution to mind wath he writes. I am affraid he has Said Something to her of Riggs & need ham[3] wich I Should be Very Sory for.

Colly has behaved Very I'll. I Allways K[n]ew him to be a Very Week Creature but Could Not Imagine he would, After wath he has Suffer'd, run in these Excesses again. Wath I have said in his favour hitherto Was Mere Compassion & humanity, wich I find Very Ill bestowed, Soe that I quite Give him Up, for it Would be Obstinacy in me to pretend to find Any thing to Say in his Favour. Mrs. Salomons is Very Unfourtunate. I dont think the Greife for the death of a Child[4] Comes near the Torment a parent Suffers for a Shamfull & Ill Conduct. And I am Heartly Sorry She has Soe great a Tryall of both.

   3 A.F. may refer to Henry Needham, an assemblyman of Jamaica, West Indies, Letter XXIII, Oct. 18, 1741. Riggs may be a relative of her deceased friend Mary.

   4 A.F. may have had in mind the death of her own son Aaron, who died on July 21st of this year at age 5 ½. *Portraits,* 214–215. As with the death of her infant daughter Sara, she does not relate this information to Naphtali.

I Must Desire you to forward a Letter to my brother Asher, for I don't know wich way to Direct it. Pray dont faill Sending of it, for its the first I have wrote him this great while. Lett me know wich Way you Direct to him, and then I'll not trouble you to doe it again. I Dont think I have anything more to Say at pres[en]t, only recommending my desire that nothing nor noe Tattle may Cause any Difference between you & your brother. Soe, wishing You health & happyness, I remain Dear child,

Your Affectionate Mother,
Abigaill Franks

New York [Monday] Nov[embe]r ye 20th 1738
Nap[htali] Franks

[On back of letter]

I bleive you did not read kensington gardens,[5] for [if] you had, you would never have Sent it. Pray Send noe more Such Idle Trash. Take Care of the Inclosed

[Section of letter torn out]

[Address]

To

Mr. Napthly Franks to be Left
att Toms Coffee House near the Royall Exchange
Corn hill

London

---

5 A *Walk in Kensington Gardens,* was listed in the Register of Books, *Gentleman's Magazine* 8 (1738), 440.

XV
[Abigaill Franks to Naphtali Franks, October 17, 1739]

New York [Wednesday] October the 17th 1739

My Dear Boy

Your brother Joyn'd the wellcome receipt of your Letter with his Safe Arriveall And, as you Very well Observe, to all our Sattisfaction, and wath Still rendered it more Soe was that he had not Lost the good Opinion his friends where [were] pleased to favour him with on his first Arriveall Amongst them. I will Assure you he has a Sincire & gratefull regard towards them all And Never mentions the many kindnesses received but with infinite Satisfaction. I have made the many inquirys You mentioned And find most things run in the Same Chanell I Allways thought they did. And I often wonder At my Self in Judgeing of Persons & things & at that distance, that I am Soe great a Stranger to & Still to Judge right. I dont Care to come to Any Perticulers Wich are all in Generall Very triffleing but must be born with. I allways have and doe Still recommend Unity. I observe wath you Say in relation to your Own history, wich is not of that indifference. However, a word to ye wise will Suffice to you on that Score and Conclude that Subject with Mum.

You tell me Moses is Very much improved. I dont know Wether you mean in body or mind. I find noe Alteration Unless it be to Understand Dressing & Diverssions better, for he did not goe Away a fooll from hence, And while with you that Continuall round of Pleassure might make a Person more gay, but Very Little improve his Understanding. However, he is Very well, & Every one thinks Soe. Wath makes me make this Small Digression is in favour of my Own Country, for at your Side of the watter You will not allow any thing right but wath has the Advantages of being bred amongst you. And for my part, if I may Judge by aperance, you have Not many more Naturall Advantages to boast of than others, for I am Sure as many Stupid Ignorant wretches has Come from England as from any where

Else. I will not put fools in the number, being want of Sence is not in our Power to choose (wath I here mention is As it regards our Own Nation).

Your Pictures Are quite an Acceptable Pres[en]t. You will make my Compliments of thanks to Mrs. Franks for those of her Family & allsoe to Mast[e]r & Miss Franks. The whole Family Was in raptures. Your Father walks abouth the Parlour with Such Pleasure a Viewing of them As is not to be Expresst. Most of your Acquaintance knew Your Picture, but I will ingeniously Own I dont find that Likeness, but it was designed for you, & that Pleases me to have it. The baby house has made your two Younger Sisters[1] quite happy, tho' Like the Golden Apple, there is Some Contention who Shall be the Sole Possesor, but I have bin Paris in this Case & tho' I have not given it to the fairest, I Adjudged it her that will take the best Care of it, & that is becky, whoe Joyns with her Sister in thanks to Miss franks for her favour.

Now Dear hertSey, Give me Leave to make an Excuse to you on Acc[oun]t of my not takeing the Pres[en]t you was soe good to Send me. My Only reason was that I think its takeing too much from You. I would have you be Assured the Tender of Your good will was Very agreeable to me, And I Give you As many thanks As if I had taken it. Your Sister Richa Indeed has taken one[2] on the score of Your Sending it to me, but Whenever Moses Sells Or Sends them back again, I Shall make her return it. I think where a Parent cant Mend A Child's fortune, they Ought to be Cautious of Deminishing, & I Shall All-

[1] The doll house was probably sent by Phila Franks, daughter of Isaac, to Rebecca and Poyer, The latter was the younger and "fairest" of the two. Phila, A.F.'s daughter, born June 19, 1722, was seventeen years old at the time, and Richa was a few years older. Richa had been born some time prior to 1717. See Rosendale, "A Document Concerning the Franks Family," 103–104, for Phila and David Franks's birthdates; Will of Moses Levy, dated July 30, 1717, later revoked, Nathan Simson Letter Books, C 104/13, Public Record Office, London (microfilm copies in the American Jewish Archives and AJHSL).

[2] One of the presents was a ring. See Letter XVI, July 6, 1740.

ways think my Self Assured of my child[ren]s duty by there Discreet & Prudent Behaviour's, wich hither to &, hope I, Never Shall have Any Occaission to Complain of.

Pray Give my humble Service to Mr. Pecheco and thank him for the Pres[en]t of the book he Sent me. Its Very Entertaining to me, for I confess it to be agreeable to my Sentiments in regard to our Religeon. Whoever wrote it, I am Sure, was noe Jew, for he thought too reasonable. You will Say Prehaps I pay a Compliment in that Expression to myself, but, I Must Own, I cant help Condemning the Many Supersti[ti]ons wee are Clog'd with & heartly wish a Calvin or Luther would rise amongst Us. I Answer for my Self, I would be the first of there followers, for I dont think religeon Consist in Idle Cerimonies & works of Supperoregations, Wich if they Send people to heaven, wee & the papist have the Greatest title too.

I should be Glad to know wath Mr. Pecheco Says to his Nephews itended Marriage,[3] for I Realy bleive it will be, but how Soon I Cant Tell. The Portugeuze[4] here are in a great ferment abouth it And think Very Ill of him, but Lett it be as it will, I bleive Rach[e]ll will not have the best of Tempers to deall with. He is goeing to make a Stay all this winter & then, prehaps, they'll marry.

   3 Isaac Mendes Seixas (1709–1782), the son of Abraham Mendes Seixas (d. 1738), a London merchant, married Rachel Levy (1719–1797), A.F.'s half-sister (see Letter XVI, July 6, 1740). It is not clear to which Pacheco A.F. refers. Rodrigo Pacheco was married to Isaac Seixas's sister Judith, and Isaac, therefore, would be Rodrigo's brother-in-law, not his nephew. It is possible that Isaac's father, who is known also as a Pacheco da Silva, had a brother to whom A.F. refers, but he is not mentioned in Abraham's will. Will of Abraham Mendes Seixas, *Wills*, 98–102. Isaac Seixas was elected constable of the South Ward in 1747, but was declared ineligible since he was not a freeman or freeholder. *MCC*, 5: 200 and 202. He was very much involved in congregational activities. Minute Book, 42, 45, and 49.
   4 This reference is to the traditional hostility between Sephardim (Spanish and Portuguese Jews) and the Ashkenazim (German and East European Jews), relating generally to religious observances, but having social overtones as well. A.F. often refers to the Ashkenazi as Tudesco, the Italian word for German.

You reffer me to the Caution in your fathers Letter with relation to Colly and Say things are Easier Prevented then mended. Good God wath An Opinion must you have of your Sisters! Sure noe woman of Common Sense Can be Soe infatuated As to throw her Self Away onpon one Whoe is the most Unaccountable Creature of god Allmightys Creation in all respects, & tho' he meets with Some Civility from Us, its not paid to his Understanding but to his want of it. Therefore You may make your Self Very Easy on that Score. He is got into the Jerseys & Promises to be intirely Guided by his Uncle. I was Very much Vexed at first that they, [in order] to Ease themselves, Should Send him to plague Us. I see noe reasson why Persons that take a wrong Method with there Chill[dren] Should throw them opon others. I told Colly he was like a bad bill in being returned opon my hands And Assure'd him if he did not mend, I Should take the Examples of his relations & Give him Quite Up. I rely Very Little on any Promises he makes, for they Seem hitherto to be All Wrote Upon Glass, & Goeing to Live where he does now will be the Only Last Method for a reformation.

I am now to Acquaint you with a Violent Secret, And that is Sollomon Hart,[5] if he Can, will Make a Match with Rachell Isaac's. My Aunt,[6] Whoe you know is a Very good Woman, asked My Opinion before She would Come to Any Conclussion. Noe one Else is Acquainted with it further then by Common report, as it allways is in Such Cases, wich I Never would bleive because I had not Soe good An Opinion of his Understanding as to Make Soe good a Choice.

---

5 Solomon Hart was *shohet* and *bodek* of the Synagogue from 1740 to 1744. Little is known of him, although there is a record of his running away from his wife sometime in 1743. See Letter XXXI, June 7, 1743, note 10; Entry of May 19, 1741, Jay Day Book, 322; Minute Book, 43–44, 47, 51, and 213. A.F.'s reference to Solomon's brother was probably Moses Hart, a well-known English merchant.

6 Rachell Isaacs may have been the daughter of Abraham Isaacs and Hannah Mears Isaacs, who may have been the sister of A.F.'s stepmother Grace Mears. In this case, Hannah would be A.F.'s stepaunt and Rachel her cousin. *Dictionary,* 65 and 110. See Letter XXI, June 21, 1741, for the death of Aunt Isaacs.

You know Very Little of Coz[i]n Rach[e]ll, but Lett me Tell you She is A Very Senciable, Discreet, Purdent, & worthy Girle. Noe Family Need be asshamed to have Soe Good a Girle come Amongst them. I told My Aunt that Since She did ask me about it, I thought She would doe Very Well if She Could see her Daughter Setled, She being an ould Woman her Self, And the Young Fellow Endeavours to Git his Liveing. Mr. Cruger[7] is Very Much his friend. I Suppose his brother will be Very Angry, but I cant think it will be with reason. They cant Expect A Woman with a Great Fortune will marry a Man that has nothing but his industry to depend on. I have not Soe much As Acquainted your Father with this, for if it Should not come to a Conclusion, Its better noe one Should know it was Ever Designed.

I send you by this three Caggs peper: one for Your Family, one for Mrs. Salomons, and one for Mr. Ab[raham] franks. Pray be Very honest And give Each there Own, for Moses Tells me You dont Deall Consentiously with them if I Sent them all to you to Distribute as You please. Capt[ain] Gill will deliver You A Small bottle of Pickle'd Cane & Cabidge. I had two bottles Pres[en]t[e]d to me, but I had the Ill Luck to break one Else you Should have had them both.

Your Old Friend Mr. Malcom goes in this Ship. He Promises himself a great deall of pleassure in Seeing You. It was a Sudain resolve; he has Mett but Very poor incouragement here. I suppose he goes in hopes of Some advantage.

I Suppose You have heard befor this of the part acted by Young Sam Levy.[8] He has, ever Since he is bin here, bin a Great plague to

---

7 Probably John Cruger, a noted merchant, and mayor of New York in 1739 and 1757, or his son Henry Cruger (b. 1707) who arrived here in 1738 from Jamaica. The latter's son Henry married Ann Delancey, daughter of Phila Franks, in 1762. *Burghers,* 85 and 139; Colonial Dames of the State of New York, *Genealogical Records* (New York, 1917), 62–64.

8 There was at least one contemporary Samuel Levy in New York at this time. A Samuel Levy was elected constable in 1736 and *parnas* of the congregation in the same year and again in 1745. The name first appears in the Minutes in 1729 and continues to appear until 1772. Minute Book, 11, 20, 30 and 35; *MCC,* 4: 346

The Letters of Abigaill Levy Franks 71

his Uncle and Aunt, but this Last was Very Unexpected. Pray give my Service to Mr. Sam Levy[9] & Tell him I am Sorry his Nephew turned Out Noe better, but I must doe Soe much Justice to the Other fooll he has here to Assure him he was not at all Privy to Any of Sam Levys affairs. And I bleive if Ab[raham] Vreest[10] had bin in town, he would have found it out Sooner & by Discovering it would have Prevented his goeing Soe Great a Length. Sam Levy is in Exile now at Phil[adelphia]. I think the best they can doe will be to order him home & Lett him play the fooll there, for then he will find enough to keep him in Countenance.

I cant Tell if I Shall have time to write to any of your Relations. Our hollydays[11] have hindered me from writting, And Gill Talks of

---

and 351. A Samuel Levy was was a member of Henry Cuyler's militia company in 1738 along with Jacob, David, and Moses Franks and Samuel Myers Cohen. E. B. O'Callaghan, ed., *Documentary History of the State of New York* (Albany, 1851), 4: 143. A Samuel Levy died in Huntington circa 1762. The inventory of his estate was attested to by Naphtali Hart Myers. Inventory of the Estate of Samuel Levy, Oct. 6, 1762, Oppenheim Collection, AJHSL. These references may be to one Samuel Levy or to several. At any rate, A.F. probably refers to the Samuel Levy who with Moses Salomons later had business interests in South Carolina which caused them a great deal of difficulty. See Letters XX, April 26, 1741; XXVII, Aug. 29, 1742; and XXVIII, Dec. 5, 1742.

9 This Sam Levy of England mentioned as uncle of Sam Levy, was possibly the brother of Isaac Levy, A.F.'s cousin. A Samuel and Hyman Levy, merchants, were listed as residing at Devonshire Court, Houndsditch, London, from 1738 to 1741. *The Intelligencer or Merchants Assistant* (London, 1738), 119; *Universal Pocket Companion: A List of Merchants* (London, 1741), 104. See Letter XVIII, Aug. 31, 1740, note 2.

10 Perhaps related to an Aaron Verse or Verss who was in Rhode Island in 1685. "Items Relating to the Jews of Newport," *PAJHS* 27 (1920), 176; or perhaps Abraham Forst, a prominent Mason: *Dictionary*, 38.

11 The holiday season was rather late that year. Rosh Hashanah [the Jewish New Year] for the year 5500 *Anno Mundi* began on October 3, 1739, and Simhat Torah [Rejoicing over the Law], concluding the Tishri festival season, fell on October 25th (N.S.) or October 14th (O.S.). A.F. wrote this letter a few days later, on October 28th (N.S.) or October 17th (O.S.).

Sailling to morrow. If I Should not, pray make My [compli]ments to them all and pray them to Excuse me & Likewise to Mrs. Compton.[12] Shee Complains Very Much of your Lost Friendship. I wonder You cant find soe much time as to See Your Old friend. I've a Complaint Against You for keeping My Letter Soe Long, for She Tells me She received it but ye middle of May. Next time I inclose a Letter I will Send a peny to pay the peny post to Carry it. Pray Send me ye 2 Voll[umes] of Hibernicus Letters[13] & ye Polite Philos[ophe]r[14] by the first Opportunity. I have Nothing More to recommend At Preas[en]t but to Assure You the Greatest Pleassure to me is hearing from you & by Allways to Convince you that I am, Dear HeartSey,

Your Affectionate Mother,

Abigaill Franks

When I write you Such
Long Letters, you must
Overlook ye blunders &
scrawlls, for I hate
writing & allways
write in Haste.

12 Perhaps Elizabeth Compton who resided in the Dock Ward in the house of George Burnett in 1732, and, in 1737, as Widow Elizabeth Compton, sold a house in Wall Street. NYAL, Dock Ward, Feb. 18, 1732; Con. Lib. 32, cp. 79. More likely, however, she was Fanny Compton, wife of Capt. James Compton, in command of the *H.M.S. Winchelsea,* who was in New York in 1735 and 1736. See Letter X, Dec. 12, 1735, note 8; James Compton to Robert H. Morris, July 21, 1737, Morris Papers; *Pennsylvania Gazette,* April 15, 1736.

13 *Hibernicus Letters or A Philosophical Miscellany* was written by James Arbuckle in two volumes. The second edition was published in London in 1734. In the British Museum catalog there are references to other works with the title *Hibernicus.*

14 A.F. refers to a book entitled the *Polite Philosopher: An Essay on That Art Which Makes Man Happy in Himself and Agreeable to Others,* written by James Forrester and published in 1734.

[Address]

To

Mr. Napthli Franks
att Toms Coffee House Cornhill near the
Roy[a]l Exchange

London

p[er] Capt[ain]
~~QDG~~

XVI
[Abigaill Franks to Naphtali Franks, July 6, 1740]

New York [Sunday] July ye 6th 1740

Dear Child

After a Teadious Expectation, Gill[1] arrived and brought Us the pleasing Acc[oun]t of your being well, wich in Some Meassure made Up for the Long time wee where without that Satisfaction, Some Vessles Arriveing Sooner to boston and Noe Letters from You Except a Very Short one by the first. It was a Very great Disapointment, Especialy to your father whoe is Very Impatiant at these things. Therefor, [I] beg You will not be Soe remiss for the futer but Send by all Oppertunitys, for in these precarious times[2] Some Vesles may

---

1 Capt. Richard Gill arrived in New York aboard the *Carolina* on June 20, 1740, having set sail from London on April 5th of that year in company with a forty-gun ship. This was a "teadious expedition," as A.F. remarks, at least two to three weeks longer than the usual voyage. Gill carried some thirty officers and military stores for an expedition to the Spanish West Indies. There were few vessels arriving in New York from London during this period, seemingly none since January 10, 1740. NOL, CO 5/1226; *Weekly Journal,* June 2 and June 23, 1740.

2 An undeclared war which had existed between Spain and England during the 1720s and 1730s, especially in the Caribbean, culminated in the "War

miscarry. I dare Say, if You could but know how much it puts him out of Temper, You would be more Circumspect & not Excuse it with being out of Town or hurry of other buisness etc, for I Imagine thats but Triffling.

    I am Very well pleased With wath your Letter Contains but Should wish to have Some more Perfect information in Some Perticulers Abouth [which you are] mum. However, Just as you pleass. Wath you purpose Abouth David Seems Very proper. The Perticulers I reffer to your father, but this I may Assure you, that I bleive he will be Very Indefatigable in buisness. He has not that Sprightly Genious that the rest have, but I dare Say he never will be guilty of a mean base Action and Is Very well liked by all he Converses with. Neither does he Drink or Game. He has a Great mind to Come to London. I Should think if he went there and Soe from thence to Philadelphia, but I Leave it intirely to your management. Your brothers are Very much Obliged to You for the Care you take of there intrest, And I hope in time they will Make a Gratefull Acknowledgement. It would please you Very much if You Could but know wath a Tender affection they all have for you, And the Little Disputes there is amongst them, whoe is Most in y[ou]r Graces. I Should think it a Great happyness If I Could once See you all togather, but its wath I noe Longer flatter myself with, for after 40[3] Age Creeps Upon Us Very fast, And Wee can purpose nothing of Pleassure to come that requires any Distance of time to Compleat. I thank you for your favours by Gill. If I can Perswade Richa to return the ring, I Shall Send it with one of Our Capt[ain]s. If not, you must make her pay for it, for She Seems Determined to keep it. Pray make me Live in the Memory of all My friends and Tell them by Gill I Shall Answer there favours. Severall things that I have

---

of Jenkins' Ear," begun by an official declaration in 1739, and merged into the War of the Austrian Succession of 1740–1748. The remainder of A.F.'s letters are written against this background of international rivalry. For accounts of New York privateers as well as the news of the war fought mostly at sea, see *Weekly Journal,* Feb. 11, May 5, July 12, July 28, Aug. 25, and Sept. 1, 1740.

    3 Born in November 1696, A.F. was at this time almost forty-four years old.

Sent for is not Come, but I shall Wave all Complaints against you & Sims[o]n Levy on that Score Untill bryant Arrives. But if I am then Disapointed, take care. Pray my service to him and wish him Success In His Legacy.[4] Your wish was Lost in Air with regard to aunt Rach[e]ll, for She is marri[e]d to Mr. Sexies.[5] They Live in the Country.[6] David hays and Family Are come to Live in town again.[7] She Letts her child [ren] come to our house, but with her Self I have noe Confab[ulation], Nor I hope never Shall, for I dont Love her. I am Sorry Soll[omon] Hart met noe better reception, for if he comes back, Rach[e]ll Isaacs and he will certainly be marrid. Uncle Ashers went Last week to Philadelphia to try wath he can doe there. Poor man he is Very unfourtunate. As for Publick News, I reffer to Moses & ye rest, Only I Tell you our City is Very Lively with all these Officeiers and beating Up for Soldiers.[8] Mrs. beckford is at last goeing to Jamiaca with wich I am not a Little pleased. She has Such an ascendant over Moses that I am quite Tired with it and have Offten wished him a[t] London again purely on that Score. Mrs. Compton makes heavy Complaints against You for not coming to See her. She

    4 Perhaps A.F. referred to a business venture between Simson Levy and N.F. which was entered into in February 1740. See Letter XXIII, Oct. 18, 1741.

    5 Rachel Levy married Isaac Mendes Seixas in May 1740. "Items Relating to the Seixas Family," *PAJHS* 27 (1920), 161.

    6 Isaac M. Seixas and his wife moved to New Jersey soon after their marriage. See Letter XIX, Nov. 9, 1740.

    7 David Hays and his wife Grace, A.F.'s stepmother, may have lived in Westchester for a while, since many members of the Hays family resided there. *Wills*, 206–207.

    8 Contemporary papers were full of news concerning military preparations and the recruiting of militia. The *Weekly Journal of* April 28, 1740, reported that "Coll. Robinson's Regiment of Foot, with Independent Companies, the Artillary Company and Company of Guards were drawn up in the Common in Battle Array," and that Gov. Clarke expressed his satisfaction with the militia. On June 23rd of that year, the *Journal* announced that 3,000 men were to be recruited and encamped at Hempstead Plains along with 10,000 men from England. It was reported in the issue of Oct. 20th that five days before, Gov. Gooch of Virginia and his militia had left New York for the West Indies.

Owns its a Great way and Cant Expect it Offten, but you have not bin near her Since you was with moses. She has bin exceeding Ill for some time, Else had bin to see you.

If noe Vessles goes from here this faull, I Shall hardly have an Opportunity to Send any peper. I wonder you did not give Mrs. Salomons the Cagg I sent her. These things are quite wrong. Was you Served Soe, You would take it Very Much Amiss. Live by that golden rule, doe As You would be don by.

Colly as Yet keeps within bounds. How Long that Exile of his will Last, I dont Say, for I did not think he would have Tarryed Soe Long. My Service to his Maiesty of Prussia.[9] Thank him for the Compliment he Makes me in Moses's Letter, but Assure him he never Will form a right Judgement of things while he is Soe much Byased by hearSay, for he is as Extravagant in my Favour As he is Prejudiced against New York, And all Upon the Same foundation, that is he knows nothing of Either, Else he would be more Moderate in his Satire or Penagirik.

I have nothing further to Add but my hearty prayers for your health and happyness. I Am, Dear HeartSey,

Your Affectionate Mother etc.,

Abigaill Franks

My Service to Miss harts. I Saw one Mr. Pope
Last Week, Whoe Pretended to be Very Intimate
with them & Mrs. Levy, but I have a better Opinion
off there Choice than to bleive he Spoke truth, for he
is quite a pettit maister.[10] Mr. Simson Levy has the
honour of being his intimate.
Sam[uel] bayard is to be marrid to Fany Moore.[11]

---

9 To whom A.F. refers by this sarcastic remark is not known.

10 A.F. probably refers to the eighteenth-century French term *petit maitre* for a fop or dandy.

11 Possibly Samuel Bayard Jr., merchant, made freeman on September 28,

[Address]

To

Mr. Napthaly Franks
Att toms Coffee house near the
Royall Exchange

London

XVII
[Abigaill Franks to Naphtali Franks, August 3, 1740]

New York [Sunday] August ye 3d 1740

Dear HeartSy

Since my Last I Dont think I have much to Say. However, as by this I have Sent Letters to all the Family that Favour me with there Corrispondence, I Imagined you would take it Unkind if you was Left without an Epistle. Therefore, to begin with the most Materiel point, wich is to Tell you it gave me a pleassure to hear from you Last Week by the Small Vessle freighted by Mr. Pecheco, to Whome pray my Compliments with thanks for his pres[en]ts of Olives & the Second Voll[ume] of des Letters Jeues.[1] I am Sorry he is Displeased att his Nephews Marriage[2] Since its don, but I am Very glad none of

---

1736, or Capt. Samuel Bayard who commanded a successful New York privateer. *Burghers*, 130; *Weekly Journal*, Feb. 11, 1740.

1 A.F. refers to Jean Baptiste de Boyer (1704–1771), *Lettres Juives, ou Correspondance philosophique historique, et critique entre un Juif Voyageur a Paris et ses correspondans en divers endroits* (The Hague, 1736). A six-volume edition appeared in 1738, and an English edition, entitled *A Jewish Spy*, was printed in 1739. The entire work was published in English in five volumes the following year. *Gentleman's Magazine* 9 (1739), 276.

2 For Isaac Mendes Seixas's marriage to Rachel Levy, see Letter XV, Oct. 17, 1739, note 3, and Letter XVI, July 6, 1740, note 6.

Us was Consulted in that Affair. Indeed, at the Very first Rach[e]ll acquainted me with Mr. Sexies Proposalls, I then told her from the Charector of the man, it was my Opinion he never intended the preformance and, therefore, beg'd She would be Very Cautious in her Conduct, but as her mother was with her, I chose to have nothing more to Say to it. I fancy Rach[e]ll Told him my Opinion, for he Never came Near Our house to See her, tho' She was here all the winter. Theire meeting Was at Mr. Levy's,[3] who had the honour of being Consulted throughout the affair, but I beg that May goe noe farther. Mr. Sexies is of an Untractable Dispossision, but I hope he will make her a good husband, for She is a Very good Girle. I dont know Where he could have mended himself in Anny thing but a fortune, but I fancy Mr. Pecheco's quarle is her being a Tudesco. The Portugueze here where in A Violent Uproar abouth it, for he Did not invite any of them to ye Wedding. I find I have dwelt Longer Upon this Affair than I Intended, but it has served to fill a space. The papers &c you sent was Very agreeable to Our Politicians. The Duke of Argyles[4] Conduct has not bin an hour in the house. Since it came, I cant help thinking but that there [is] a Mixture of Pride as Well As Patriotism in his Conduct. Its certain According to our Speculations [h]ere [that] Matters have bin Very Wrong Concerted, for if Admirall Vernon[5] had bin Assisted [in] a Just manner, the Spanish West Indias

---

3 Possibly A.F. refers to her brother Isaac, who by his will left his entire estate to his children Asher and Esther. In it he provided, however, that in the event of their death, his estate was to go to his half-brother Samson and his half-sister Rachel Seixas, an indication of his attachment to Rachel. See the Will of Isaac Levy, *Wills*, 158–160.

4 John Campbell, the second Duke of Argyle (1678–1743), a very factious Scottish dissident with a long career of parliamentary arguments, joined the advocates of a war policy against Spain in opposition to Robert Walpole, prime minister. He was dismissed from the many offices he held and became one of the intriguers who finally succeeded in causing Walpole's resignation. Foord, *His Majesty's Opposition*, 124, 142, 145, 203, 204, and 208.

5 This is a reference to the unsuccessful attack made upon the Spanish West Indies by Admiral Edward Vernon (1684–1757) in 1740. Though he was initially

would by this have bin Very much demolished, [if] not the best part in the possession of the English, for there Fear was great; but now they have had time to recover, our forces will find a much Warmer Reception. Wee have five Companys now Compleat incampt on our Commons[6] And Expect two or three more in a Very Little while. If they Should be Disappointed, its bleived Upon any Such Occaission again they would not find the Americans soe Readily Disposed to fallow the beat of a drum.[7]

You will receive Letters from all the Family by this and Consequently [al]l the News, wich, by the by, is not of Any Consequence further than Assureing you of there [Love] And Good Wishes, in wich I heartly Joyn With them all. My Compliments to Messrs. Ab[raham] & Aaron Franks, Sim: Levy &c &c. Mr. Pittman Sent me

---

successful in his assault on Porto Bello in 1739, the campaign quickly bogged down. The New York journals, like A.F., were deeply concerned with West Indian affairs and tended to blame the defeat on a failure to combine land forces under the command of General Thomas Wentworth with the sea forces under Vernon. *Weekly Journal,* July 28 and Aug. 18, 1740.

6 A.F. refers to the militia encamped in the Field or Commons, a tract of land including present-day City Hall Park. She seems to be paraphrasing the *Weekly Journal* of Aug. 4, 1740, which reported: "We have now five Companies Compleat here commanded by Capt. Clarke, Cosby, Provoost, Cuyler and Stevens, who are all encamp'd on the Common and every Day exercis'd and it is thought will make as good as appearance as any on the Continent of America." See also issue of June 23, 1740. There were several militia companies in New York during 1737–1738. Jacob, Moses, and David Franks were members of Capt. Henry Cuyler's Company along with Samuel Myers Cohen, Samuel Levy, and Gerardus Duyckinck. Seemingly, they were not with the Company in 1740, but no records are available for this date. Joining the militia was a very common practice, partly social in nature. Among A.F.'s contemporaries who were members in 1737–1738 were William Bryant, Moses Gomez, Richard Gill, and Joseph Simson. E. B. O'Callaghan, ed., *Documentary History of the State of New York* (Albany, 1851), 4: 138–147.

7 There is evidence to support A.F.'s fears, for on Sept. 8, 1740, the *Weekly Journal* ran a notice requesting information concerning deserters from Capt. Provoost's Company.

from Lisbon Some Brazill Snuff. Moses Tells me Your Uncle Aaron Likes it Very Well. Therefore, Shall Send him a little, but if he dont Like it, Say nothing abouth it and Give it Whoe you please. I Shall next Month Git the pepers ready and Send by the first Opportunity. You never Lett me know the Jest that I Suppose was made on my Sending the Apples. God bless and [ke]ep you. I am, My Dear child,

Your Affectionate mother,

Abigaill Franks

[Co]lly[8] came to Town a Fryday night to See [his] brother, but I Shall Soon Send him to the [w]oods Again.

[Address]

To

Mr. Napthaly Franks
Att Toms Coffee House Cornhill
near the Royall Exchange
London

---

8 Colly had at least three brothers, Moses, David, and Solomon Moses. Will of Isaac Franks, Derby 243, PCC. In Letter III, Oct. 7, 1733, A.F. refers to a cousin Abraham Salomons, who possibly was also Colly's brother. There is some evidence that Moses was in the colonies at this time for he was in South Carolina in March 1741. Misc. Records, Vol. 69B, 1736–1740, p. 449, Probate Court Records, Charleston, South Carolina. In A.F.'s next letter (Letter XVIII, Aug. 31, 1740), she writes that she will take care of Moses Salomons, indicating that Moses is indeed the brother she refers to here.

XVIII
[Abigaill Franks to Naphtali Franks, August 31, 1740]

My Dear   New York [Sunday] ye 31th Aug[us]t 1740

You Very rightly Judged that hearing from you would be Very Agreeable to me, As your Letter realy was Soe that I received Last night by Via Boston, As I Judge your Love and Duty from your Conduct. I can Eassily Imagine the Satisfact[io]n it must Give you to receive the information of our health, in wich I bless god. This Leaves Us praying the Allmighty to preserve you in the Same and All other Felicity. Its A Month Since I wrote to You in this Same Ship, wich Wee Expected then to have gon in a few days. As I Am not at the pains to Copy my Letters (they not being of any Consequence), I have forgot wath I filled the paper with, but I bleive I wrote wathever I Could Gather in order to Make a full Sheet, And As Nothing Matteriell has happen'd Since in Our Politicks, I Shall Wave Saying any thing Upon that Subject. They are in a State of Indolence Untill they Shall hear from Your Side of the Watter. It was Wrong Conducted to raise men Soe Long before the[y] went Upon the're [their] Enterprise, for they Desert as fast as they Are Listed.

I Observe wath You Say in Some Affairs, wich I should be pleased You Would be more Perticuler Upon in Your Next, for I have not a Spirit of Divineation, And UnLess I have Some Loose hints, I am as far from the mark As ever. I shall take Care of Moses Salomons And Use him as kind as Possiable. I can but I hope Mrs. Salomons will not take it AMiss that I cant Lodge him in my house,[1] but I Shall take Care he Shall be in ye Neighbourhood, for Every room in Our house is fill'd. The Girles are Oblige'd to Lay in the Nursry, there not being

---

1 For A.F.'s residence, see Letter XXXI, June 7, 1743, note 5. The crowded conditions may have been due to the renting of some of the rooms in her home. One boarder, Hugh Brady, resided there up to 1746. See *Post-Boy,* Oct. 27, 1746.

a Spare room for them. My Compliments to All friends. Tell Mr. Sim Levy his friend Mr. Paterson is A Very agreeable Gent[lema]n. I am Sorry Mr. Is[aac] Levys Son[2] turns out noe better. I am Surprised after behaveing Soe Ill, they have the Assurance too goe to there relations When there is the Army and Navy to goe too, but they are Soe Stupid to think all Villiany is to be forgiven, Provided they can call themselves good Jews And Not bring that Last Shame, As they Term it, Upon there Parents, As if Religeon gave a Sanction to wicked[ne]ss. I Would Not have you Mind Any thing he Says Either in praise or Dispraise, for he is a Vile Lyar And Not to be Countenance'd in Any thing. Its wath I am Averse too, to Say these Ill Natured things of any one, but he realy Deserves it, and, therefore, I thought it Proper to give you A Caution. Not that I imagin You will Converse with him, but Others of his Stamp may, & he may be Mischeavous. I have not Seen him, but I here he has Excercised his Tallent with regard to My Brothers at Phil[ade]l[phia],[3] Whoe Used him but too well.

[On back of letter]

I Shall Take Care [to] Send a Good Parcell of peper with bryant and with *[torn]* Promise and my Prayers for you, I bid you adieu Dear child. Your Affectionate mother,

Abigaill Franks

[Address]

To

Mr. Napthaly Franks
Att Toms Coffee House Cornhill

2 Probably the Sam Levy, son of Isaac Levy, A.F.'s cousin, mentioned as being of ill character in Letter XV, Oct. 17, 1739, notes 8 and 9.

3 A.F.'s brothers in Philadelphia at this time were Nathan, Asher, and Isaac, and half-brother Samson. In this year, Nathan Levy bought a lot on the Delaware River. Con. Lib. 2, cp. 80, Department of Records, City Hall, Philadelphia.

near the Royall Exchange
London

XIX
[Abigaill Franks to Naphtali Franks, November 9, 1740]

New York [Sunday] ye 9th November 1740

Dear HeartSey

I have had the pleassure (tho' at Second hand) to hear from you. It was a Very great Disapointment to Us and a great a fault in you to be Soe Negligent. Severall Vessles have Arrived at boston, Philadelphia, and from Bristol but nothing from you, wich, however, I would Willingly Excuse, but a Vessle Directly to this and Noe Letter is Unpardonable. Your father, I bleive, will make you Soe many reproaches on that Score that I shall Wave Saying anything further, but beg you to be more Carefull hearafter, for indeed you have for this Some time past Gave frequent Occaissions for Complaints of this Nature. As You have Letters Soe often from here, I fancy I Shall Acquaint you with nothing new but to make this a Little Longer than barely to Tell you wee are well and Wishing this to meet you in the Same. I shall give you a Short account of my Short Journey to the Jerseys, where I went to make a Vissit to Mrs. Sexies[1] and All[s]oe to Meet my brother Isaac Levy who is goeing to London—wich Last was the Strongest Motive that Drew me from home. I hope you may have a happy meeting, And As you are Very well Acquainted with him, I need say nothing to recommend him to You only this: if your

---

[1] The Seixas residence in New Jersey was probably in Greiggstown, Somerset County, where the couple had a "plantation" of 120 acres and a "good dwelling house." In 1744, this property was advertised for sale with the note that David Hays (Rachel's stepfather) was living on the premises and that Isaac then resided on Stone Street, New York. *Weekly Post-Boy,* Jan. 2, 1744.

treatment to him is not Very Civill and Such as he both Deserves and Expects, he will have Sense Enough to resent it, and in Wich I Shall allsoe bare a part. I Give you this hint because I cant Tell but you may have that Civill Quality Soe Inherent to the Jew Gente[ma]n of your Side of the Watter, of Treating Persons with Indifference that have not Vast fortune's. I was five days with Mr. Sexies and Am Very glad I took the resolution to Goe, for it has Very much Al tered my Opinion of him. I was Surprised to find A person of his Temper Soe much Mended and Capable to Conform with Soe much Ease to the Station of Life he has entered into. I mean with regard of keeping a Small Contry Store and Attending those Triffleing People with Soe much patience. I bleive Mr. Pecheco will Scarce think his Nephew would Ever have Weighed a pound of Sugar in the Jerseys with a Contented mind. They Seem to be Very happy in each other, And I hope they will allways Continue Soe. They both Send there Compliments to you. Rach[e]ll Says She is Very Sorry you have forgot her.

Mrs. Hays Death[2] has bin Very Sudden. If there be Such a thing as Dying of a broaken heart, it was her Case. Noe one Ever had Soe much reasson to ressent her Conduct, for the fellow She Marrid treated her Exceeding Ill, and She was Slighted by all her Acquaintance, Soe that her Cup was filled Up with bitterness, and to a woman of her Spirit, I am amazed She bore it Soe Long. Sam[son], hettey, & Joe goe to Philadelphia, hannah is to be with Mrs. Mears, & Little Miriam is to be put at board Some where.[3]

---

2 Grace Mears Hays, A.F.'s stepmother, died on October 14, 1740. She was just two years older than A.F. *Portraits,* 225.

3 Grace Hays had eight children by Moses Levy, her first husband and father of A.F., one of whom died in infancy. Those mentioned by A.F. were Samson (1722–1781); Hetty or Esther (b. 1721), who was living in Philadelphia in 1744; Joseph (1728–1772); Hannah (1723–1751), and Miriam (1720–1748). Her two other children seem to have made their own way. Rachel (1719–1797) was married to Isaac Mendes Seixas, and Benjamin (1726–1802), later a prominent merchant and teacher. David Hays (d. 1778) seems to have had no children with Grace and continued his career as a merchant. PAJHS 33 (1934), 210; *Dictio-*

The Letters of Abigaill Levy Franks 85

My Compliments to Mrs. Salomons. I dont write to any but your Self by this, for I have wrote twice to all my Correspondents Since I have received any from them. (And to Use the Term of merchants, I hate given Long Cr[edit] for Letters.) I hope by ye Post to hear her Son[4] is at Phil[adelphia], where he will Meet Moses & Phila,[5] whoe, I Suppose, will accompany him here. Pray take care that Mrs. Salomons has her peper this time. I have sent 2 Caggs, and if that is not Enough, I will Send you more next time. There is one to Mr. Pecheco to whome pay my Respects; Allsoe to Mrs. Franks and Family, Mr. Ab[raham] Franks and Family, Mr. Aaron Franks, David Salomons & Sisters, Mr. Sim[son] Levy, Isaac Levy and his Family. I cant find

---

nary, 88–89 and 91. According to known sources, Miriam was twenty years old at the time, and A.F.'s remarks about "Little Miriam" seem strange, unless she was being sarcastic.

There is an interesting description of Hetty in the "Journal of William Black, 1744," edited by R. Alonzo Brock in the *Pennsylvania Magazine of History and Biography* 1 (1877), 415–416. This account, dated Philadelphia, June 5, 1744, reads: ". . . I went to Mr. Levy's a Jew and very Considerable Merch't, he was a Widdower and his Sister Miss Hettie Levy kept his House. We Staid Tea and was very agreeably Entertain'd by the Young Lady; She was of the middle Stature, and very well made her Complection Black but very Comely she had two Charming Eyes, full of Fire and Rolling, Eyebrows Black and well turn'd, with a Beautiful head of Hair, Coal Black . . . She was a Lady of a Great Deal of Wit, Join'd to a good Understanding, full of Spirits, and a Humour Exceeding Jocose and Agreeable." The editor of the "Journal" identifies the Mr. Levy as Samson Levy, a subscriber to the dancing assembly of 1748, but it was much more likely Nathan Levy, who in 1744 was a well-to-do merchant and widower, whereas Samson at this time was only twenty-two years old.

4 This is probably Coleman Salomons since his brother Moses is seemingly in New York, though not at A.F.'s house. See Letter XVIII, Aug. 31, 1740.

5 This is probably Moses and Phila Franks. Just why the pair went to Philadelphia is not known. Moses seemingly went on business, and Phila accompanied him. It is also possible that Phila went to meet Oliver Delancey, her future husband. They were married two years later, perhaps in Philadelphia, and carried on their courtship away from the city. See Letters XXX, April 1, 1743, and XXXI, June 7, 1743.

I've anything More to Say. By farmer I shall write again, Soe take my Leave with My Constant prayers for Your health and happyness. I am, Dear child,

                Your Affectionate mother,

                    Abigaill Franks

If you Chance to See Mrs. Compton, Remember me to her and her mother.

                [Address]

        To

    Mr. Napthaly Franks att
    Toms Coffee House ComhiII near the
    Royall Exchange
                    London
    p Capt Bryant

XX
[Abigaill Franks to Naphtali Franks, April 26, 1741]

                New York [Sunday] Aprill ye 26th 1741

Dear HeartSey

Since I rec[eiv]ed yours by Capt[ain] Leake of the 14th Jan[uar]y, Wee have had the pleassure to hear from you by farmer, who arrived Yesterday, And wish the rest of the Ships may be here Very Soon, by whome you have made me Expect a Long Epistle. I am Allways glad to hear from you by any means and can Excuse your not writeing in Perticuler to me when you have other buisness to take care of, for I am Assured its Neither want of Duty Nor Affection there, for You need not Give Your Self any Concern on that Score. But Lett me recommend Your Constant Care in Writting to your father, whose Impatiance at any Disapointm[ent] of that Nature Gives him an Uneasiness that I am Very Glad I am a Stranger to. I offten Tell him I would rather be Accused of Insensibility then have my Passions Under Soe Little command as he has. You Supose Very Justly in regard to the Hurry of buissness Y[ou]r father and his 2 Sons are in. Pray god they may have Success, And I wish the Same to you, for I find You are Diping in the New York trade, but I reffer to your father on that Subject. I Observe David is Designed for Jamiaca,[1] on wath Scheme I am yet a Stranger to. If it be to his advantage, he Shall Goe, but if its Only an Uncertain Project, he had better Stay Where he is And Not, As Sam: Levy and Moses Salomons,[2] to goe and buy a 1000 b[arrel]s Rice. If they Are to doe Nothing Else (As All those Places are Very Expencive), they may gitt five pounds and Spend Seven. However, I Shall Wave my Opinion Untill I am better informd, but this I am Certain, David will be Very Glad to goe, And As he is Very Temperate, I am Under noe Aprehension of the West indias not Agreeing with him.

You mention nothing Concerning Our Joynt ticket (in your Last), Soe I Suppose its a 0. I never make any Account of those things And, there fore, am not Disap[oin]t[ed].[3] Moses Salomons Made but a

---

1 This seems to be another reference to the government contract made between Naphtali and Simson Levy as Victualler of His Majesty's Navy carrying supplies between New York and Jamaica. See Letter XXIII, Oct. 18, 1741, note 4.

2 A.F. probably refers to Samuel Levy and Moses Salomons, who apparently left New York soon after the latter arrived in 1740. See Letter XV, Oct. 17, 1739, notes 8 and 9. As of the following year, they were in South Carolina. The rice is an obvious reference to the purchase of a staple crop in that colony. They remained there long enough (at least two years) to run up a considerable debt, just as A.F. had feared. On March 20, 1741, the pair executed an indenture of £2,605. 6. 8 to Daniel and Thomas La Roche, South Carolina planters. See Letters XXVI, June 3, 1742; XXVII, Aug. 29, 1742; and XXVIII, Dec. 5, 1742; and Misc. Records, vol. 69A, 1736–1740, p. 6, Probate Records, Charleston, South Carolina.

3 A.F.'s reference is undoubtedly to a lottery ticket. Games of chance, horseracing, commercial speculation, and lotteries had an almost irresistible appeal for the eighteenth-century Englishman and to a lesser extent for the colonists.

Short Stay with Us, but whilst he did, he made himself Very Acceptable. I think him A good Nature'd and Well behave'd body, And you may Assure your Aunt I Shall with pleassure doe Any thing to Serve him. I am Very much Obliged to Your relations for there Civility to my brother. Pray make my Compliments to Your Uncles, Messrs Ab[raham] & Aaron Franks. To the rest of the Family I have wrote my self. Mr. Sexies & Aunt Rach[e]ll Salute You. He was in town 3 weeks agoe. I would Willingly be informed how matters are between him and his Uncle. He requested me to mention him to his Uncle, Soe I Laid hold of the Oppertunity of thanking Mr. Pecheco for some books he Sent me And a Letter, or Else I Should have Convey'd my thanks thro' your means.

All my Letters Are Under Mrs. Peirce's[4] Care. She Desire's You would Goe and See her on her Arrivall. If you Can Perswade ye Ladys of y[ou]r Fam[i]ly to goe, pray doe, but dont Ask it as a favour from me. They Proffess a great Friendship for Our Family. Amongst many Civilitys, I'll Give you one instance: Capt[ain] Pierce[5] had, Some

---

To the Frankses, however, there was an added inducement. In 1719, Isaac Franks and Moses Hart astonished London by winning £20,000 in the government or state lottery. V. D. Lipman, *Three Centuries of Anglo-Jewish History* (London, 1961), 59. This lottery, usually held at the Guild Hall, was not abandoned until 1823. A. S. Turberville, *English Men and Manners in the Eighteenth Century* (Oxford, 1926), 88–89. It is probable that A.F. had invested in this state lottery, although she could have tried some private or semi-private venture such as the drawing held on December 8, 1740, in the Bridge Lottery, Stationers' Hall. *Gentleman's Magazine* 10 (1740), 621. In 1762, David Franks was one of the managers of a £3,000 lottery held to obtain funds to erect a lighthouse at Cape Henelopen. *New-York Mercury,* Jan. 4, 1762. See also Letter XXXI, June 7, 1743, note 11.

4 Mrs. Mary Pearse was the eldest daughter of Lewis Morris and wife of Capt. Vincent Pearse. In 1742, the couple became involved in a scandal which resulted in Capt. Pearse citing his wife in court for adultery and his naming one Reynolds as co-respondent. Lewis Morris to Mary Pearse, May 22, 1742, and June 17, 1744, Morris Family Papers, Rutgers University Library; McAnear, "An American in London," 171 and 368.

5 Vincent Pearse (d. 1745) was the captain of the *H.M.S. Flambrough,* which

time a goe, Information of a Large q[uanti]t[y] of Powder & Other Dutch goods. Great part was Landed abouth Our Wharfe.[6] He Sent his Lieut[enant] abouth Ten at Night to Mr. franks to Tell him if any of it or all belonged to him, to Secure it, for if it was not his, he would Seize it, wich he did, for it none belonged to Uss. I beg you would not take Notice of this to any one. In my Opinion, it Was Very Civill. Mrs. Ashfield[7] Dyed Yesterday morning. As I Expect Letters from you & must Soon Write Again, I Shall Conclude this With My Wishes for your happyness. I am,

> My Dear boy,
> Your Affectionate Mother,
> Abigaill Franks

My Compl[i]me[nt]s to Mr. Isaac Levy and Familly.
Tell Mr. Sim: Levy I Pitty him for the Noise & plague he Must Undergoe to have my Brother Lodge in the Same house with him.[8] My Compliments to Uncle Ab[raham's] Family.

---

arrived in New York on August 25, 1738, and was stationed in Turtle Bay. Stanley N. Katz, "An Easie access: Anglo-American Politics in New York, 1732–1753," diss., Harvard University, 1961; *Weekly Journal,* June 16, 1735, Aug. 28, 1738, and March 12, 1739; *Acts of the Privy Council of England, Colonial Series* (London, 1910), 3: 32. Pearse seemingly became a merchant and was involved in the sale of pipe stoves. *Weekly Journal,* Dec. 1, 1740. He was also the owner of the fifty-ton scow *Restoration* and the eighty-ton ship *Canary Merchant,* both of which left for London on May 12, 1741, undoubtedly one of them carring Mrs. Pearse with A.F.'s letters. Since she was to deliver the letters personally, specific directions, i.e., Tom's Coffee House, were omitted. NOL, CO 5/1226. A.F.'s comments about Capt. and Mrs. Pearse are a good example of the friendly relationships between the Morris and Franks families.

6 This wharf was possibly behind the property owned by J.F. on Duke Street in the Dock Ward and could be Coenties Slip. See Letter XXXI, June 7, 1743, note 5.

7 Mrs. Isabella Ashfield died April 25, 1741 at the age of sixty-seven. Tombstone Inscriptions, unpublished manuscript; TVR. See Letter VI, June 9, 1734, note 19.

8 Simson Levy, merchant, resided at Corbet Court, Gracechurch Street, Lon-

[Address]
To
Mr. Napthly Franks
London

XXI
[Abigaill Franks to Naphtali Franks, June 21, 1741]

New York [Sunday] June ye 21th 1741

Dear Child

The greatest Sattisfaction I can have is to hear from you, wich of Late you have bin Very Carefull to Lett us have by all Oppertunitys and beg you will make it your Practice that your Father may have noe more Cause of Complaint. You give me Some pain in Makeing Soe many Excuses for not writting me by All Oppertunitys. I have Severall times told you its wath I dont nor Cant Expect when you have other buissness to Mind. I am not Soe Tenacious of a Compliment due to me, Soe I but hear from you any ways I am Satisfyed. Its the heart and Not the hands that Carrys a Weight with me, and I have noe reasson in the Least to Distrust Your Love or duty. Theirfore, I Would have you be Very Eassy on that Score and Only write me when you have nothing of more Consequence to Imploy your time. I have received the Medcine you Sent Am Concern'd they Should make Such a doe abouth me. I knew nothing of theire writing for any thing or would have hindered em. Its my Opinion as a person grows in Years, they Contract Infirmitys that will hardly be removed. And as I have, thank god, Allways had a Great Share of health, I must now begin to Expect those Little Ills humane Nature is Liable too And therefore Would not be Troublesome farther then there is a Ne-

---

don, at this time. *Universal Pocket Companion: A List of Merchants* . . . (London, 1741), 104.

cessity for to remove a preas[en]t pain. Nothing in Life Should in [sic] ingage me to Confine my Self to any Rule by way of Prevention. People must be Very fond of Life to make it a trouble to them to prolong it. My Physick is Temperence & Content, wich I would Prescribe to all the world And would be the best Preventing dose they Could Swallow. Indeed I take your advice in ye Pyrmont watter,[1] because I Love the Drink, but I've noe Opinion that it will any ways Cure the Weekness I have in my Joynts. Its a pain to me to write, I have such a Trembleing in my hands. Thats another Infirmity age is Drawing on me.

Your father is Very full of buissness. I never knew the benifit of the Sabath before, but Now I am Glad when it comes for his Sake, that he may have a Little reLaxation from t[ha]t Continuall Hurry he is in. In short, its a Very great Fatigue And makes him Very Peevish to those he imploys. In the Family he is the Same good Nature. Still I offten, when I here him Lowd Amongst them, take part Against him, and then its over for a While. You have in Severall of Yours insisted on davids going to Jamiaca[2] but never Gave the reasson why, Soe that your fathar has Not Yet resolve'd opon his goeing. At preas[en]t that place is Soe Unhealthy that I had rather he Should Stay and goe in the Faull, but if ye Gent[le]m[en] from Jamiaca Should write for him, he Shall Soon be Sent thither. He is Very willing to goe, and if Secrecy is required, you may depend Upon him. Pray Wait on Mrs. Peirce and ask his Charecter, for he was a great Favourite.

Mr. Nap[htal]y Myers,[3] I bleive, will doe Very well here, & if he

---

1 Pyrmont water is a type of medicinal liquid similar to seltzer, Islington, or chalybeate, all of which were popular in the eighteenth century. *A Treatise on the Nature, Properties, and Medicinal Uses of Pyrmont, Spa and Seltzers . . . Being a Proper Supplement to Dr. Russel[l]'s Dissertation the Uses of Sea Water, & c.* (London, 1762). A.F. seems to have been suffering from rheumatism or arthritis.

2 See Letter XX. Seemingly, David Franks was still in New York.

3 Probably Naphtaly Hart Myers (c. 1711–1788), who was newly arrived from London and who became a merchant in New York City, as well as Newport

answer the Charector you give him, he may be Assured of any friendly office in the Family. He Lodges at Judah Hays,[4] who Lives in Mrs. Sims's house[5] Just by Us. As you will receive many Letters from the Family, You will hear all the Citty News, wich at preas[en]t is Somwath Mellancholy.[6] Wee are much Disapointed in the Carthagena Expedition.[7] I hope they will retreive theire glory by Somthing Else Very Soon.

---

and Philadelphia. In 1756, he was elected president of Shearith Israel. He died in London in 1788. Minute Book, 49–51.

4 This is an interesting reference since Judah Hays is mentioned in advertisements appearing in the *Weekly Journal* of May 4, 1741 and June 29, 1741, as being removed to Joseph Murray's house "opposite to Cortlandts' Market, here Persons may [be] supply'd with All Sorts of Goods, wholesale or retale." Perhaps the newspaper referred to his business, not his residence address.

5 Mrs. Sims, was probably Mary Simmes, widow of James Simmes. Her house was in "Pearle" Street. *NYHSC*, 3 (1895), 175.

6 It is interesting that A.F. does not specifically discuss the so-called Negro plot of 1741, although it is probably the "mellancholy" news she refers to. The newspapers of the period were very concerned with the details of what was supposed to be an attempt on the part of slaves and Catholics to somehow destroy or overthrow existing government and society. Many slaves were tried and some fifty executed in the largest and most hysterical conspiracy trials in the history of New York. A number of slaves belonging to Jews were implicated in the "plot," including Windsor and Herefor belonging to Samuel Myers Cohen, Jack of Judah Hays, Lewis Gomez's Cuffee, and Mordecai Gomez's Cajve. One of Jacob Franks's slaves was involved, but his name is unknown. It may have been Caesar or Dublin, two of Franks's slaves. Moses owned a slave named Samson at this time. *Weekly Journal,* June 15, June 22, and June 29, 1741; *PAJHS* 27 (1920), 384–385. For reference to J.F. as slave owner and trader, see Nathan Simson Letter Books, C/104-13, Entry of May 1, 1710, Public Record Office; NOL, CO 5/1220, April 14 1720; NOL, CO 5/1222, Oct. 11, 1717, and April 14, 1718; NOL, CO 5/1224, Oct. 21 1730; NOL CO 5/1225, May 3, 1731; NOL, CO 5/1226, June 10, 1738; NOL, CO 5/1228, June 3 1729.

7 Admiral Edward Vernon's expedition to Cartagena was followed with great interest by New Yorkers. Rumors of victory and defeat attracted much attention. At first the news was good, but by June and July reports of failure, heavy losses, and rumors of portending attacks by Spain against Long Island were

Pray without faill Send a Grate to burn Coall in our Little parlour. You know how Large the Chimney is and Lett that be a rule. Take care that its not too Small. Lett there be Very Little brass abouth it. Send all Convienencys with it for a Coall fire. I dont Understand givin[g] Proper Directions, theirfore Leave it intirely to your Care. Dont Serve me as you And Sim[son] Levy have don Very offten of Late, Not Send the things I Send for. Send me with Capt[ain] Bryant A genteel Snuff box and the Price to be 40 S. Sterling. Dont faill. Its for a Lady I have a great freindship for, and I Would not have her Disapointed. Lett it be the same fasshion Miss Franks sent me.

My Compliments to Mrs. Franks. I dont write her by this, being I have wrote her by Mrs. Peirce, And I Am Unwilling to be troublesome to my friends. Thank Miss Franks for the Snuff box and Picture She Sent me. I Should be Very glad if I could find any thing here to Send her. My best regards to her and her brother. Mr. Myers Speaks of all the Family with great regard, but in Perticuler gives miss a Charming Charector. The Apples and other things you wrote for Cant be had Untill the faull, when I Shall take Care to Send them, and then I Intend to Send You Some preserve'd peaches, & Strawberys. My Compliments to Mr. Abraham Franks And Mr. Aaron Franks And Allsoe to all my inquireing Friends. I Shall hardly write you by farmer, who goes at the same time as bryant. I Should be Glad to know how my brother Isaac is Liked in there Private Opinion. I dont heed much wath Is Said to me on that Score. Pray be mind full of the things I wrote for and Send em without faill. I Gave Mrs. Ross a fan As if it Came from you, for wich She is Very thankfull. Send her a Small preas[en]t by the Next Ship. Your Brother moses has Soe much to doe before the Ships goe that he bleives he Shall hardly have time to write, therefore desires you would not think him remiss if it happens that you have noe Letter from him by these Oppertunitys and begs you would Likewise Excuse him to all his friends if he does

---

circulated. This was part of the background of the "Negro Revolt" discussed above. *Weekly Journal,* May 31, June 22, June 29, and July 6, 1741.

not write. He Sends his kind Love to You all. I cant find Any thing More to Say, and I need make noe Excuse for the Shortness of my Letter. Therefore, Shall take my Leave. May the Allmighty god keep you to Long Life, happyness & a good Conscience is the wishes of My Dear boy.

Your Affectionate Mother,
Abigaill Franks

[Address]

To
Mr. Napthaly Franks
London

XXII
[Abigaill Franks to Naphtaly Franks, September 6, 1741]*

New York [Sunday] Sep[tember] ye 6th 1741

Dear HeartSey

I have the pleassure to Tell you wee heard from you of the 25th of June and And [sic] Are in dayly Expectation to hear again by a Ship hourly Expected, who, I pray god, may Comfirm the Last of its haveing parted with you inoying a Perfect Tranquility of mind and body, wich is a Very Sinciable Joy to me and all the Family. This Letter goes to Boston to Capt[ain] Warren,[1] whoe Saii'd hence Ten days agoe,

---

* On the outside of the letter there is added a note to Naphtaly by his brother.
1 Capt. Peter Warren (1703–1752) commissioned in the Royal Navy in 1727, married Susanna Delancey, daughter of Etienne and sister of Oliver Delancey. A resident of New York when not on sea duty, he had many real estate holdings in the city, including a residence in Greenwich Village known as the "Glass House Farm." Indenture dated June 18, 1731, and notes, Peter Warren Papers, NYHSL. While in command of the *H.M.S. Squirrel* he sailed to the West Indies

And As I Neglected writting then, I beg you would Make my Compliments to all my friends and pray them to Excuse that Omission. I have wrote twice Very Lattly to them all and want of Subject and Capacity to Entertain in this Epistolary way agreeably Makes me allways put of[f] writting to the Very Last, And then the Consequence is the Ship Saills without my Dispatches. And to Tell you the truth, it never gives Me any Great Concern, for I Detest writing, tho' I would Very Unwillingly be rude or thought Ungratefull for theire many favours. Therefore, I Desire you would Sofften it in the best manner you Can.

News & buissness you have from all the rest of the Family, Soe to Avoid repeatition I Shall Contract in a Small Space wath I have to Say, wich is to recommend Mr. Sam[uel] myers[2] to Your Friendship and that of all your friends, And as by theire repeated Assurances I have the Vanity to bleive they have a Friendship for me, I Shall Esteem all friendly Offices Discharged to him as if Emeditly Conferd on my Self. My best regards to Uncle Abraham Franks. I Send him a Little Snuff and Very Little indeed. I Should not have Sent Soe Little, but it Was all Capt[ain] Warren Gave me. I did not Care to Mix it with any Other that he might have it pure, as it was Designed a Preas[en]t from a Spanish Governor to a french Governor

---

in 1741 where he captured a number of Spanish vessels. He returned to New York late in June and then, as A.F. indicated, went to Boston some time in August. *Weekly Journal,* May 20, 1741, and Oct. 18, 1741; Elizabeth Delancey to Cadwallader Colden, June 1, 1741, Cadwallader Colden Letters, Box XI, NYHSL. In 1742, Warren was stationed in New York aboard *H.M.S. Launceton. Weekly Journal,* Aug. 16 and Oct. 18, 1742. He became Admiral of the Red in 1748, but not governor of New York as he had expressed a desire to do. He died in England in 1752. Notes, Peter Warren Papers, NYHSL; Robert Hunter Morris to Lewis Morris, April 2, 1742, Morris Papers. When A.F.'s daughter Phila married Oliver Delancey she became Warren's sister-in-law.

2 Samuel Myers Cohen ran advertisements in the *Weekly Journal* of Aug. 25, 1740, and Sept. 1, 1740, telling of his intended voyage to London and requesting that all persons indebted to him "are desired to take Notice thereof and pay their respective Ballances." He seemingly left shortly after these notices ran.

in one of the Prises Capt[ain] Warren Took.³ Tell my brother Isaac I have wrote him three Letters, and If he Desire I Should Continnue writting, he Must be my Director or Else I [s]hall fall in my Old Way of Silence. I have desired Mr. Nap[htal]y myers to write for Some things wich I hope you will not faill Sending by first Oppertunity. According to the Custom of this Season⁴ I Shall End my Letter with my prayers that ye Allmighty Disposer may write you in the book off Life, Happyness, and Every Other Felicity You wish or want. I am, My Dear child,

Your Affectionate Mother,

Abigaill Franks

Dear Isaac I Shall pray heartly for you
next Wensday, for I know you are Very Sick
When you cant Eat. My Dear brother Nat[han] is
under Great Affliction for the Loss of
poor bila.⁵ I was Very much Concen'd, but

3 Probably A.F. refers to a captured Spanish privateer that received a good deal of comment. *Weekly Journal,* Oct. 18, 1741; Elizabeth Delancey to Cadwallader Colden, June 1, 1741; *Gentleman's Magazine* 11 (1741), 388 and 697.

4 As A.F. indicates, Yom Kippur fell on Wednesday, September 9, 1741, according to the old style or Julian calendar which A.F. used. Eleven days are added to obtain the corresponding date on the modern Gregorian calendar, making it September 20th. This is one of the few references A.F. makes in her letters to religious observances.

5 Little is known of Nathan Levy's family life in Pennsylvania. The Bila whom A.F. mentions may have been his first wife or perhaps a child. On September 25, 1740, he was given permission from the Proprietor Thomas Penn to have a thirty-foot-square family burial plot "wherein the child of Nathan Levy was buryed." This was probably on Spruce Street. Thomas Penn to Benjamin Eastburn, Sept. 25, 1740, Pennsylvania Manuscripts, 1684–1772, Vol. 7, HSP. Similar permission was granted in September 1738. Wolf and Whiteman, *History of the Jews,* 24–25. Nathan married again early in 1743. See Letter XIX, note 3. His second wife, Michal Levy, upon his death, was granted Letters of Administration on June 29, 1754. Letters of Administration, Vol. F, p. 527, Philadelphia Register's Office, City Hall.

The Letters of Abigaill Levy Franks

She is happy and Wee must Submit.—I hope you will Soon return back to him. Adieu my dear brother. Yours—

                Ab[igail] Franks

[On outside]

The Sickness rageing att philad[elphi]a, they here will not Lett me go home to my abode. 12, 14 and 16 diy a day sometimes.	D[ea]r Brother Y[our]s most affec[tionatel]y, D. Franks[6]

                ****

[Address]

To
Mr. Napthaly Franks
Att
London

XXIII
[Abigaill Franks to Naphtali Franks, October 18, 1741]

New York [Sunday] October ye 18th 1741

Dear HeartSey

    I wish Writing was As Great a pleassure to me as receiveing a Letter from You is, then You should not Soe offten have Cause to Complain of my Omission, tho' I think I Write by Every Oppertunity that goe's Directly to London. However, if I dont, I have you allways at heart, and if there was not Soe many Others in the Family who are allways

---

6 Although A.F. makes no comment, David Franks must have gone to Philadelphia some time after June, the date of the last letter.

writting to You, be Assured I Should be more Carefull. I am Convince'd your Complaint will Cease in Your Next, for I have wrote this Summer Severall times to you and all my friends. Therefore, [I] dont write to anny of them by this, but beg you to make my Compliments to Mrs. Franks, her Son & Daughter, to Mr. Ab[raham] Franks & Family, & Mr. Aaron Franks. I thank you for your Care in the Medcine. I thank god I have had noe Occaission to make Use of it Yet, for I never have those Severe fitts of the Cholick but in the winter, but As I intend not to Expose my Self Much to ye Cold, I hope to Git the better of it. I have my health Perfectly well And dont know any thing I wish for but the happyness of Seeing you, wich I begin to fear I never Shall, for I dont wish you here, And I am Sure there is Little porbability of my Goeing to England. If parents would Give themselves Leave to Consider the many Difficulties that attends the bringing up of Childeren, there would not be Such Imoderate Joy att there birth. I dont mean the Care of there infancy—thats the Least—but its affter they are grown Up and behave in Such a maner As to Give Satisfaction, then to be bereaved of them in the Decline of Life, when the injoying of them would be Our Greatest happyness, for the Cares of giting a Liveing Disperses Them Up and down the world, and the Only pleassure wee injoy (and thats intermixt with Anxiety) is to hear they doe well, Wich is A pleassure I hope to have and that all the blessing & Felicity Attendent on the good & Virtueous may be your Lott.

As buissness is not my Province, I have Very Little more to Say to you. Pray Tell my brother Isaac he Was Very Anxious abouth the Sheet of paper he Sent me by the Nightingale that he Desired You & David Salomons to Lett me know of it. I think he might have the goodness to wrote by this Last Ship, but I Shall Write him noe more Untill I hear from himself. Hanah Levy & Jos[hua] Isaacs[1] will be

---

1 Hannah Levy (1723–1751), A.F.'s half-sister, married Joshua Isaacs on December 16. See Letter XXIV, Dec. 13, 1741. At her mother's death, a year earlier, she went to live with her uncle Judah Mears. See Letter XIX. Isaacs, a merchant

marrid in a few weeks. Its my Opinion [that] She will be Well Settled. Tell Isaac [that] My brother Mickll[2] is Very Much Displeased with it and will not Speak to her, becauss She would not please him and have Ralph Jacobs[3] to Whom he had Promised her.

I am Very much Concerned for Simson Levy. I wish he may not meet with Some Loss. It seems a Very odd affair to Send Such q[uan]t[itie]s of things that Mr. Needham Never wrote for; it engroses all Conversation.[4] Mr. Levy Might have Live'd the Age of an antidill-

---

and inhabitant of New York City and Raritan, New Jersey, died three years later in 1744.

2 Michael Levy (b. 1709), A.F.'s brother, was a New York merchant and part owner of the *Prince Frederick:* NOL, CO 5/1225, Sept. 26, 1733. Two years prior to the date of this letter he had been indicted for assaulting the high constable of New York, Henry Breasted. Minutes, Court of General Sessions, Vol. 1722–1743, p. 276, NYCCO. He may have gone to Jamaica, B.W.I., as a result of this indictment. See Letter XXVII, Aug. 29, 1742.

3 Ralph Jacobs (1711–1796), inhabitant of Rye, New York, was in business partnership with Jacob Hays, dealing mainly in dry goods. Jay Day Book, III, 116, 157, 162, 168, etc. Jacobs later married Sarah Simson, who died on September 16, 1762. *New York Mercury,* Sept. 23, 1762.

4 A.F. may refer to a contract made by N.F. and Simson Levy in February 1740 with Alexander Roberts, London merchant, by which they chartered the ship *Charming Nightingale* for a nine-month period beginning February 14th of the following year for a trip from London to New York or Philadelphia and thence to Jamaica and from Jamaica directly back to London. Simson and N.F. had contracted with the Commissioners for Victualling His Majesty's Navy to supply food for the naval forces stationed in Jamaica and needed the ship to fulfill the terms of their contract. According to a complaint later brought by Roberts, the ship set sail from London in May 1741 and arrived in New York some time in July, where it was loaded by J.F. and Moses Franks as factors of N.F. and Levy for its trip to Jamaica. It left New York at the beginning of August and arrived in Jamaica on September 25, 1741. Henry Needham was to load the ship in Jamaica with sugar for its return trip to London. As A.F. indicates, Levy also used the vessel to ship a number of items directly to Needham without the latter's request. When the ship left Jamaica it sailed for New York rather than London as had been agreed with Roberts. During the trip to New York the ship was lost at sea, and Roberts in 1746 sued Levy and N.F. The latter

vian And Never have bin Soe much Talked of if Con: Philphs[5] had not Made him her Dupe in this Affair. That Any one Could be perswaded to bleive a Gent[lema]n would make Such an infamous Creatur his wife, As he Calls her to Mr. Needham, that Very thing has more Exassperated him than All the Other Extravagence. I Very much fear he will have a Dear bought Experience. I fancy the Lady will make a broaken Voyage. Our Young Fellows have neither Estate nor Gallantry Enough to Answer her Expence. She may Sing adieu Flateaux Esperanc'e.[6]

The Pickles & Sweet meets are ready, but your Father will not Send them by this, being he Ships nothing Else on board. Pray give my humble Service to Mrs. Peirce, the Capt[ain] & Miss Waggate. Pray Tell Mr. Sam[uel] myers I wish him well & Desire to Live in his Memory and the rest of My Enquireing Friends. The Spectacles you

---

had taken out an insurance policy against the loss of the *Nightingale,* the proceeds of which he shared with neither Roberts nor Levy. A.F.'s concern about the business affairs of Simson were justified since he became bankrupt the following month and absconded to avoid his creditors. In February 1742, N.F. and two other merchants, as assignees of Levy, gave Samuel Bayard, Jr., and John Livingston a power of attorney to obtain all debts due Simson Levy from J.F., Abraham Isaacs, Samuel Levy, Jacob Levy, Moses Salomons, Henry Needham, John Chambers, James Cuyler, and Stephen Van Cortlandt, all of New York, and Moses Levy of Rhode Island, and Abraham Minis, George and William Wood, and Capt. Heron of Georgia. Con. Lib. 32, cp. 282. Obviously, Levy's business organization had been far-reaching.

5 Teresia Constantia Phillips (1709–1765), a well-known and notorious woman of the world, claimed that at the age of thirteen she was "violently seduced" by Lord Chesterfield. She was married and divorced on a number of occasions, and her notoriety was reported in Henry Fielding's *Andrea.* She left England for Jamaica in 1754, although it was possible she was in Jamaica earlier. A.F.'s letter seems to indicate that she convinced Simson Levy that she was married to Henry Needham, but nothing has been found to substantiate this event. *DNB,* 15: 1099–1100; *Daily Advertiser,* Nov. 16, 1733; Dobree, ed., *Letters of Stanhope, Earl of Chesterfield,* 1: 175–176.

6 A.F. apparently is referring to *adieu flatteuse esperance,* which means "farewell flattering hope."

Sent are to young. None Under Sixty fits my Eyes, but dont send any more, for I can better Sute my Self here. Little Poyer Sends you her Love and Duty. She is a charming child for her age. She is Just Now beging me to Lett her write you a Letter. I Say this Puerly to pleass her. May the Great and good god bless And Preserve you to Long Life, health & a good Name is the frequent prayer of My Dear boy.

Your Affectionate Mother,
Abigaill Franks

Mr. Nap[htal]y Myers Expresses much Love and regard to you. He is a Very good body & Deserves the good will you have for him.

[Address]

To
Mr. Napthaly Franks att
Toms Coffee House near the
Royall Exchange
London

XXIV
[Abigaill Franks to Naphtali Franks, December 13, 1741]

New York [Sunday] December ye 13th 1741

Dear HeartSey

Since my last by Clarke, I have had the pleassure of y[ou]rs p[er] bryantt, wich you Will bleive was Very Agreeable to me and All the Family, tho' they think it a Little Negligent in you not to Answer the many Letters they write. I Confess its a Very weak Excuse You Make in not haveing time, for there is noe Necessity to tarry Untill the Ship is Upon goeing, being they dont relate to buissiness and, therefore, might be Answered as soon as received. If the Date is Something Old, its not a farthings matter. However, they have good Nature Enough to Excuse it, as You'll find by there Continuing to write to you by all Oppertunitys there is. My Civill brother Serves me the Same, but if he gits Another Letter from me, he Shall Eat it. Pray Tell him Soe And wish him Joy on his Sister hannahs marriage with his Old friend Jos[hua] Isaac's.[1] And pray make an Excuse for me to Dear Mrs. Salomons & Coz[i]n David for not Answering there Letters by this, for wee are all Employed in Assisting hannah to git her things ready Against the day, wich is next Wensday. My brother Nathan has bin soe good to furnish her with All her Little Nesscessarys Upon this Occaission, And to Save Expence wee have all Lent a helping hand to make em up, Soe that I've noe time to write but this Afternoon. I Send by bryant Some pickles for y[ou]r Family, Mrs. Salomons & Mr. Ab[raham] Franks. Allsoe a box with Sweetmeets wich Contains 4 pots, one for Mrs. Salomons, one for Mr. Abraham Franks, one for Miss Phila Franks, and for your Self one pot with Green Sweetmeets, 3 with peaches, & 2 with Straw berys, wich I hope may Come Safe & Use'd with pleassure. Pray make my Compliments to all friends. I wish the Multiplicity of y[ou]r Affairs would have Premited you to have Sent the box I beg'd Soe Earnestly for, but I find if I Am not to be Disapointed, I must Apply to Mrs. Salomons. I find Her to be the Only person your side of the Watter that is willing to Oblige, for You too Frequently Neglect Sending ye Triffles I Write for, wich I Could instance in Many things. Therefore, whenever I Send for any Thing, I Never Speak of it that noe One may know my Disapointment but my Self.

I am Very Sorry Our Country woman Mrs. Pierce has made Such a faux pas.[2] She has quite made me a Sceptick. I Shall allmost doubt all Appearances of Virtue. I had a Letter from her but Am Wavering wether I Shall Answer it, tho' I Would Unwilingly be rude, being She bought some things for Us and took Great Care to Send e'm.

[1] See Letter XXIII, Oct. 18, 1741, note 1, and Letter XXV, Dec. 20, 1741.
[2] Mrs. Pearse's faux pas refers to her involvement in adultery and divorce. See Letter XX, April 26, 1741, note 4.

Her Affair has Quite Laid [low] the Talk of Mr. Needham & Simson Levy.[3] I doe in my Conscience bleive Mr. Needham Only Employed Levy that he Might have Some one to doe his Dirty affairs with this woman, for he has not Left his first factor, whoe I Suppose Would not interfere in Supplying that Jade, for noe man thats in buissness and has any regard to his reputation Would, & As he found Mr. Levy good nature'd and thoughtless, he has honourd him with that Scandleous Commission, wich one or other of e'm will pay Very Dear for. I hope it will fall Upon Mr. Needham, tho' Mr. Levy Richly Deserves it for Consenting to be imployed at first for Such A Creature. Wee have made Use of the grate, but I Would rather had one with barrs. It's Just dark, and your Father is Calling for Tea Soe that I must break of[f], but not without my prayers for your happyness. I am, my Dear Child, Yours Affectionatly,

Abigaill Franks

If you are acquainted with Mr. Pittman,
give my Service to him and thank him for the Snuff
he sent me. I Shall Answer his Favour by bryant.
Mrs. Bickley Dyed Last Week.[4]

[Address]

To
Mr. Napthaly Franks att
Toms Coffee House Corn Hill near
the Royall Exchange
London
Capt[ain] Farmer

3 See Letter XXIII, Oct. 18, 1741.

4 Mrs. Elizabeth Bickley, widow of Max Bickley, former merchant and attorney general of the province, drew her will on November 18, 1741, which was proved nine days later. She "dyed" sometime between the two dates. It was, therefore, a little longer ago than last week as A.F. indicates. *NYHSC* 3 (1895), 338. The note and the address seem to be in the hand of Richa Franks.

XXV
[Abigaill Franks to Naphtali Franks, December 20, 1741]

New York [Sunday] Decem[be]r ye 20th 1741

Dear HeartSey

I wrote you Last Week by farmer. Since that wee have had the pleassure to hear from You by Via Boston & hope wee Shall Soon have that Satisfaction again, there being more Vessles Expected. As for Our man of war & Store Ships, its thought they will not come in this winter, for As they have bin Out Soe Long, its bleived they have bin on the Coast And Meeting with a Little blowing Weather. They, being Strangers, would not Venture but went of[f] again, tho' the Weather has bin Soe Very favourable for the time of Year that wee have Constantly had Vessles in Every Week. One Came in this day from bristoll And brought Severall London Letters. Should have bin pleased to heard from you. I Send You by bryant 2 Cags with peper & one with peaches and one with peper for Mr. Abraham Franks And one for Mrs. Salomons. Alsoe a box in wich is one Jar Sweetmeets for Mrs. Salomons, one for Mr. Abraham Franks, one for Miss Phila Franks, one for your self with 3 Cups of Preserved peaches & 2 with Strawberys. These Last You must turn Upside down out of the Cups, being I put Some Currant Jelly opon them becuse I had Spilt the Syrup of them. Your Sisters Could Git Noe Squriles[1] this time, but I have bespoke some flying ones Against Next Spring. My Compliments to Mrs. franks. I dont write her by this for I have wrote her twice Since I have rec[eiv]ed any from her: My Love & Service to Mr. Ab[raham] Franks &c. to Mr. Aaron Franks, Mr. Harry Franks & Miss Franks.

---

1 Squirrels had a vogue in the eighteenth century as pets. Flying squirrels, native to North America, are mentioned by Capt. John Smith, who called them "assapanick." These animals float through the air by an extension of skin connecting fore and hind limbs.

Mr. Jacob Levy[2] Gives his Love & Service to you. He is an Obligeing, good Natured, pritty behave'd young man As Ever I Mett with, but he and his Aunt Disagree Very much, And between Us, I Would Not have it spoke of again. An angel Could Not Agree with her. Uncle Isaac Levy Can Tell you her Triffleing manner, but I beg you will not Say this to Any one, for She and I agree mighty Well. I Never Contradict her; And indeed I don't offten See her Nor any of our Ladys but at Synagogue, for they are a Stupid Set of people. But Mum for that. Hanah Levy was marrid Last Week,[3] And I hope she will doe Very well. If you are Acquainted with Mr. Paterson (or Else Desire Mr. Simson Levy to doe it), Make my Compliments to him, And Tell him I wish him Very Well & Soe does Every branch of my Family. Your friend, Mr. Nap[htal]y Myers, makes himself Very Agreeable And Usefull in the Family. I dont att All doubt of his doeing well here, for he is Very frugall & carefull.

Since I Wrote ye above Your Father has Rec[eiv]ed y[ou]r Letters by Capt[ain] Cary, Wich Confirms my Wish in hearing you was Well. May the good God have you in his Care & bless & Prosper you is the Constant prayers of My Dear Child.

Your Affectionate Mother,
Abigaill Franks

[Address]
To
Mr. Napthaly Franks att

2 Jacob Levy, a merchant, returned to England in 1742, but shortly came again to New York. See following Letter XXVI, June 3, 1742. He probably married Rachel Myers Cohen, *née* Michaels, the widow of Samuel, in 1744, since he was involved in litigation in the Mayor's Court as one of the executors of Cohen's estate in that year. *Levy v. Eisetse et al.* (1744), MCM file 1742–1748, p. 193; *Levy v. Petersan* (1745), ibid., p. 266; Con. Lib. 32, cp. 471; Con. Lib. 38, cp. 282; *Wills*, 66.

3 Hannah Levy and Joshua Isaacs married December 16, 1741. This is the third mention of the marriage by A.F. See Letters XXIII, Oct. 18, 1741, and XXIV, Dec. 13, 1741.

Toms Coffee House Corn Hill near the
Royall Exchange
Capt[ain] Bryantt   London

XXVI
[Abigaill Franks to Naphtali Franks, June 3, 1742]

New York [Thursday] June ye 3d 1742

Dear HeartSey

I can with truth return you your Own Expression where you Tell Me wath a Senciable Pleassure you have in receiveing Letters from me, for Bleive me, to hear from you and to hear you are well give's me more Joy then I can well Express. Indeed I dont fly in those Exstasys Soe Naturall to Some, for wich I have offten bin Accused of Insensiblity, but I know I am as warm & Sincire in My Love and friendship as Any, but have all ways Endeavoured to have them bounded by Some reasson, & therefore by habit when Ever my Joys flow Upon Me, I cant help being Very Grave, for its an Observation that Extreems Cant Last, And therefore I hope your ressentments & Wishes of revenge are allmost over. You will Easily Imagine I mean Sim Levy from all Appearances, and I know you have much Reasson to Detest his base Actions, And Every honest person Ought to Shun him, but to Decend Soe Low As to Call names and be Soe Very Violent as You Are is inexcuseable. He is not to be Excused in any shape, for its Evident this Affair was all Designed. Indeed I Offten wondered When I heard in wath manner he Lived (Wich Seemed to be in a Very Profuse way), he could not support it, And If you that was with him would have given your Selves but Leave to have Considered, the Consequence might Soon have bin Deduce'd without goeing into A Long Lesson of Mathematicks. But its Over[1] & My Wishes are Dia-

---

1 A.F. probably refers to the partnership between N.F. and Simson Levy, which ended when the latter became bankrupt and absconded. See Letter XXIII, Oct. 18, 1741, note 4.

metricly Oposite to yours, for I hope he may make it Up for the Sake of Isaac Levys Widow and child [ren][2] And for poor Sam Levy Who Will be Very much Distrest, for I bleive all he has Will hardly pay the demands Upon him on the protested bills, And to Loose all his Suport in the Decline of Life is Terriable. I wish he Was Safe here that wee Might know how matters are Setled & wath Is to be don with Moses Salomons, who I bleive will be Obliged to Stay Longer Att Carrolina[3] than he Likes. I had a Malencholy Letter from him some time agoe. I hope Something may be don to Make him Eassy, for its hard he Should bare Soe Great a Punishment for anothers fault. Pray god Gaurd Us from All Such Tryalls. I am Very much pleased with the Porposall you make of David's Entering into partnership with my brother nathan,[4] but your Father will give a More Ecsact

---

2 There were several contemporary Isaac Levys, and which one A.F. refers to is not clear; however, it is probably Isaac Levy, her cousin, a London merchant and son of Joseph Levy. See Letter III, Oct. 7, 1733, note 10. His relationship to Simson Levy is not known.

3 Samuel Levy and Moses Salomons, who had been in partnership in Charleston, S.C. since March, 1741, had run up a considerable debt. Misc. Records, Vol. 69B, 1736–1740, p. 449, Probate Court Records, Charleston, S.C. Moses Salomons, in addition, was indebted to Simson Levy, whose assignees demanded payment. Con. Lib. 32, cp. 282, Feb. 9, 1742. This debt was also shared by Samuel Levy. A.F.'s concern over Moses Salomons was finally put to rest by J.F. and their son David, when they remitted payment for various bills some time prior to November 1743. J.F. and David Franks wrote to Moses' principal creditors Daniel and Thomas Laroche of Charleston in order to clear Moses of this "unfortunate affair." Ibid., Vol. 69A, p. 4. For A.F.'s continued concern see Letters XXVII, Aug. 29, 1742; XXVIII, Dec. 5, 1742; XXXI, June 7, 1743; and XXXII, Nov. 22, 1743.

4 David Franks and Nathan Levy finally entered into a partnership sometime in August 1742, although it was not formalized until March 1743. See Letter XXIX, March 14, 1743; and "Ledger of Daniel Gomez, 1739–1765," *PAJHS* 27 (1920), 247. They traded in tea, pepper, sugar, dry goods, iron, and cordage. Among the ships owned by the pair were the schooner *Drake* (1744), the sloop *Sea Flower* (1745), the brigantine *Richa* (1746), the *Myrtilla* (1748), and the ship *Phila* (1750). After this date the entries appear in the name of David only. These include the ship *Parthenope* (1751), the ship *Delaware* (1773), and the ship *Mars*

Acc[oun]t of it; therefor, I Shall Wave that Subject. I am Very much of your Mind with regard to Sam[uel] myers Goeing to London (for I doubt not the Unhappy Sins of his youth was Called to rememberance by the Good-natured Jews whose greatest Pleasure is Scandle), but it was, I fancy, the Abundant Pride of Heart to Show the Difference between former & Present Circumstance. However, he behaves Very Well and is much Esteemed in his way And has allways bin the most Gratefull Person I ever knew, Dayly recounting the Benifits rec[eiv]ed from Us, Soe that I am Very Glad he met with that Civill Treatment he did from you &c for wich he is Very thankfull. I *thank* you for the pres[en]t of the Handk[erchief]s. You take Care to keep me fine; you dont Consider I Grow Old; however it happens to be Very grave. You have Again forgot to send the box, tho' you have charged 40s. for it; allsoe the first Voll[ume] of the Annals of Europe[5] is not Come, & you have charged for two. I beg You would not be Soe remiss in my Mighty Affairs. If my requst is not Amiss, I Should be Glad You would be Civill to Jackey Levy,[6] for he realy is A Very good Lad. He goes to try if he can meet Any Little Incouragement to Come back Again, wich I hope he may, for I Shall

---

(1775?). He also owned the *Gloucester* (1772) with Moses Franks and Isaac Levy and the ship *Belle* (1774) with Moses Franks. "Jewish Owners of Ships Registered in Philadelphia, 1730–1775," unpublished manuscript in the Oppenheim Collection, AJHSL. David Franks and Nathan Levy also owned the ship *Union*, William Bryant, master. Entry of Sept. 3, 1748, NOL, CO 5/1226. For litigation involving David and his uncle, see *Nathan Levy and David Franks v. Patrick Nealson* (1746), MCM, Vol. 1742–1748, p. 359. For references to their partnership, see another unpublished manuscript in the Oppenheim Collection, AJHSL, entitled "Newspaper Notices of and by Jews in Pennsylvania 1735–1760."

Prior to Nathan Levy's partnership with his nephew, he had been in partnership with his brother Isaac. They were proprietors of a store on Front Street in Philadelphia in 1735. Ibid.; Wolf and Whiteman, *History of the Jews*, 26–27.

5 A.F. refers to George Gordon's *Annals of Europe*, which was published in eight volumes in London during 1739–1745. The first volume contained extracts and copies of treaties, public papers, and pamphlets.

6 Jacob Levy did return and, upon his return, married the widow of Samuel Myers Cohen. See Letter XXV, Dec. 20, 1741, note 2.

Allways be Glad to See him. Our Pre[sen]t Governor[7] sends two of his daughters home by bryant. The Eldest is a fine woman, Very Like Mrs. Beckford. They will be Very glad to See you, and if to be don, Carry Some Ladys of your Acquaintance with you. They will stay in London Untill the Spring. Wee dayly Expect the Other Governor[8] with Capt[ain] warren. If I can help it, I will not be a Courtier again, tho' dont think I was a Courtier in the Sence its Generly rec[eiv]ed. No. I will Endeavour to be Civill, but I have not soe much Complisance as to flatter & Cringe, not Even if I was dependant. My Sould could not Stoop Soe Low as that. I have an honest Surliness in my Disposission that I bleive would make me not Very Agreeable with Some your Side of the watter.

Wee have horrid Acc[oun]ts from the fleet at Jamiaca,[9] & your Politicks at home is in a fluctuating way. I agree with you that the Late Minister will think himself Very happy if they Leave him at Quiet, tho' If he can Answer for his past Conduct, he Ought not to be backward. But if he has Comited Mistakes & Injured his Country, I am a Spartan & would have him Suffer, for his Mismanagement Could not be An Error of the mind, being his Opposers Pointed at the many mistakes & how they might be rectify'd, and if he thro' wantoness of Power would not receed, why Let him take the Consequenc. Noe Evill Minister Should be Screend from Justice.[10]

---

7 The then lieutenant-governor was George Clarke, who with his wife Ann had eight children, four sons and four daughters. The daughters were Mary (Molly), Letitia (Ann), Penelope (baptised 1723), and Elizabeth (baptised 1725), E. B. O'Callaghan, *Voyage of George Clarke, Esq.* (Albany, 1867), lxx–lxxv.

8 George Clinton (c. 1686–1761) was appointed governor on May 21, 1741, but did not arrive in New York until Sept. 22, 1743. Lamb, *History*, 2: 589; *NYHSC* 3 (1895), 404. New Yorkers expected Clinton to arrive with Capt. Peter Warren on his ship *H.M.S. Launceton* sometime beginning in the spring or summer of 1742, as A.F. suggests. *Weekly Journal*, April 12, 1742.

9 New York journals were quite concerned over reported ship losses in Jamaica and the Caribbean and with rumors of Spanish attacks upon Georgia and the Carolinas. Ibid., March 8, May 24, and May 31, 1742; Amos A. Ettinger, *James Edward Oglethorpe* (Oxford, 1962), 241–244.

10 The "Late Minister" is Sir Robert Walpole, who resigned his office of

Pray make my Compliments to Mr. Aaron franks. The Snuff you Sent Last was Very good. I have A botle of Brazile.[11] If you Like it, Lett me know and I'll Send it you by the next, for its to triffling to Send it for a pre[sen]t, and I use nothing but Scoth Snuff of wich I am become a great taker. Your Sister Richa, I Suppose, will Tell you the Lucky Escape she had, wich has given me Soe Much fear that I Shall not Eassily Give any of them Leave to goe by watter. Pray heaven keep Us from all Disasters and Premitt You Long to Injoy Life & happyness is my Ardent prayers. I Am, my Dear child,

Your Affectionate Mother,
Abigaill Franks

Mrs. Ross sends you her Love blessing & thanks.

[Address]

To
Mr. Napthaly Franks
To be Left att Toms Coffee House Corn hill
Near the Royall Exchange
London.

XXVII
[Abigaill Franks to Naphtali Franks, August 29, 1742]

New York [Sunday] August ye 29th 1742

Dear HeartSey

Not hearing from you for Some time and, therefore, of Consequence the wanting Subject to Say Something is the reasson that I

---

prime minister in February 1742 because of parliamentary discontent over his conduct of the war as well as his domestic policies. Foord, *His Majesty's Opposition*, 200–216; *Weekly Journal*, April 12, 1742.

11 Brazil water, a red-orange dye, extracted from South American trees; the number of washings determined the tint.

have not wrote by Severall Oppertunitys. And Your Father Constantly writting, Whoe Amongst the rest of his Affairs Mentioned the Only thing I Could have Said, that wee where all well and Joyne'd In the Same Sentiments And wishes for you And the rest of Your relations, to Whome I pray you to make my Compliments Sutable to there Severall Stations, for I Shall write to none by this Opportunity, haveing wrote by bryant, whoe, I hope, has Mett with a Successfull passage, for these are Perillous times to goe to Sea in.

You have before now heard of the Descent the Spaniards made on Georgia And the Probability they had of Suceeding, And if they have, its Supposed theire next Attempt will be on Carrolina.[1] I am in pain for poor Moses Salomons. This Goverment buissness has bin Very Unfortunate to him. I Long to know wath is to be Don for him. Its Terriable he Should Suffer for anothers Villiany Soe Severely. Mr. Levy[2] is return'd and I bleive finds himself Very Much Embarasse'd. Good God wath a Chain of Missfortunes Dishonesty & Extravagance brings along, Where it involves the Inocent with the Guilty. I wish for a Vessle from England to hear from You, for wee have bin a Long time in a State of darkness in relation to this dark buissness, And how or when it will be Cleared Up, god knows. As for news, Wee have Very Little & that is Disagreeable with relation to our West india Expeditions, for its bin most Shamefuly inactive. Its Suprising the admirall & Generall Are not Called home to Answer to the many things Laid to there Charge, for tho' they Could not Command Success, it was in theire power to Conduct right & Endeavour for it, wich is Very Obvious they have neglected. Its Very plain theire Missmanagement has given Courage to the Spaniards, who, if they

---

1 A.F. expresses her continued concern caused by the rumors of Spanish invasions against Georgia and the Carolinas. Although the attacks centered on St. Simon's Island in Georgia, the Spaniards under Don Manuel de Montiano, governor of Florida, were repulsed on July 7, 1742, at Bloody Marsh by forces led by General Oglethorpe. Ettinger, *Oglethorpe*, 241–245; *Weekly Journal*, Aug. 9 and Aug. 16, 1742.

2 Probably Samuel Levy, who had been in South Carolina with Moses.

had not there hands Soe full in Europe, Might be Very TroubleSome in America.

Its bin An Exceeding hot Summer and Somwath Sickly,[3] but I hope the Aproach of the Cold Season will Abate it. Uncle Ashers has bin Very Ill, but by the Last post they thought him some thing better. He made Us a Vissit Abouth 3 months agoe and Lookt as Young & as Well as Ever he did. I hope this post will bring the agreeable Acc[oun]t of his recovery. Ben & Jo' Levy[4] would meet with a Considerable Loss in him, for he has them Under his Care & is the most proper Person they Could be with. My brother Mic[hae]ll has allsoe had his Seassoning at Jamiaca,[5] but by the Last Ships wee heard he was Prity well recovered. And I hope he will doe well there. If you can Spare Soe much time to write him a Letter, he will take it as a favour, And I Should be Very much Oblige'd. I Suppose david has Given You an Acc[oun]t of the Method he & Uncle Nathan is to Enter in to buissness,[6] but I have Some Concern on that Score, wich I have not

---

3 As A.F. remarked, the summer of 1742 was exceedingly hot and "Somwath Sickly." On August 2, 1742, the *Weekly Journal* carried a notice that "Last Week also a Woman died very suddenly as she [was] washing Cloathes near Fresh Water. Some believe her Death to be occasion'd by the excessive Heat we had for some days last Week." Elizabeth Delancey in a letter written to her parents, Mr. and Mrs. Cadwallader Colden, on Sept. 9, 1742, reported the distemper in the city and that some had died of it. "The chief sickness is in the fly [Smith Valley]. I haven't heard of any on our Street . . . She commented that she thought of leaving the city if sickness spread." Delancey Papers, MCNY.

4 A.F. probably refers to her half-brothers Benjamin and Joseph Levy. Asher may have been taking care of them, since they were then orphans.

5 Probably A.F. refers to Michael's business activities in the island as well as, obliquely, to the N.F.–Simson Levy episode. The New York–West Indies trade had been lucrative for many years and did not cease with the declaration of war. Great profits could be made even though it involved disobeying or circumventing English law. Methods varied, but they were often effective. For a discussion of this trade, see Richard Pares, *War and Trade in the West Indies, 1739–1763* (London, 1963), especially 395–396 and 432–435.

6 See Letter XXVI, June 3, 1742, note 4, with regard to David Franks's partnership with his uncle Nathan Levy.

The Letters of Abigaill Levy Franks 113

Communicated to Any one but Shall now to You. It is with regard to Mr. Pecheco. You know he is Concerned Greatly with Uncle Nathan. Now if Mr. P——Should be any ways involved, I would Gladly know if it would Noe Way Affect them at Phil[adelphi]a, for then David would be As bad off as Moses Salomons & soe from the prosspect of great benifit, it would be the reverse. Wee are in dayly Expectation of Capt[ain] Warren With the Governor. The thought of A change Give's Great pleassure to the Unsteady Multitude. I wish they may not have the fate of the Frogs in the Fable.[7]

Since I wrote the Other Side, wich was before dinner, the post is come from Phila[delphia] And brought the Mellancholy Acc[oun]t of Uncle Ashers death. Poor man, Affter a Series of Misfortunes wich he was Just beginning to Overcome, was takeing from the pleasing prosspect of this world to a State of bliss, where all is at reast & Care's Preside noe more. He Desired to be buiry'd at Phil[adelphi]a: Uncle Nathan is Much Concerne'd, & soe I bleive will Uncle Isaac be, to Whome pray pres[en]t my Love. I intended to have wrote to him but this has made me Soe Low Spirited that I cant Settle my Self to write. Therefore pray him to Excuse me. I wish you all well with a Long & happy Life attended with a Good Conscience ("for that is to the Soul wath health is to the body").[8] I Am Dear Child,

Your Affectionate Mother,
Abigaill Franks

To Dye is Landing on Some Distant Shore
where billows never break nor Tempest Roar.
Before you Feell the Friendly Stroaks, its O'er.

---

7 A.F. refers to *Aesop's Fables*, where the frogs repeatedly asked Jupiter for a new king, only to find themselves worse off with each change. Sir Roger L'Estrange, *Fables of Aesop and Other Eminent Mythologists: with Morals and Reflexions*, 2nd edition, corrected and amended (London, 1694), Fable XIX, "The Frogs Chuse a King," 19–21.

8 For the "good conscience" reference, see above p. 5, n. 10.

The brave thro' thought the Fears of Death defy,
and Fools to blest insensibility.⁹

[Address]

To
Mr. Napthaly Franks att
Toms Coffee House Corn Hill near the
Royal Exchange
London

XXVIII
[Abigaill Franks to Naphtali Franks, December 5, 1742]

New York [Sunday] Decemb[e]r ye 5th 1742

My Dear HeartSey

With the Agreeable Paragrah you End your Letter, give me Leave to begin in wishing you and the Dear partenar of your happyness[1] Endless Joys & Felicity. May your Years be Years of Successive Joys, And that Indulgent Heaven may be your Gaurdian & Protector, And

---

9 A.F. quotes from memory. Cf. Sir Samuel Garth (1661–1719), *The Dispensary: A Poem in Six Cantos* (London, 1726), Canto III, verses 225–229:

To Die, is Landing on some silent Shoar,
Where Billows never break, nor Tempests roar.
Ere well we feel the friendly Stroke, 'tis o'er.
The Wise thro' Thought th' Insults of Death defy,
The Fools, thro' bless'd Insensibility.

1 A.F. refers to N.F.'s marriage to Phila Franks, daughter of the late Isaac, the brother of Jacob, on October 24, 1742. *Gentleman's Magazine* 12 (1742), 602. The periodical indicated Phila's financial worth at £30,000. Phila's "Eassy Fortune" was considerable for she received a large legacy from her father. See Will of Isaac Franks, Derby 243, PCC.

that the prosspect you have of happyness may be increased beyond your wishes. I have Wrote Miss Franks by this, wich I beg you would Deliver with the Most Tender and kind wishes from A heart that She Lays Very near too. Bleive me, my dear heartSey, the Sence of the Eassy Fortune You receive does in noe maner Eaquall the Sattisfaction I have to hear Every one that has the pleassure of knowing Miss Franks Say the most kind and agreeable things of her, Wich must make the marri'd State Very happy, for without the Ingredient of good Sence & good Nature, it Must be Very Insiped, for I think there is required the Same Maxims & Reasson to Make a Friendship in Mariage as in any other Article of Life. And As you Say you are now blessed with the Uttmost of your wishes, I dare Say You will Endeavour to Live Up to the Charector You have allways Injoye'd of being Guided by Reasson and Lett that charming Guide be your Director in Every Minutt Circumstance. I can Say noe more but recommend to you the Example of the best of Fathers, And then I dare Venture to pronounce your wife and You will be intituled to the Filch of bacon.[2] I thank you for your Physickall Prescriptions from time to time, but I have at preas[en]t noe Occaisson for any. I bless god I have a good Stock of health and an Eassy Mind, wich Latter would be now Very much Increassed if I had the pleassure of being with You, And its A Desire that runs thro' all the Family. I Observe Some Perticuler remarks in y[ou]r Letter wich is Very Naturall to Persons of the Dispossision You mention. Howe[ve]r I beg you Would in your turn Supress a resentment and Carry Every thing Very fair & Eassy, for the many troubles they have mett with would Sower A person of a more

---

2 Here again A.F. commits a kind of malapropism. She uses the word "Filch," when she means a flitch of bacon, which is the side of an animal, usually a hog, salted and cured. She refers to the use of this item as a reward to any man and woman who do not repent of their marriage after a twelve-month period. John Ray, *A Compleat Collection of English Proverbs* (London, 1768), 265. Cf. "The bacon of paradise for the married man that does not repent." Robert Christy, compiler, *Proverbs, Maxims and Phrases, Classified Subjectively and Arranged Alphabetically,* 2 vols. in 1 (New York, 1903), 1: 535, no. 23.

Steady & Even Temper. Therefor, I beg & pray you to be quite Passive there. I need not recommend a dutyfull regard to Mrs. Franks, as you have bin allways happy in her Freindship. I hope it will continue. The Many Obligations You are Under to Your Uncle Aaron Joyntly with the Rest of Our Family puts me to the Same want you Say You are in, And that is Suteable Expressions of Gratitude for the Multitude of Favours rec[eiv]ed from him. Pray make my My [sic] Compliments to him As Expressive as you can with My Wishes of Joy on t[hei]r part & Miss Franks And allsoe to Good Mr. Abraham Franks, And Tell him I have the pleassing hopes of a Favour from him by the Next Oppertunity. The things you Sent by Capt[ain] Coolidge & Griffits Answered the Intent And Claim my thanks. As you Observe Joseph & Parson Adams are Very Amuseing; that Auther makes Parson Adams Speak Smart things with great truth & Simplicity.[3] You are not Soe Carefall to Send the Many Little things that are Printed as You Used to be. I have Seen Severall wich I Should have bin Very Well pleased with that you have bin remiss in Sending, for they Are all readers in the house & writers. I hope next Spring to Send you a Letter wrote by Little Poyer whoe has Just begun to Learn. Wee have Just now rec[eiv]ed Letters from Moses Salomons. Poor Youth, he is in Uneassy Situation. I Am Surprized Nothing is don for him. I dont think he meets with kind Useage. You all Are Senciable (that) its a Misfortune a person of more Experience than he might have mett with. Keeping him att Carolina cant mend but make matters worse. Its a Very E[xpe]ncive place, tho' he Endeavours to retrench his, for he Lives with a Gen[tle]m[an] in the Country. You wonder I never took Notice of the Propossall And Call it a Foolish one. I never incourage'd It, but I Could not Perceive Soe much Folly in it. Its a thing Very Naturall to Like an agreeable Person, And If I am not Mistaken, there was a reciprocall return. However at preas[en]t the

---

3 A.F. refers to Henry Fielding's *History of the Adventures of Joseph Andrews, and of His Friend Mr. Abraham Adams,* published in two volumes in 1742 in London.

prosspect is far off. I know not how he Apeared in England, but here he bhave'd mighty well And was thought Soe by all his Acquaintance. I can Assure you he is a great Favourite of Mine, And I am Very much Concern'd for his misfortunes.⁴ But Now, pray Tell me, doe you Expect Your Sisters to be Nuns? For Unless they can Meet with a Person that Can keep them a Coach & Six, I Supose they must not think of Changeing there Condition. I am noe Stickler for Marrying at a Moments warning. Neither Would I consent to Any worthless body that Makes an Apearance, but If chance Should Pres[en]t a Worthy Person (tho' there is noe prospect of it here), I would not give Up my Power (of Bestowing of my child[ren] to make them happy) to any ones Caprice. And Prehaps if Mr. Sallomons had Made Use of the Authority he Ought in his Family, Soe Cruell an accident⁵ had never happened as he mett with before he Dyed. Not that I have Any prosspect at preas[en]t of there being marri'd, but this is by way of Speaking my mind. There is david Gomez⁶ for this Some Years has had an Inclination to Richa, but he is such a Stupid wretch that if his fortune was much more and I a begar, noe child of Mine, Especialy one of Such a good Understanding as Richa, Should Never have my Consent, And I am Sure he will never git hers. I Should be glad if

4 A.F.'s concern for Moses Salomons is evident. A reference to him appears in almost every letter, beginning in 1741.

5 A.F. probably refers to J.F.'s sister's husband. Perhaps one of his daughters married a Christian and it is this which she considers "Soe Cruell an accident."

6 David Gomez (1697–1769), son of Lewis Gomez, was a New York merchant, perhaps of not too great a fortune. He lived in his father's home until at least 1734, and the assessed valuation of his property was one-tenth that of his father. NYAL, Feb. 27, 1734, Montgomerie Ward. From 1734 to 1740, he was in partnership with his brother Mordecai and Paul Richard, a mayor of New York City. See entries of May 3, Aug. 23, Nov. 7, and Dec. 20, 1734, Sept. 4, 1735, May 14, 1736, and April 6, 1738, NOL, CO 5/1225; July 31, 1740, NOL, CO 5/1226. For family relationships, see Con. Lib. 32, cp. 100; for business relationships Con. Lib. 32, cp. 213; for his purchase of land and house on Queen Street Con. Lib. 32, cp. 117. He later married Rebecca DeLeon Sielva of the Barbadoes. *Wills*, 125–127.

you would take care and Write offtener to y[ou]r brother david. He thinks himself Ill Used and Slighted, for he very Seldom has a Letter, and he Says when You doe write, they are Soe Short that he is quite out of Temper with it. I impatiantly wish to hear from You Again, for then I Expect to hear your wishes Compleated, and ye pleassure I Shall have to receive a Letter from Dear Miss Phil[a] will be an adition to it. May kind heaven Showr Its choicest blessings on you is the Constant wishes, My dear child, of your Tender And Affectionate Mother,

Abigaill Franks

Man, the first happy Favourite above,
When Heaven Endow'd [him] with a Power to Love,
his god nea'r thought him in a blessed State
Till Woman made his happyness Compleat.[7]

[Address]

To
Mr. Napthaly Franks att
Toms Coffee House Corn Hill near the
Royall Exchange
London
Bryant

---

7 This passage has not been identified.

XXIX
[David Franks to Naphtali Franks, March 14, 1743]

Philad[elphi]a [Monday] March 14th 1742-3[1]

Dear HertSEY

(Coppy)

My writeing to you this time is to Acquaint you of My father & Brother Sending Me a Bill Exchange[2] of £150 Ster[ling], dayted 24th Feb[rua]ry last, Payable to My Self on Uncle Aaron, w[hi]ch Bill I have Indorst over to Thomas Hyam[3] or order for Value rece[ive]d of Lynford Lardner.[4] My father desired Me to Acquaint you *[missing]* go, which I cant do as the Busyer does not *[missing]* them on Acco[un]t of Oppertunity's not allway's offering *[missing]*. The following is a Paragraph of a letter rece[ive]d from My father dated March 9 (by Brother Moses's Man, Samson).

["]I wrote you yesterday p[er] Post Since w[hi]ch I have takein a Resolution to Send Samson to you with Inclos'd 1st & 2d Bill's Exchange, one for £200 Ster[lin]g & the other for £100. dated New York March 9, Payable to your Self, w[hi]ch I desire you to dispose of out of hand for the highest Exchange for Jersey Money, for I am in want of Money & not able to raise Any at Present but under the Exchange

---

1 This letter and the one following are the only known letters from David to his brother Naphtali. Written from Philadelphia, they are among the earliest extant letters written by Jews in that area.

2 A bill of exchange is a written order made by one person directing another to pay to a third party a certain sum of money. The third party may order it paid to whomever he wishes. *Black's Law Dictionary* (3rd ed.), 221.

3 Thomas Hyam (c. 1679-1763) was a Pennsylvania banker, merchant, and business agent for the Penn family. Leonard W. Labaree, ed., *Papers of Benjamin Franklin* (New Haven, 1962), 5: 29n.

4 Lynford Lardner (1715-1744) held several administrative posts in Pennsylvania including Receiver-General of Quit Rents and Keeper of the Great Seal of the Province. Ibid., 3 (1961), 12n.

& that Not for what I want. But as I hope you will be able to gett 60 p[er] C[en]t or would not do it. But [I] would rather take Money upon Int[e]rest than to Sell t[he]m under 75 p[er] C[en]t Exchange, so that you will Indorse s[ai]d Bill's & write y[ou]r Brother My reason of Sending them to you.["] W[i]ch Bill's of £200 & £100 I have this day Sold and Indorst over to Thomas Hyam by order of Lynford Lardner who Bought t[he]m. I shall Send Samson back to Morrow so that he'll not be from N[ew] Y[ork] a week. New is None & as to Business very dull. I have nothing in the world hardly to do. I cant get any Money in to Make Any remittance as I indended, but hope Soon to do it. The Arti[c]les betwene Uncle Nathan & My Self are drawn & Shall Signe them Next week.⁵ I forgot to Acq[uain]t you with the Rece[i]pt of ye 28d Sep[tembe]r. I thank You for Y[ou]r advise & Shall do My Utmost to Please you & Make return's as Soon as I can. If I am to go to India, I should like to go before I am too old. As I Suppose you are before this time a Marrid Man, I wish you both Joy & all the happiness you Can desire. My love to My New Sister. I really wish I could come & Spend one winter with you. I quite want to See England. I shall always think I have seen Nothing till I have bin at London.⁶ It's very likely if Uncle Nathan does not goe, I may have leave, if you think fitt to Stir in it. My Duty to Uncle Abraham & family & Uncle Aaron & to all My relations remember Me in due order. Pray be So good to Send Me Riders Brittish Merlin⁷ for the

---

5 This letter dates more exactly the agreement of partnership between David and his uncle Nathan Levy which A.F. discusses in Letters XXVI, June 3, 1742, and XXVII, Aug. 29, 1742.

6 Despite his desire to see London, David did not go to England until after the Revolution. He died there in 1794. See his will, Holman 366, PCC. A David Franks died in Philadelphia in 1793 during the plague, but this was probably not the son of A.F. Lyman H. Butterfield, ed., *Letters of Benjamin Rush* (Princeton, 1951), 2: 714–715.

7 *Rider's British Merlin* was an almanac first issued in London in 1733 and then almost annually through the early nineteenth century.

last Year & this Year. It's an almanich. Uncle Nathan & family desires to be remember[e]d to you & Be assur[e]d.⁸ I am

> D[ea]r Brother,
> Sincerely y[ou]rs &c &c &c
> D[avid] F[rank]S

XXX
[David Franks to Naphtali Franks, April 1, 1743]

April 1st 1743

Dear Brother,

The other Side is Coppy of my last via Cork, Since which have had nothing to Say, but t[ha]t all the family in N[ew] York were well last fryday the 27th, but in very great uneasiness & great Concern on Acc[oun]t of Philla's being Marry'd to Oliver D Lancy. She has been Marriy'd in Sep[tembe]r Last ye 8th, & not a Soul Knew of it till Last week when she absented herself & went to his Country house¹ where she has Remain'd Since & not been in town. I was very much Surpris'd when I heard it, as I Suppose my Father will or has before this time acq[uain]t[e]d you with the particulars. Am told he is & my Mother in great greif about [it].

This week we Rec[eive]d Uncle Isaacs Letter of 4th Jan[uar]y wherein he acq[uain]ts us of the orders we shall Receive about purchaseing from the privateers. They are Soon Expected in. One of the

---

8 This word has recently been identified by Mark Stern, biographer of David Franks.

1 This note of the date of his sister Phila's marriage is the only known reference to the time of its occurrence, which strangely is rarely, if ever, mentioned by contemporaries. The country house mentioned was probably in Greenwich Village. See the following letter for A.F.'s reaction to the marriage.

Ships was Randsom[e]d[2] for 90,000 p[iece]s of 8/8. All here are well & Desir'd to be Remember[e]d to you & beleive me Sincerely,

D[ea]r Brother Hertsy,
y[ou]r most affec[tionat]e Brother & obeid[en]t Serv[an]t
Davld Franks

Flour 7/9 to 8/[3]
Bread 9/
Exch[ang]e 7/2
Wheat 2/9 to *10*[d]
To Mr Nap[htal]y Franks

[Address]
To

Mr. Napthaly Franks
   att Tom's Coffee house
   near the Royall Exchange
   Cornhill
London

5
via Cape fear p[e]r Capt[ain] Cornish

---

2 This reference probably is to the capture of several ships by New York privateers during King George's War. See Letter XXII, Sept. 6, 1741, note 3.

3 These were the current selling prices at Philadelphia for the commodities listed. *Pennsylvania Gazette,* April 18 and May 5, 1743.

XXXI
[Abigaill Franks to Naphtali Franks, June 7, 1743]

Dear HeartSey
                    Flatt bush[1] [Tuesday] June 7th 1743

My Wishes for your Felicity Are As great as the Joy I have to hear You Are happyly Married.[2] May the Smiles of Providence Waite allways on y[ou]r Inclinations And your Dear Phila's, whome I Salute with Tender affections, pray[in]g kind Heaven to be propitious to Your wishes in makeing her a happy mother. I Shall think the time Teadious Untill I Shall have that happy Information, for I dont Expect to hear it by the return of these Ships[3] and, therefore, must Injoyn Your care in Writting by the first Opportunity (after the birth of wathever it shall please god to bless you with) Either by Via Carrolina, barbadoz or any other. I am now retired from Town and would from my Self (if it Where Possiable to have Some peace of mind) from the Severe Affliction I am Under on the Conduct of that Unhappy Girle. Good God, Wath a Shock it was when they Acquainted

---

    1 Flatbush, Brooklyn, was the site of a country residence of the Frankses, although there is no record of their owning property there. They may have rented or been summer guests. A.F. may have been living away from town and not using her Harlem residence in order to obtain privacy as a result of Phila's marriage. (The city was also the scene of a yellow fever "epidemical," which spread along the docks facing the East River. See Cadwallader Colden's account mentioned in note 4 to Letter XXXIV, Dec. 4, 1746.) Flatbush at this time was used as a resort area. Gov. George Clinton wrote in 1751: "I am at Flatbush with family . . . we ride, & Shoot & dance & sing & live as Merry as possible." George Clinton to Robert Hunter Morris, Aug. 18, 1751, Morris Papers. Years later, in 1781, Rebecca Franks, daughter of David and granddaughter of A.F., resided in Flatbush where her neighbors were the Van Hornes, her close friend being Cornelia Van Horne. Rebecca Franks's letter, dated Aug. 10, 1781, HSP.

    2 See Letter XXVIII, Dec. 5, 1742.

    3 A.F. was probably referring to Capt. John Griffith on the *Britannia* or John Bryant on the *London,* both of whom were reported cleared for departure on June 27, 1743, in the *Weekly Journal* of that date.

me She had Left the House and Had bin Married Six months. I can hardly hold my Pen whilst I am a writting it. Itts wath I Never could have Imagined, Especialy Affter wath I heard her Soe often Say, that noe Consideration in Life should Ever Induce her to Disoblige Such good parents. I had heard the report of her goeing to be married to Oliver delancey,[4] but As Such Reports had offten bin of Either off

4 The marriage on September 8, 1742, of Phila with Oliver Delancey (1718–1785), son of Stephen Delancey and youngest brother of Susanna Warren, is something of a mystery. Seemingly the event should have been the talk of the town; yet contemporary journals, diaries, newspapers, and letters are strangely silent. A rare notation of the marriage is found in a letter of Henry Beekman to Gilbert [Livingston], dated March 20, 1743: "It is reported that Oliver D. Lancey is mary'd to Mr. Franks daugh[ter] Vaylo a Juew." Beekman Papers, NYHSL. The marriage was a shock to A.F. It was the one event she dreaded most. Intermarriage was to Abigaill, as sophisticated and as worldly as she seemed, a calamity. This seemed to be her greatest fear in the colonial wilderness. Although the event is not specifically referred to in the extant letters, her son David also intermarried. He was betrothed to Margaret Evans only six months after this letter was written. See Letter XXXIII, Nov. 25, 1745, note 1.

Oliver may possibly have married Phila for the legacy left by her uncle Isaac, but more likely it was for affection since he must have realized that the family could have refused to give her the dowry. Also Oliver, coming from one of the most noted New York families, must have met opposition within his own family for marrying a Jew. On Phila's part, the number of eligible Jewish young men in New York was small. Even A.F. had little regard for them. See Letter XXVIII, Dec. 5, 1742. Moreover, many, if not most of A.F.'s friends, were non-Jews. Phila may have met Oliver at the home of his eldest brother, Peter Delancey, who owned a house in the Dock Ward directly adjoining the Frankses. Phila, who was born June 19, 1722, was about twenty at the time of her marriage, and Oliver, born on September 16, 1718, was about twenty-four. *PAJHS* 1 (1893), 103–104.

Some time after their marriage, Oliver and Phila lived in the Delancey country seat, near present day 12th Street, west of Ninth Avenue in Greenwich Village. An interesting account is given of the area by Dr. Alexander Hamilton, a Maryland physician traveling through the northern colonies, who on June 22, 1744, wrote: "Art twelve oclock we passed a little town, starboard, called Greenwitch, consisting of Eight or ten neat houses, and two or three miles above that on the same shoar, a pretty box of a house with an avenue fronting the river belonging to Oliver Dulancie." Bridenbaugh, ed., *Gentleman's Progress*, 52.

your Sisters, I gave noe heed to it further than a Generall Caution of her Conduct, wich has allways bin Unblemish[e]d, And is Soe Still in

---

Just prior to the Revolution, the couple lived in Bloomingdale, another suburb of Manhattan. In November 1777 their house was burned by American rebels. D. A. Story, *The Delanceys* (Canada, 1931), 75. The assumption that the couple lived in Fraunces Tavern is not correct and arises from the fact that a Frances Delancey resided there. Bayard Genealogy and Family Notes, 5, a typescript in NYHSL.

If contemporary reports are to be believed, Oliver was something of a "tough." He was indicted shortly after his marriage, on November 3, 1742, for assaulting Judah Mears, the brother of A.F.'s stepmother. Minutes of General Sessions, Vol. 1722–1743, p. 320, NYCCO. In 1749, Gov. George Clinton wrote that Oliver and his friends had attacked a poor Dutch Jew and his wife, broke their windows, and swore that they would lie with the woman. Using indecent language, they warned the couple not to bring charges since they were members of prominent families. George Clinton to John Catherwood, Feb. 17, 1749, *Doc. Rel.*, 6: 471. Later in the same year, Clinton reported that Oliver had stabbed and killed a Dr. Colchoun in a drunken brawl. Ibid., 513. In an election held the following year, the governor wrote that Chief Justice James Delancey had his "two Bullies, Peter and Oliver, to frighten those, that his artful! Condesention & Dissimulation could not persuade to vote their conscience." George Clinton to Robert Hunter Morris, Aug. 29, 1750, Morris Papers. Of course, it must be remembered in evaluating these reports that Clinton was a bitter enemy of the Delanceys, and these letters may have been written to embarrass them. Peter Warren, writing in 1750 to Oliver, informed him "you must give me leave in confidence to tell you that the name of Delancey has been so Injuriously and Scandalously represented that at present there is no possibility of doing you any service in a Public Way." Warren to Delancey, Aug. 11, 1750, Peter Warren Papers, NYHSL. The note obviously refers to the Delancey-Clinton controversy.

Oliver also appeared to be something of a "dandy," spending considerable time and money on the wigmaker and barber. See William De Witt Day Book, 1739–1752, NYHSL. On April 2, 1743, "Mrs. Dience" (probably Phila) paid 10 shillings for a "towr" and £1 for a "wigg for her selfe." Ibid.

For genealogical material, see John Watts notes, Delancey Papers, MCNY. The marriage produced seven children, two sons and five daughters—Ann [Mrs. Henry Cruger], Susanna [Lady Draper], Stephen, Oliver, Phila [Mrs. Payne Galway], Charlotte [Lady Dundas of New Brunswick] and Maria [Mrs. Robert Dixon]. Phila was the godparent of the daughter of Pierre de Joncourt and

the Eye of the Christians, whoe allow She has DisObliged Us but has in noe way bin Dishonorable, being married to a man of worth and Charector. My Spirits Was for Some time Soe Depresst that it was a pain to me to Speak or See Any one. I have Over come it Soe far as not to make My Concern Soe Conspicuous, but I Shall Never have that Serenity nor Peace within I have Soe happyly had hittherto. My house has bin my prisson [5] Ever Since. I had not heart Enough to Goe Near

---

Jeanne Couillette, born May 26, 1749, who incidentally, was called Phila. *Collection of the Huguenot Society* 1 (1886), 224.

Oliver not only was a merchant with a store in the house of Myndert Schuyler but also was a land speculator. G/AM, no. 37, 75 and 138, Peter Warren Papers, Sussex Archaeological Society, Lewes, England; *Gazette,* May 16, 1748; Jay Day Book, 312; Stephen and Oliver Delancey Papers, Bound Volume 1647–1804, items 20, 24, 28 and 39, NYHSL; Index, Grants of Land under Water Bureau of Topography, Room 2040, Municipal Building, New York City; Request of Richard Lush for location of Oliver Delancey land in Otsego County, Jan. 20, 1792, Commission of Forfeiture Papers, Clerk's Office of the Court of Appeals, Albany. He served in the British Army during the Revolution as an officer, and had a distinguished military career. Prior to the War, Delancey served as a member of the Provincial Assembly. *Valentines Manual* (1864), 575.

5 Samuel Myers Cohen and Rachel, his wife, deeded two adjoining houses to J.F. and his wife. The property located on the north side of Duke Street had been deeded on Aug. 4, 1727, to Rachel who was then the widow of Samuel Levy [A.F.'s uncle] by Jacob Bratt and Nicholas Ayres. The property was bounded on the east and west by that of Lawrence Wessels and Abraham Splinter and on the north by Slyck [Mill] Street. Con. Lib. 12, cp. 356–358, Office of the Secretary of State, Albany; Con. Lib. 31, cp. 185–191. This property, located in the Dock Ward, was close to the Synagogue on Slyck or Mill Street. Leo Hershkowitz, "The Mill Street Synagogue Reconsidered," *AJHQ,* 53 (1964), 404–410. The Franks residence in the Dock Ward in 1733–1734 was close to those of Robert Livingston, Abraham Depeyster, Adolph Philipse, Frederick and Jacobus Van Cortlandt, and Stephen Bayard, all wealthy and influential men in the community. NYAL, Feb. 24, 1733, and Feb. 18, 1734. This was probably J.F.'s residence and his place of business, which was at Queen Street: an advertisement in the *Weekly Journal* of March 17, 1735, mentions that the house of the goldsmith, James Heister, is opposite to Mr. Franks, merchant, in Queen Street.

In 1740, J.F.'s property is described in the Will of Jacobus Van Cortlandt as

the Street door. Its a pain to me to think off goeing again to Town, And If your Fathers buissness would Premit him to Live out of it, I never would Goe Near it Again. I wish it was in my Power to Leave this part of the world. I would come away in the first man of war that went to London. Oliver has Sent Many times to beg Leave to See me, but I never would, tho' now he Sent word that he will come here. I dread Seeing him and how to Avoid I know noe way. Neither if he comes can I Use him rudly. I May Make him Some reproaches, but I know My Self soe well that I Shall at Last be Civill, tho' I never will give him Leave to Come to my house in Town. And as for his wife, I am Determined I never will See nor Lett none of ye Family Goe near her. He intends to write to You and My brother Isaac to Endeavour a reconcilation. I would have You Answer his Letter, if you dont hers, for I must be Soe Ingenious [as] to conffess nature is Very Strong, and It would give me a Great Concern if She Should Live Un happy, tho' its a Concern she does not Meritt. As to the Other Affair you wrote me Abouth, You may be Very Eassy on that head. The Person Concern'd will give You All the Sattisfaction you desire. Wath you say abouth y[ou]r Sisters comeing to England, I shall Very readly agree to it and the Sooner the better, if it was only a Means of her not Seeing the Other, wich She will hardly be able to avoid Unless She intirely Excludes her Self from all Company, wich She has don for this three months past, tho' Phila has not bin in Town[6] Since she Left Us, but

---

occupying the westernmost position of a double house (probably the two adjoining houses referred to in the Cohen deed) in the Dock Ward bounded by the houses of Samuel Bayard and Peter Delancey. The rear lots were divided by a partition wall which went down to the wharf, probably Coenties Slip. The double house is now 80–82 Pearl Street. Will Liber no. 13, 552–561, New York Surrogate's Office, 31 Chambers Street, New York City; *NYHSC* 3 (1895), 310.

From 1744 to 1770 the Franks residence and/or business address is placed in Dock Street by newspaper advertisements. *Revived Weekly Post Boy,* May 7, 1744; *Gazette,* Dec. 24, 1750, March 31, 1760, Aug. 15, and Oct. 3, 1763, Feb. 20, 27, April 9, and May 14, 1764; *Mercury,* May 9, 1757, and May 12, 1766; *New York Journal,* May 10, 1770.

6 Phila, as this letter and David's of April indicate, lived at home for six

has (wathever I have forbid) found means to Send Messages, for as they Lived Very Affectionately. It Subsists Still, And I am Sure She will find all the means she can to See Richa. I thank you and your Dear Phila in the behalf of your Sisters & My Self for the Profussion of Preas[en]ts sent Uss. I Shall make mine Up but cant Tell when I Shall Wear it, for in the mind I am in now I have noe Inclination for dress or Visiting. Ye Girles will Make theres Up as Soon as they goe to Town, wich will be ye Latter end of the Summer. They was Just in mourning for my aunt Isaacs[7] whoe had bin Just Dead when they received them. The reasson why I did not Write to Mr. Aaron Franks was not from [lack of] a Due Sence of Obligations and Gratitude, but from an Apprehensiveness of being Trouble Some. You may Assure him I am Sensiable of the many kindnesses and Favours rec[eiv]ed from him, And it gives me pain to Express my Gratitude, because wathever I Can Say falls Short of wath is his due from my Family and my Self, tho' If I can bring my mind into any State of Ease, I Shall write him by this. I wish I could find Any thing Agreeable to send to my Dear Phila. Moses Sends her a pott of Sweet meets and mordechay Gomez's wife[8] has Given me a Small pot for You, wich I dare Say is Exceeding Good, And I hope You may Use it with pleassure. All Friends Say many kind things to You And wish you a great deall of Joy. I shall take Care and Send Some quaills next faull and secure them better than ye Last. Make my Compliments to Uncle Abraham Franks with thanks for his kind Letters, wich I Shall not Answer by this And, therefore, Desire you would make an Excuse for me. Your

---

months after secretly marrying. She left home in the latter part of March 1743, and probably went to Delancey's home in Bloomingdale. Henry Beekman to Gilbert [Livingston], March 20, 1743, Beekman Papers, NYHSL.

7 Aunt Isaacs, see Letter XV, Oct. 17, 1739, note 6.

8 Rebecca DeLucena married Mordecai Gomez on May 4, 1741, after his first wife Hester Campos had died. Mordecai held considerable property in the city and had an extensive mercantile business. For Mordecai and Rebecca's marriage contract, dated April 30, 1741, see Con, Lib. 32, cp. 205. For Mordecai's Will and further biographical information, see *Wills*, 84–91.

brother david I hope will doe Very well. The Ship is not yet Arrived at Phil[ade]l[phia]. As to w[a]th you Say Concerning My brother Nathans Marrying,[9] your reassons are perfectly Just, but then on the Other hand it is a great Disadvantage for a man to keep house without a good Mistress, Soe that a Wife to him is a Nesscessary Evil. My brother mich[a]ell keeps his health And Good Charector, wich is to me a great Satisfaction. Sol[omon] Hart is absconded in Very Unhappy Circumstance. His wife and child is with [*about two words made illegible by the fold*], wich is all they've got for the honor of being Allyed to M H[ar]t. Its Commonly Said the rich man is gods Steward. M H[ar]t is a Very Saveing one whoe will Lett a brother Perish when Such a Truffle as £200 might make him happy.[10] The married Sister wrote him She had some Tickets in the Lottery,[11] and if She

---

9 Nathan Levy's first wife may have been Bila, who died in September 1741. See Letter XXII, Sept. 6, 1741, note 5. This is a reference to Nathan's second marriage to someone whose first name was Michal.

10 Solomon Hart, a merchant and *shohet* [ritual slaughterer] of Congregation Shearith Israel, married Rachel Isaacs sometime late in 1740. As A.F. indicates, he ran away in 1743, and by the following year he still had not returned. Peter Jay sued Solomon in Mayor's Court in 1744, and the records indicate that the defendant was not found. See Letter XV, Oct. 17, 1739, note 5, and Letter XVI, July 6, 1740; *Jay v. Hart* (1744), MCM, vol. 1742–1748, p. 85. The M. Hart whom A.F. mentions was undoubtedly Moses Hart, a wealthy London merchant and Solomon's brother. A Solomon who is known to have been the brother of Moses Hart died in England in 1768. Moses Hart was the father of Simha Hart Franks, N.F.'s mother-in-law, and therefore N.F.'s grandfather by marriage. At his death, he did not leave a legacy to N.F.'s wife or any of her brothers or sisters. This led to a complicated legal case that eventually reached the House of Lords. Norman Bentwich, "Anglo-Jewish Causes Célèbres," *TJHSE* 15 (1946), 112–120. A printed copy of the judgment is in the archives of the American Jewish Historical Society.

11 The government lottery of 1743 had among its prizes two of £10,000 and four of £5,000. Eighty thousand tickets were sold at £10 each. A total of £304,230 was to be awarded. The drawing took place on November 21, 1743, but was apparently not of any help to Solomon. *Gentleman's Magazine* 13 (1743), 161 and 611. Moses Hart had previously won a lottery and Solomon's sister may, therefore, have had hopes of winning. See Letter XX, April 26, 1741, note 3.

got a good Prise, she would Send him a pr[e]s[en]t. If the prayers of the poor Prevaill, She may have Success if Sol[omon] Hart puts Up prayers for her, being he is Realy Poor & Needy.

Now Lett me Say Something for the Distress wee are more nearly Concern'd in, and that is poor good moses Solomons. Is that Unhappy Youth to Spend the best part of his Life, as it Where, in a Goall? For Such may be Termed the Confin[e]d Life he is in att pr[e]s[en]t. Wee rec[eiv]ed Letters from him Last week, wherin he Complains Pittyously of the Ill Treatm[en]t he meets with from his friends, whoe he hardly hears from, and when he does, never Lett him know wath will be the Consequence of his Detention or wich way he may be cleared. Its Very Severe that he Must be the Victim of anothers Villiany. The manner in wich he Committed his Error was wath a person of Greater penatration in buissness might have fell into. His Letting Mr. [Sam] Levy come off was noe fault, because Mr. Levys pretence was to Come here in order to make Up his Own Affairs that he might the better be inable'd to assist in Dischargeing there Joynt Debts: wich I am affraid he has not much in his power to per form.[12]

12 See Letters XXVI, June 3, 1742; XXVII, Aug. 29, 1742; XXVIII, Dec. 5, 1742; and XXXII, Nov. 22, 1743. J.F. wrote in a letter to Moses Salomons, dated Nov. 25, 1743, that the latter would shortly be on his way to London and from thence to India, "where you soon make up your lost time." Misc. Records, Vol. 69A, 1736–1740, p. 4, Probate Court Records, Charleston, South Carolina.

On the commercial activities of Jews with India in the eighteenth century and on, including persons bearing the names of Franks, Hart, and Solomons, see Walter J. Fischel, *The Jews in India: Their Contributions to the Economic and Political Life* (Jerusalem, 1960), 174–175 (Hebrew), which lists a number of Ashkenazi and Sephardi merchants maintaining ties between India and England and dealing in diamonds and coral. These traders had branches in London and in Madras, and Fisehel gives data on the activities during the first half of the eighteenth century of individuals bearing such names as Aaron Franks who lived in Madras and who may have been related to the Frankses in England. Aaron Franks asked for permission in 1728 to travel to Europe because his affairs required it. Marcus Moses, his partner, petitioned "to return to England by one of the slops bound thither this season." Persons bearing the family names of Hart, Solomons, Salvador, Franco, de Castro, Espinosa, Nunes, Moses, and Pacheco were among the merchants in the Madras area. Shortly before coming to these

Your Father will Give You a farther Acc[oun]t of this Mellancholy affair, wich I wish may in some Meassure be Happly Terminated. My Compliments to Mrs. Compton & Capt[ain] Riggs. I beg they will be Soe good to forgive me that I dont Answer there agreeable Favour by this: my Spirets is too Depresst to write. It is with reluctancy I doe write to Any one at pr[e]s[en]t. Therefore whoever I Omit, You must Excuse me to them. I think I've Spun this to a Considerable Lenght and shall Conclude with the Repetition of my prayers for Your Health and Happyness. I am,

My Dear Son,
Your Affectionate Mother,
Abigaill Franks

---

shores, Michael Gratz "probably, early in 1758 or late in 1757, . . . sailed for India, seeking joint account with his London kindred." William Vincent Byars, *B. and M. Gratz: Merchants of Philadelphia, 1754–1798* (Jefferson City, Mo., 1916), 12. Meyer Schomberg in his diatribe against some London Jews (*TJHSE* 20 [1964], 102 [sheet 6–7]) condemns those Jews who on the Sabbath day are overmuch concerned with matters financial, in these words: "In addition, they walk on the day of rest by design in the street of the changer which is called Exchange Alley, to enquire and find out on that day from merchants and brokers if there has been a rise or fall in the price of India *(Hodu)* securities which are called 'India Bonds,' or of the India *(Hodu)* securities which are called the 'southern sea' or South Sea notes of the treasure-house called *'Banco.'*" The interest of Jews of London, Amsterdam, and New York in India trade continued during the eighteenth century. See, for example, Walter J. Fischel, "From Cochin (India) to New York: Samuel Abraham, the Jewish Merchant of the 18th Century," *Harry Wolfson Jubilee Volume on the Occasion of His Seventy-Fifth Birthday: English Section, Volume 1,* ed. Saul Lieberman and Leo W. Schwarz (Jerusalem, 1965), 255–274, and the "Log Book of the Ship Samson," *PAJHS* 27 (1920), 239, which is inscribed "Isaac H. Levy's Journal, 1798," and shows conditions, etc., of a voyage between New York, Madras, and Calcutta. The sloop started back from Madras to New York on October 17, 1798, but by March 6, 1799, had not yet reached New York. Compare Walter J. Fischel, "The Indian Archives: A Source for the History of the Jews of Asia (from the Sixteenth Century On)," in *The Seventy-Fifth Anniversary Volume of the Jewish Quarterly Review,* ed. Abraham A. Neuman and Solomon Zeitlin (Philadelphia, 1967), 210–224.

P. S: Nap[htal]y Hart myers goes on Very well.
He had noe View but the Discharge
of His duty when he Offered his Service
to Come over to be with that poor Unhappy
Youth, whoe I Hartly wish may be Reinstated
to his health both of body & mind.[13]

XXXII
[Jacob Franks to Naphtali, November 22, 1743]

New York [Tuesday] Nov[ember] ye 22nd 1743

Dear Son,

On ye 4th Ult. I answerd Severell of y[ou]rs Received This Summer, which I Deliverd to Capt[ain] Osberon, who was to go Passanger from boston with ye Gosport Man of war,[1] & I allso wrote you ye 11th Ult. & sent ye Same to go with said Man of war, but she being sailld, Mr. Salomon Isaacs[2] writes Me, was put on board a Mast Shipe, but for fear have here Inclosed a copey of what I wrote you & hope you May be able to Git us said Com[m]o[dities], Since which have had ye Satisfaction of y[ou]rs of 13th & 14th Septem[be]r with ye Inclosed Invoices & bills of Loading for Tea on board of Bryant

---

13 A.F. here reflects her sentiments with regard to Moses Salomons. Her reference to "Hart" and "Hartly" is another example of her play on names and words.

1 On May 26, 1743, the *H.M.S. Gosport,* Capt. William Ellis, master, arrived at Sandy Hook after convoy duty in the West Indies. While in New York, Ellis was removed from his command and Capt. Stourton was appointed commander. *Boston News-Letter,* June 9 and July 7, 1743. The ship arrived in Boston on July 14, 1743. Ellis died one month later on August 12th. *Weekly Post-Boy,* Aug. 13, 1743.

2 Solomon Isaacs, brother of Joshua Isaacs, a merchant formerly of Freehold, N.J., was living in Boston in 1737 and probably remained there until at least the time of this letter. He died in Charleston, South Carolina, in 1757. *Portraits,* 317; Barnett A. Elzas, *The Jews of South Carolina* (Philadelphia, 1905), 28–29, and 40–41; *Wills,* 103–106.

& Griffith, which have received in good ord[e]r & have Disposed of Eight Chests to good people at Three and Six Months Cr[edit] & at 6£, though expect to receive some of ye Mony Much sooner, & By Bryant or Griffith will Send you ye Ac[coun]t [of] Sales of ye Last Teas & Some Returns on ye same. Fault is found again t[ha]t ye Tea Does Not draw a high Couller, for t[ha]t is ye Tea Likt in this place. As you Must belive, It is all ways a great Satisfaction to Me & family to here from you. I realy Think your neglect of given Me ye Same Very Much, for by Many wessells Arrived this Sum[me]r & fall at boston & Philad[elphi]a, & Likewise by Mr. Scoots wessell[3] Directly here, [and I] had Not a Single Line from you by any of t[he]m. Not so Much as a News Pap[e]r (except by Scots shipe), which I think very hard & there hope you will not serve Me So again. I think y[ou]r Uncle Isaac or D: Salomons Might have wrote Me a few Lines by t[he]m. Wee are all, Thank god, in good health, hopeing This will find you & y[ou]r Phila & ye rest of our Relations in ye Same, to all whom [I] shall, please god, write & ans[we]r their fav[ou]rs by ye Next shiping, which will Soon be there, being No Less t[ha]n five wessels bound to Londo[n]. Wee are Now Loading ye buildings for Jamaicoa. One shipe is allready sailed, two Now a Loading, & shall Load ye New wessell of Mine with ye rest. I Compute ye Cost will be ab[ou]t £3000 our Currancey, on which have allready Drawn £ 2300, & ye bread wee are Now a shipeing will amount to ab[ou]t £ 1500, both of which will soon be Completed, when shall send y[ou]r Uncle & y[ou]r self bills for ye same & hope shall Draw very Little on y[ou]r Uncle for ye Same & shall in all Respects use my honest Endeavo[u]rs to give you both all ye Encour[a]g[emen]t t[ha]t Lays in My Power to Continue the Tea Trade.[4] Oliver Delancey

3 Perhaps Joseph Scott, a New York merchant, but more likely either John or Robert Scott, London and Jamaica merchants. *State Papers,* 43: 260.

4 J.F. dealt in all types of commodities. An advertisement in the *Gazette* of April 16, 1739, told of the sale of nails, spikes, scythes, spades, frying pans, anvils, vises, anchors, small swivel guns, and "Several other sorts of Iron-Work." Also included was Bohea tea. See also *Weekly Journal* of April 21, 1739. He also traded

has bin with me (being ye first time since t[ha]t unfourtunet affair hapned) Ab[ou]t ye £1000 Left Phila.⁵ I showed him & gave him a Copey of t[ha]t part of y[ou]r Uncles will. All I can Say ab[ou]t It is & beg t[ha]t If It can be Don so as he may have It, for y[ou]r Uncle Aron to doe It, for to Me It seems It is best as age befalls me. He now writes to Mr. Baker⁶ to speak to y[ou]r Uncle Aaron ab[ou]t It, & he will give Security t[ha]t If Ever Brother Aaron is oblidged by Law to allow ye said £1000 to ye Heir at Law, t[ha]t he will t[he]n Repay ye Same. It may seem Strange to you t[ha]t I should Desire ye same, but If you concedor wee live in a Small place, & he is Related to ye best family in ye place, & though y[ou]r sister has Accted so very UnDutyfull, yet It would Give Me & family a great Deall of Trouble was she to be Ill Used by her husband or Relations, which at present is other ways. But should he be kep from Said Mony (If it can with Safety be paid), It might be other ways. He Seems to be a Carefull Young Man & will Not spend his estate, all which I would have you Mention to y[ou]r Uncle Aaron to whom I write a few Lines by this opp[ortunity] & shall be Heartily Glad to here y[ou]r Uncle Aaron Complys with My Request. Am Told Phila writes you by this shipe. I have hardly had ye Sight of her since she Left ye family. Am assured she heartily Repents what she has Don & Therefore offten am Inclined to See her & give her Liberty to Come to See us, but can

---

in rum, wine, rice, and skins. See entries of June 5, Sept. 18, and Oct. 20, 1739, Jan. 24 and 31, and April 21, 1740, in the NOL, CO 5/1226. On July 26, 1742, J.F. exported three cases of tea to Jamaica and on August 10, 1742, he shipped one box of tea to Newfoundland via the sixteen-ton sloop *Oglethorpe,* Samuel Tingley, master. NOL, CO 5/1226.

5 By his will, Isaac Franks bequeathed £1,000 to Phila Franks to be paid to her when she became of age or married, whichever sooner occurred, provided her marriage was with the consent of her uncle Aaron Franks, the executor of the will, and her father. Will of Isaac Franks, Derby 243, PCC.

6 This probably refers to either Samuel or William Baker, both of whom were London merchants closely connected with the New York trade. In 1741, the Common Council asked them to purchase a "large fire Engine" and later in the year a "Good bell." *MCC* 5: 22 and 45.

Not Bring y[ou]r Mother to It. Therefore, Desire you to ans[we]r her Letter & to write y[ou]r Mother Ab[ou]t her. As to y[ou]r Sister Ratcha, she is as good a Child as Ever Lived, yet am Resolved she shall go for London, if Peace, by first good Opp[ortunity][7] & hope you or Relations will [not] be against ye same. I adwise wee have Not had a Line from ye Commis[sioner]s by our wessells. At ye Same time am pleased to here by y[ou]rs t[ha]t they are Satisfied with our Proceedings & Inclosed you have Copey of what wee Now write t[he]m, & you will Deliver ye Packet of Advert[isemen]ts Directed for you at ye N. York Coffee house,[8] Deliverd to Capt. Clarke. I have sent D: Salamons at his Broth[e]r Moses Desire £100 St[erling] by This Op[portunity] & shall This week write to him ab[ou]t what you & y[ou]r Uncle Mentiond & wish he was Clear. I shall Not have above £400 our Mony when all Debts come In of his, & great part of his goods I Sold but Lattly. When ye Ac[coun]t [is] finished, will Send a Copey to his Brother David t[ha]t he may see I Don him Justice. Shall send ye Acc[oun]ts Relating to My Demands for ye goods, sunck at Georgia[9] p[e]r Next Op[portunity]. Inclosed you have ye Portested bill of ye Generall, for he was gon from Georgia before ye

---

7 Richa did not leave for England until June 20, 1769, a few months after her father's death. She was the administrator of his estate. *PAJHS* 22 (1914), 39–51; Letters of Administration, Vol. 1768–1774, Jan. 31, 1769, New York Surrogate's Court, 31 Chambers Street, New York City.

8 The New York Coffee House was known by 1761 as the New England or Quebec Coffee House. Its early address is not known, but it was probably near the Royal Exchange. In 1767 it was at 7 Sweetings Alley and/or Sweetings Rents. Lillywhite, *London Coffee Houses*, 407.

9 For reference to business arrangements between J.F., his son Moses, and his brother-in-law Aaron, see three bills of exchange of £300, each dated New York, June 14, 1743, made by J.F. and his son to the order of Aaron. Box 10, item 184, James Alexander Papers, NYHSL. For an account of the affairs of Moses and David Salomons and of J.F.'s attempts to help the former, see Misc. Records, Vol. 69A, 1736–1740, Charleston, S.C., pp. 4 and 6; note, dated Nov. 26, 1743, Vol. 69B, p. 449. For further reference to business losses of J.F. and his son Moses as Victuallers to the Navy, see *Weekly Journal*, Oct. 7, 1743; Con. Lib. 32, cp. 471.

bill got there & am in great hopes t[ha]t Parliament will doe us Justice in said affair[10] & shall be Glad to here you have Recoverd ye Mony of Capt[ain] Roberts. There is yet a Ballance Due to me from Col[onel] Cochran. Pray use ye Encl[ose]d to Recover ye same for me. Y[ou]r Brother David was gon to Georgia & am concerned to find It is Not in his Power to Comply with y[ou]r Ord[er]s.

Samuell Levy has not made any Pay[men]t to his Cr[edit] at Carolina. He keps in ye Country, but Inded am Told it is Not in his Power. Our New Gov[erno]r[11] Seems to be a good Sort of a Gentleman, but by what I find, his Cheif Delight is in Drinking, & If he keps on as he has hereto done, he will Dispatch him Self. But kep it to y[ou]r Self; at Least Let Not My Name be Mentiond Ab[ou]t It. As [to] Mr. Asyne, he is [a] great [*shoteh*=fool] but on y[ou]r & My Relations Recom[me]nd[ation] have & shall Comply with y[ou]r request. If there be any fault with ye horse, y[ou]r B[rother] Moses is to blame. Inclosed is a bill of Exchange & Letter of Advice for £50 St[erling] on Mr. John Hanbury,[12] which when Paid please to Cr[edit] ye Acc[oun]t of T. S. C. for £30 St[erling] & ye £20 Pay to Isaac Levy, ye Servant, by ord[e]r of y[ou]r B[rother] David. Some

---

10 The general referred to by J.F. is James Oglethorpe, against whom charges of defrauding his regiment and failure to pay numerous bills of exchange were brought by the War Office. J.F.'s account was probably among the unpaid bills. Oglethorpe left Georgia on July 23, 1743, to answer these charges, but he was acquitted in June 1744. In March of that year. Parliament granted to him the sums he had expended in the defense of the colony in an amount in excess of £60,000, as J.F. had hoped. Ettinger, *Ogelthorpe*, 250–252. J.F. apparently continued to do business with the general after this date, for on December 26, 1746, J.F. recorded a note that had been made by William Horton in Frederica, Georgia, on November 4, 1746, certifying a debt due him by Oglethorpe in the sum of £318.8.3 for "flour, biskett, and Molasses delivered into the Magazine by Mr. Thomas Sumner in Nov. 1744." Con. Lib. 33, cp. 92.

11 George Clinton arrived in New York in September 1743. See Letter XXVI, note 9.

12 John Hanbury (d. 1758), a Quaker and London merchant, was governor of the Hamburg Company and a purchaser of land from the Ohio Company. McAnear, "An American in London," 383; *State Papers*, 43: 260.

of his goods Mr. N. Myers has yet Unsold. I daily Expect another bill from him as allso from Mr. Gray.[13] All other perticulers shall ans[we]r at large in my Next. You are Mistaken ab[ou]t My Insurance to Georgia; ye Insurars Risque was over 24 hours after ye Sloops Arrivell at Georgia, but as Generall Ogelthrope would Not let ye wessell Unload, I can Not think but they must stand to ye Loss, for t[ha]t is ye Restraine of Princes. Howeaver, shall Like It Much better to git ye Pay[men]t with you t[ha]n to go to Law with My friends here, who ye Insurars are. I wish y[ou]r Tea Trade to boston may Ans[we]r. Tea, am Told, Sold there Lattly for 24£ Ready Pay. Guns are in great Demand here & would have sold to great advance. Messrs. Crawley[14] Desapointed Me very Much by not Sending t[he]m as they promises Me, and They Give Me Their Reason. Have wrote t[he]m ab[ou]t [the guns] again, So Desire you to Speak to Mr. Allen ab[ou]t ye same. If they will not Engage to Send t[he]m by ye Return of ye next wessell, t[he]n Desire you to Engage for a Large percell of Swevels. Would have 50/2, 30 three & 20 four pounders & with shott sutable to t[he]m, t[ha]t is If ye war Continues. Else Send only ye Swevell,[15] which will all ways Sell. I could have had Ready Mony for ye quantity I now write for, but fear other people now have wrote for Some. If you find they have, t[he]n Send but the half. You may Send t[he]m on y[ou]r own Ac[coun]t, If you think Propper. Shall be Glad to here you have bought ye branches. If not would have you Send, as wrote you already, a Small p[air] of *ez hayyim* for ye *sefer*.[16] Y[ou]r Mother

13 The Mr. Grey referred to is possibly a member of the firm of Grey and Meynard, Agent-Victuallers to the Navy in Port Royal, Jamaica. *Weekly Journal,* Oct. 17, 1743.

14 Ambrose and John Crowley were ironmasters and successors of Ambrose Crowley, Sr., and were also well-known London merchants. Lucy Sutherland, *A London Merchant* (New York, 1962), 153 and 156.

15 J.F. refers to the size of cannon, which was determined by the weight of the shot. Those mentioned were too small for carriage mounts and, therefore, considered swivel guns, which were used on ships or for quick firing elsewhere.

16 See Cecil Roth, "Ritual Art," *Jewish Art: An Illustrated History* (New York, 1961), 318, where he discusses the *ez hayyim* [tree of life *(Proverbs* 3:18)] or

& Sister will write you p[er] Bryant they Give Their Love to you & to ye rest of our Relations, & Pray Excuse me to t[he]m all for Not writing at present, for have Realy no time without ye Shipe Stays a day or two Longer. Allso Excuse me to y[ou]r Uncle Isaac, with my Love & Service to t[he]m all is what offers at present. Wishing you & y[ou]r Phila all ye happiness this world affords & Remain,

   Dear Son,
        Y[ou]r Most affactionate Father,
           Jacob Franks

My Respects to all friends.
Wee daily Expect wessells from
Jamaicoa, when hope to have
further ord[e]rs from ye agents who
are yet & hope all ways will be
our very good friends.

---

wooden staves which served as rollers. To two of these staves, the Scroll of the Torah [The Five Books of Moses written in Hebrew on parchment] used in the synagogue service would be attached, respectively, at either end. Among Ashkenazi Jews, the term *ez hayyim* is applied to the wooden staves and to their metal ornaments, the Torah finials at both ends of the staves, which could be plated in silver or gold, or made removable. The removable finial ornaments, also called *rimonim,* made of silver or gold in Amsterdam, London, and the Hague at the end of the seventeenth century and during the eighteenth century, in the possession of the Spanish and Portuguese Jews' Synagogue in Bevis Marks, are described in *Treasures of a London Temple,* which is a descriptive catalog of the ritual plate, mantles, and furniture of that synagogue, compiled by A. G. Grimwade and others, with an introduction by Dr. Solomon Gaon and a foreword by Lionel D. Barnett (London, 1961) [pp. 4–5 of the introduction; catalog of the *rimonim* (bells for the Scrolls of the Law), pp. 26–37; plates XI and XII for illustrations of some of these *rimonim*]. We may assume that J.F. was interested in acquiring a pair of removable metal *rimonim* from abroad, the work of skilled craftsmen, artistic silversmiths working with silver or gold, since it would have been a simple matter to make wooden staves or rollers in this country.

[In another hand]
Pray my respects to Mr. Hart.[17] I shall answer his favour p[er] Bryant.

M.F.

[In another hand]
Mr. Nap[htali] Myer Gives his Service to you & will write you p[er] Bryant.

[Again in hand of Jacob Franks]
I can but take Notice of what M. Salomons writes Me in a Letter I Received from him few days before. Capt[ain] Griffith Came in from London, which Realy Gave Me Some Concern as I had No Letters from London for Some time before. What he write is t[ha]t he had Rec[eiv]ed a Letter from his Brother David, who Tells him t[ha]t his affairs would have bin Made up before had Not an Accedent happned to his Uncle Aaron Alone & Desires Me to Let him Know what it was, but as y[ou]r Letters by Griffith Makeing No Mention of any thing Like It made me Easy, but at ye Same time think It is a very Od way of writting. If any Thing was in, It Pray Let Me Know It.

XXXIII
[Abigaill Franks to Naphtali Franks, November 25, 1745]

New York [Monday] Nov[embe]r 25th, 1745

Dear HeartSey

I Received y[our]s by bryant And Wadle. The Latter was only an abrievia[tio]n of the former. All the Sattisfaction they gave me was to hear from you and that you Was in health, wich Was A Great pleas-

---

17 Moses Franks probably referred either to Aaron Hart (d. 1762) or to Moses Hart (1670–1756). *Wills,* 113–117.

sure to me for in the Midst of my many griefes.[1] I am not Insensiable to the Happyness and Wellfare of those I hold most dear. As to wath relates to buissness, I have Soe little knowledge of It that I Leave the Explainat[io]n of it intirely to y[ou]r Father but this: Give me Leave to Say that I think your Fathers Treatment from you & your Uncle, Especialy from the Latter, is more Like a Slave than a Freeman. Its

---

[1] A.F.'s grief may have been occasioned by Phila's marriage to Oliver Delancey, as well as David's marriage to Margaret Evans (1720–1780), a Christian, on December 17, 1743, and the baptism of David's daughter on April 12, 1745. There is no specific reference to the latter marriage in the extant letters of A.F., but the letters of 1744 are missing. Margaret Evans was the daughter of Mary and Peter Evans, Register General of Pennsylvania. John Moore, the husband of Frances Moore, A.F.'s close friend, was the brother of Mary Evans. John and Frances Moore were thus David's uncle and aunt by marriage. Perhaps it was through A.F.'s friend that David met Mary. They were married and lived in Philadelphia and had five children. Abigail, born on January 6, 1745, was baptized in Christ Church on April 12, 1745, and died September 11, 1798; Mary (known also as Polly), born on January 25, 1748, was baptized at Christ Church on April 10, 1748, and died August 21, 1774; Rebecca, born in 1760, died in September 1823; Jacob, born January 7, 1747, was baptized at Christ Church on April 20, 1747, and was living in 1781 at Isleworth House in England with his father. In his will, dated July 30, 1785, and proved July 22, 1794, David Franks bequeathed the major portion of his estate to his children Jacob, Abigail, Rebecca, and Moses. It is possible that David Franks also had a son John, but there is little evidence to support this, and it is more likely Jacob was also known as John. Raised as Christians, Abigail and Rebecca married Christians of prominent families. Abigail married Andrew Hamilton, son of the noted attorney of the same name, and Rebecca married Col. Henry Johnson. Their son Henry married into the Frederick Philipse family. Charles H. Hart, "Notes and Queries," *Pennsylvania Magazine of History and Biography* 34 (1910), 253–255; Septimus F. Nivin, *Genealogy of Evans, Niven and Allied Families* (Philadelphia, 1930), 16; *PAJHS* 4 (1896), 197; Burial Records of Christ Church, 1709–1785, p. 547, and Baptismal Records of Christ Church, 1709–1768, pp. 311, 339, and 351, Christ Church Library, Philadelphia; Will of David Franks, Holman 366, PCC; Daiches-Dubens, "Eighteenth Century Anglo-Jewry," 159. There is an occasional reference to the date of David's marriage as October 1744. *Pennsylvania Archives*, 2nd series, 11 (1890), 92.

Very likly ye returns is not Soe Soon as they Ought to be, but I Suppose Moses has Cleared that Point in Some Sort. This I know, all that is Transacted is with a View to make remittance. I know not wich way they might be made quiker Unless you would have your Father take money Upon intrest than where would be the advantage to him. It might to you & Your Uncle, but If I have a right Way of thinking, It would be of more benifitt to him to be without the Consignment. However, I hope You will Soon be make Eassy, And If I durst Offer my advice to Your Father, I would Decline receiveing any more buissness that would Subject me to those reproofs & reproaches. I say'd nothing when the Last Tea came in wadle, but if your Father had my Spirit, I would have Sent it Directly to Philadelphia. Dont think I take it Amiss, Your Uncles demands for wath is his Just due; its the Manner its don Piques me. Good God to Accuse him of Dishonesty And Tradeing with his money with an Intent to Defraud him, for I can take it in Noe Other Sence, is to me insuportable. Then he is takeing to task In the Manner And Method he does his buissness, As if he was to be kept In Leading Strings all his Life. I think he is the best Judge how to manage his buissness. He has Followed it Long enough to know wath he is abouth And, I dare Say, Understand it As well As any merchant in this place. Not that I think he is Above being advised, but then Lett it be in a Candid friendly manner but not in a Lordly Imperious Way. By all thats Sacred, if my Father was to write me in ye Manner y[ou]r Uncle does to his brother, I would Send his Scraps of Letters back. Dont think me Ungratefull or that I have not a Sence of Obligations Due to y[ou]r Uncle. I Own I have A Very Just Sence of them And Should think it the greatest happyness of My Life if I could in any Shape Shew it, for I detest the thoughts of Ingratitude And Should hate My Self if I thought I could be in any ways guilty of Soe detestable A thing, but I cant bare to See the Many Insults y[ou]r Father receives. Indeed its from his Own brother and therefore I never Say any thing to him abouth it, but None of my Own relations Should dare to Use him thus, be his dependance Never Soe great. I say with Cowly (where I to Curse the Man I hate, Lett attend[an]ce & dependance be his Fate).² I waite with Impatience to hear from Moses, for I bleive you have had Some bickerings. However I wish all May be ended Amicably, for it would be a great Distress to me to find any Disagreement between you. I charge you wath ever happens to keep nothing of that kind a Secreet from me. As to wath you Say of david, doe Just As you think proper.³ For my part, if I cant throw him from My heart, I Will by my Conduct have the Appearance of it. Its a Firey Tryall. You are Noe parent⁴ And therefore Can be Noe Judge. Pray heaven Whenever You are, you may be a happy one. I Am in hopes Your wishes for one May be Compleat, Especialy as you say your wife is fond of children, for you may be Assured I Have her Content as Much at heart as Any of my Own children, and I dont know wich of them has a Greater Share of my Affections. Mrs. Warren writes She will be here in the Spring. If She goes then to England, I bleive Richa will not goe with [her], for now Moses is Gon, She has Noe one to Goe with her, Soe that Scheme of her coming is Over. I thank you for the books You Sent. I would Willingly [have] Sent Mrs. Franks Some Green Sweetmeets, but Could git none that was Very Good. The News from Our parts I reffer to

2 The quotation is from "Several Discourses by way of Essays on Verse and Prose," by Abraham Cowley (1618–1667) in his *Collected Works*, 11th ed. (London, 1710), 2: 685. The quotation should read "If there be Man (ye Gods) I Ought to hate Dependance and Attendance be his Fate."

3 Perhaps A.F. refers to a gift which N.F. sent his brother David on the occasion of his wedding. A silver bowl made in London with the coat of arms of Franks and Evans engraved thereon is presently in the Metropolitan Museum of Art. Yvonne Hackenbroch, ed., *English and Other Silver in the Irwin Untermeyer Collection* (New York, [1963]), plate 112. A pair of tea caddies made by Paul Delamarie embossed with the arms of Franks impaling Franks may have been given as a gift to Naphtali on his marriage. *Sotheby and Co. catalogue,* May 2, 1963, 32. See illustrations. See also Jessie McNab Dennis, "Lamerie Silver for the Franks Family," *Metropolitan Museum of Art Bulletin*, new series, 26 (Dec. 1967), 174–179.

4 See Letter XXXIV, n. 1.

Others. I have nothing to add but My Prayers for Your happyness and with my blessing I Conclude,

> My dear child,
> Your Truly Affectionate Mother,
> Abigaill Franks

Mr. Napthaly Franks

[Docket]
Ans[were]d p[er] Myers
ye 23 Ap[ri]l 1746

XXXIV
[Abigaill Franks to Naphtali Franks, December 4, 1746]

New York [Thursday] Decemb[e]r 4th 1746

Dear HeartSey

As all Civilized Nations pay respect to A Father, I did not know wether it Was Soe proper to begin my Letter in the Familiar manner [as] I Used to doe And Call you plain HeartSey, but As my Learning is Not Arrived to the pitch of giveing proper titles, I chose not to Expose my Self but keep to the Old Method. Therefore, in the Most Affectionate Manner receive my Congratulation to You and My dear Phila on the birth of Your Son,[1] whoe I hope May Live a blessing to his parents. I should Now think it the Greatest Happyness to be with you. Your Sister Richa is quite wild Abouth it. She Says She is

---

1 N.F. and Phila had at least four children—two sons, one of whom was Jacob Henry Franks (1759–1840), and two daughters, Charlotte and Abigail (d. Dec. 27, 1814). Parish Register, Mortlake, Surrey, England. Daiches-Dubens, "Eighteenth-Century Anglo-Jewry," 159. The son died in infancy. See above, Letter XXXIII.

Sure It would be better taken Care of if She was with it. In Short, the Joy is thro' the Whole Family, because they know it gives You Soe Much Satisfaction. Pray god You may Always have your Desires Compleated in that Dear child & Every other blessing. I rec[eiv]ed Severall of your Letters And in Perticuler A Long One by Mr. Myers. Wath You write Abouth buissness I reffer answering to that intirely to Your father, whoe I hope will Soon Compleat Your Desires and Expectations on that Score. I am Sure he does all he can to Advance Moses Intrest[2] & Satisfy Your Uncle & y[ou]r Self with remitances. Moses, Who has bin here Soe Latly, Must be Able to Acquaint you the Constant Care & Aplication of Your Father. It will Give Me the Only wish I have to See all made Eassy on that Subject. I find you All Accuse me on wath you call pride and Arrogance. In Mr. Myers I have Wrote to Isaac & Moses; therefore, Shall Say noe More Abouth

---

2 A.F. refers to J.F.'s unsuccessful attempts to have New York merchants use Moses Franks as their agent in England. J.F. continued his efforts on his son's behalf. On July 26, 1749, Moses in a letter to William Alexander wrote: "By a letter rec[eiv]ed from my father he informs me that he has waited on you with applications on my behalf for your Services; and that you had been so obliging to promise him to favour me with your Commands as occasions offerd." This seems to have been merely a civil reply on Alexander's part, since there is no evidence to show that he used Moses as his agent. As A.F. indicates in the following letter, such evasive answers were fairly common. Box 1, William Alexander Letters, 1744-1798, NYHSL.

Despite these difficulties Moses did succeed in becoming a successful merchant. His business career, covering some forty years, was varied, but generally involved the colonial trade. He was associated prior to the Revolution with Adam Drummond and Arnold Nesbitt in supplying His Majesty's forces. He was also a partner in the firms of Amherst, Plumsted and Franks and Colebrook, Nesbitt and Franks. Undoubtedly a help to his business career was his marriage to his cousin Phila Franks, daughter of Aaron Franks. King George III to Henry Fox, April 7, 1762, Emmitt Collection, NYPL; Frances Dublin, "Jewish Colonial Enterprise in the Light of the Amherst Papers (1758-1763)," *PAJHS* 35 (1939), 1-25; Virginia D. Harrington, *The New York Merchant on the Eve of the American Revolution* (New York, 1935), 113, 116, 239, 262, 292, 299 and 327; Lipman, *Three Centuries*, 59; Marcus, ed., *American Jewry*, 374-380.

it, but that without the Spirit of Divination I can Tell whoe you Mean to be that Somebody wrote in Large Characters in Your Letter. However, I am Very Eassy [that] I neither Cherished Nor Initiated in the Mystery of Pride. He brought it with him from a Land flowing with things of that Sort in all Shapes. If he does Amiss, Lett him bear the burthen of his Sins. For my part, while he is Civill, I Shall not I Shall not [sic] Change my Conduct. As to Rach[e]ll Hart, I wish it far'd better with her, but It Has bin Soe Offten the Subject of My Epistile's that I am Tired And Shall Say noe more, Only I hope She will Not bring her Missery back Again Among those that Are in Very Little better Circumstances, for none of her relations Can Give her any Assistance. It pleasses me Much to find You are in Such Unity, And I agree with you that it is A happyness when it Subsist Amongst Relations, for the Psalmist Says

> how Vast must there advanage be
> how Great there pleassur prove
> whoe Live Like bretheren
> & Consent in offices of Love[3]

---

3 Cf. Psalms 133:1. The impact of biblical Hebrew poetry, including the Psalms, upon the English language is alluded to in Joseph Addison's *Spectator*. See *The Works of the Right Honorable Joseph Addison*, with notes by Richard Hurd, D.D., 6 vols. (London, 1854–1856), 3: 383, where Addison states: "Our language has received innumerable elegances and improvements from that infusion of Hebraisms which are derived to it out of the holy writ." Abigaill Franks, who here quotes from the Tate and Brady metrical version of the *Psalms*, and who read the *Gentleman's Magazine*, would have found numerous references to studies, interpretations, and translations of Hebrew Scriptures and paraphrases of various Psalms in that periodical. See, for example, the following random references in the *Gentleman's Magazine:* 3, no. 25 (Jan. 1733), 37, where the writings of Homer are compared with those of Moses for sublimity; 5, no. 7 (July, 1735), 358, on rhyme used by Hebrew and Persian poets; ibid., on versions and translations of the Psalms; 4, no. 1 (Jan. 1734), 44, Psalm 139, paraphrased; 6, no. 10 (Oct. 1736), 609 and 610, 97 on Hebrew poesy and the translation thereof, and on Psalm 129, respectively; 6, no. 11 (Nov. 1736), 642, 644, 645 and 646, 97 on Psalm 129, the poetry of the Psalms, the translation of Psalms 1 and 2, and on

I thank God Wee Are in Perfect health & have passed A pleas[an]t Summer At Harleam,[4] but, However, I dont Like that Moveing. I Should Like to make the Country My Constant Aboad; the town has Noe Enchantments for me Like old Barzali,[5] I I [sic] have Lost the Taste of Mirth & Mussick. I have Sent Some of the things you wrote for. The Other things that I have not Sent I must have time to git, but You may be Sure You Shall have them next Summer, and wish With all my Soul I Could find Something of More Consequence to Oblige you with. Cramberies Are Very Scarce. The Small pox keeps the Country people & ye Indians from Town,[6] Else Should have Sent a Larger Q[uan]t[ity]. These I Got in Quarts from Severall persons. I have had the Compli[men]t[s] of half the Synagogue to Wish me Joy and there Compliments to You. A kiss to the Dear Mama & Son.

Balaam, respectively; and 7, no. 1 (Jan. 1737), 12–14 and 147–148 on the Hebrew language and Hebrew poetry; 9, no. 4 (April 1739), 190, on the use of Hebrew particles; and 18, no. 5 (May 1748), 201–204, and no. 6 (June 1748), 249–251, on Hebrew, the primitive tongue.

4 During 1746 and part of 1747 another smallpox epidemic swept New York. James Alexander to Cadwallader Colden, Jan. 20, 1746, *Colden Papers* 3: 190–191. A.F. probably went to Harlem because of the epidemic. She was not the only one on the move. The Assembly met at various places during the year, including the home of Mordecai Gomez in Greenwich Village, where they met in February 1746. *Journal of the General Assembly . . . 1743–1765* (New York, 1766), 2: 98. For accounts of the epidemic, see John Richard to Henry Van Rennselaer, March 15, 1747, Van Rensselaer–Fort Papers, NYPL. For one of the best descriptions of the disease and of yellow fever, which Cadwallader Colden, one of the foremost colonial scientists, found common along the waterfront where "all the filth and nastiness of the town and street is emptied," see letter of Cadwallader Colden to John Mitchell, Nov. 7, 1745, Box 11, Colden Letters, NYHSL.

5 A.F. refers to II Samuel 19:35–36.

6 See letter of John Stolle to James Alexander, Oct. 13, 1746, Box 10, James Alexander Papers, NYHSL, in which the writer stated: "Send the returns and other papers which I left with you, as I do not Care to Come to York my Self by Reason of the Small Pox."

With My Wisshes of Numberless blessings to You all, I am, My Dear Son,

> Your Affectionate Mother,
> Abigaill Franks

Mrs. Ross thanks you kindly for your preas[en]t and Sends her Compliments of Joy to You & Mrs. Franks.
HeartSey Franks

[Address]
To
Mr. Napthaly Franks
London

XXXV
[Abigaill Franks to Naphtali Franks, January 1, 1747][1]

New York [Thursday] Jan[uar]y 1st 1747

My Dear Heartsey

The Receipt of Your Letter by Clark[2] gave me much Concern, Especialy As It was Such An Affliction to Your Dear Phila. But it's the Will of that Divine Power to wich all must Submit and say with

---

1 This letter is a later acquisition, thanks to Mr. Bryant Lillywhite of Surrey, England. See Leo Hershkowitz, "Another Abigail Franks Letter and a Genealogical Note," *AJHO* 59 (1969), 223–224.

2 The *New-York Weekly Journal* of January 5, 1747, noted that "Last Tuesday Night [December 30] arrived here the Scow Sally Capt. Ferdinando Clarke in almost Seven Weeks from London." Abigaill probably did not get the letter until Wednesday, December 31, or even January 1, and she answered immediately.

Aaron, "it's the Lords doeing and Wee must be Silent."³ I had wrote a Letter to your Wife by this, wich I would Gladly gave taken back again, being it was a Letter of Congratula[tio]n and will Renew her Greife. But I Could not git it, being the bag was gon.⁴ I hope this May find her Perfectly recovered. My Love to her, wishing You all the Health & happyness You desire. As to the other parts of Your Letter, I shall Answer by the Next, haveing noe time, Capt[ain] Bryant Waiting for this. My Love to Issac & Moses.⁵ I shall Allsoe Answer theirs Next Week Via Irland. My Compliments to All Friends. May the Allmighty Preserve You to Long Life & Felicity is the Constant prayers of,

Dear HeartSey,
Your Affectionate Mother,
Abigaill Franks

Pray be Very Civill to Capt[ain] Bryant,
For he is Very Obligeing.

[Docket]

My Mother Ans[were]d the 19 Ap[ri]l
1747—p[er] M Ludlod
[Address]

To
Mr. Naphtaly Franks
In Biliter Square

Merchantt

---

3 Abigaill probably refers to Aaron's silence at the death of his two sons, Nadab and Abihu. See *Leviticus* 10:2–3.

4 Abigaill clearly had written to congratulate Phila before learning of the death of her infant son.

5 Abigaill refers to her brother Issac and Moses, her son.

P[er][Capt[ain]
Bryant

London

2/FE⁶

XXXVI
[Abigaill Franks to Naphtali Franks, January 4, 1748]

New York [Sunday] Jan[ua]ry 4th 1748

Dear HeartSey

Since My last, Wee have not Had the Satisfaction to hear from you, but hope that the Expected Ships may git in before the Weather is Colder or Else Our Expectations must be given Up for this winter. I hope when Wee doe hear from You that it May Answer Our Tender wishes for Your happyness, wich is My Continuall prayers. I Should be glad if you would Allways, while you are Out of Town, Send Every week a Letter to be Sent by Ships that are Constantly bound here to Some ports, for Your father is Soe Disapointed that it puts him quite Out of Temper. By the Way of Bristoll & boston there is Constantly Oppertunitys, and the dutch Ships Generly bring Letters from london. Pray be more Carefull for the futre. I have Sent You Some Locust trees & Some tulip trees,[1] some peper peaches

---

6 This postmark on the letter indicates that it was received in the General Post Office, Lombard Street, on February 2, 1747, a rather quick voyage, and was not hand delivered by Captain Bryant.

1 A.F.'s sending of trees perhaps reflected N.F.'s scientific interest. On May 3, 1764, he was elected a Fellow of the Royal Society. He appears to have had an interest in botany. Redcliffe N. Salaman, "The Jewish Fellows of the Royal Society," *MJHSE* 5 (1948), 154. The interest in American flora and fauna is reflected in the work of such scientific inquirers as the Swedish botanist and traveler Peter Kalm (1715–1771), *Travels into North America* (London, 1772), and the first American botanist, John Bartram (1699–1771), *Dictionary of American*

And Cramberys. Quailes Are Very scarce; the Last Hard Winter Destroyed many, And the few I had, Ceaser[2] Lett fly. Watter Mellon & Cabage Seed I sent by Some Ship Last faul. If there is Any thing Else that You can think Worth Send[ing] for, pray doe, And I Shall with pleassure procure them for you. Pray Send me some brockley, Colli flower, & artychoak Seed, but I Desire they may not be Sent by the Way of boston or Cape breton. The tea that I thought was not Sent Last Year I found Last Week in a Closet in the store,[3] where I had Safely put them Up when I went in the Contry, thinking they had bin Spanish peas and barley, for that Lay at the top of the box, & I Never Imagined that any tea would be put at the botton, soe that my accusation was Wrong for wich I Ask pardon. As to procouring Commiss[io]ns for moses, I dont find It Can be Soe Eassily don, for merchants dont Care to Leave there Corrispondents. Your father has Spoke to Severall. They Promise Civily, and that is all,[4] Soe that he

---

Biography, Vol. 1, Part 2 (New York, 1957), 26–28. J. H. Plumb, *England in the Eighteenth Century (1714–1815)* (Baltimore, 1965), 18–19, discusses the acquiring, enlarging and improving of landed estates. "Trees, plants and fruits which have been thoroughly assimilated into the English garden were then new and strange."

As owners of estates, affluent British Jews, no doubt, were interested in experimental gardening, and Abigaill Franks, who from time to time would send various American plants and seeds to Naphtali her son, aided him thereby in cultivating this avocation. Moses Hart's residence was known for its fine gardens. See Daiches-Dubin, "Eighteenth Century Anglo-Jewry," 148. See also the picture of "Isleworth House (The Franks' Family Home) 200 Years Ago" (ibid., facing p. 152).

2 Caesar was undoubtedly a slave owned by the Frankses, who, along with many of their Jewish and non-Jewish neighbors, held slaves. Caesar may have replaced a slave named Lucena (possibly a way of deriding Abraham de Lucena [d. 1725] who was J.F.'s adversary) who was implicated in the Negro revolt of 1741. A Caesar also played an important part in that revolt. *PAJHS* 17 (1920), 27 and 34–35; see Letter XXI, note 6.

3 Possibly in the shop owned by J.F. on Queen Street. See Letter XXXI, June 7, 1743, note 5.

4 See Letter XXXIV, Dec. 4, 1746, note 2.

must turn to Somethig in Europe, for I dont Care to have him back here, for all his Company Git drunk from Sunday Night Untill Saturday morning, & tho' I Should be Very glad to See moses, I still think My Self happy t[ha]t he is Out of this degenerate place.[5] As Soon as You Receive the Cramberys, put them all in Watter and Pick the Wither'd ones out, And then they will keep Very Well. Its a Jest to say they rot, for that they Very seldom doe. I wish You may Make Use of them With pleassure & that You may Meet with Content in Every thing you wish or desire. I am With Tenderness, Your Affectionate Mother,

                                                    Abigaill Franks

Very Cold[6]

[Address]
To
Mr. Napthaly Franks
Billeter Square[7]
London

---

5 This is one of many comments by A.F. on the degeneracy of New York City specifically and colonial atmosphere generally.

6 The *Evening Post* of Jan. 19, 1747, carried an account of the burning of the roof of the City Hall during "intensely cold" weather.

7 This Billeter Square location indicates that N.F. had changed his coffee house address after his marriage and now was more readily to be found at this address. The later letters are not addressed to a coffee house. Billeter Square, a fashionable area of London near Fenchurch Street, was also the residence of N.F.'s uncle Aaron Franks, and had been the home of Isaac Franks.

XXXVII
[Abigaill Franks to Naphtali Franks, April 29, 1748]

New York [Friday] Aprill 29th 1748

Dear HeartSey

Dont think I am Makeing a Trifileing Excuse to Avoid writting, for bleive me I advance nothing but truth when I Tell you the Ship Sailling a week Sooner than Was Expected prevents me where nature and Friendship calls to Answer the Many Agreeable Letters I have rec[eiv]ed, for I would Equaly endeavour to Avoid the Imputation of Neglect & Ill Manners as I would being to[o] troublesome. Therefore, Desire You to make my Compliments to all my friends And Tell them I hope Very Soon to have an Oppertunity to Discharge my duty in a Perticuler Manner to them all. If the Ship Tarrys Untill Sunday, I Shall find time to Write Dear Phill: & moses. He, I find, is Very much pleased with the Diversions of bath; in Short, You must Settle him Amongst you. He is quit[e] spoilt for a Ressident in ye willds of America. My Phila, I hope, has her health quite Established And wish her all the happyness She Desires and merits. I Send you by this 2 boxes with Aple & Rassberys & one box with Strawberys. Moses wrote for the Latter And hope they may pleass. In the faull Ships I shall Send You Some fine Peaches put Up in a Very Perticuler maner with Directions. I did not Expect the Nutt trees would doe, for they will not bear transplanting. You must plant them from the Nut it Self, Soe that If You Incline to have any, Lett me know & I will Send Some. Pray Lett me know if my brother Isaac is Dipt in the Lake of Oblivion, for I have not heard from him this Long while. If he can hear, pray make me Live in his memmory. Wee shall remove for the Seasson Out of Town. I Confess I have a Dislike to that hurrying Up and down and Only Comply with it to Oblige you all. As to News I Never dable in it. The Situation of America with relation to ye war[1]

---

1 The War of the Austrian Succession, to which A.F. refers, finally ended in 1748, only to be followed by the Seven Years' War which began some eight years later.

is much as it was. I should be rejoyce'd to See Isaiah's Prophecy ful-
filld, that all warlike Instruments where Converted to Implements of
Husbandry.² I have nothing more to Say (but that in my Next I shall
Look over your Last Letters), and If any thing Requires An Answer,
I shall take care to doe it. Being in some hast[e] at preas[en]t, I wish
health & happyness to you, My dear Phila, Mosses, &c &c. I Am, my
dear child,

Your Affectionate Mother,
Abigaill Franks

Becky & Poyer commend theire Love's
to all Under your Roof.
Mr. Horsmendon Is to be married to Mrs. Vessey.³

———

[Docket]
Ans[wered] p[er] Bryant⁴ 27 June 1748

———

[Address]

To
Mr. Napthaly Franks
London

---

2 A.F. is obviously referring to Isaiah 2:4.

3 Daniel Horsmanden (1694–1778), a Chief Justice of the Supreme Court
and noted New Yorker, had a long and varied political career. Mary Vesey, the
daughter of Lawrence Rheade, was the widow of Rev. William Vesey who died
sometime between May 1 and July 21, 1746. She married Horsmanden on May 8,
1748. Register of Marriages, 19, TVR; *NYHSC* 4 (1896), 86; *Dictionary of American Biography*, 9: 237–238 (see also Letter II, note 5).

4 N.F.'s reply to this letter, sent at the end of June, arrived in early September.
Evening Post, Sept. 12, 1748.

XXXVIII
[Abigaill Franks to Naphtali Franks, October 30, 1748]

New York [Sunday] October 30th 1748
Dear HeartSey

Its one of my first pleassure's to Hear from you. I cant Say I have as much in writting, because its wath I never Like't, tho' I have as much Sattisfaction in Converseing with You in this manner As Possibly any thing of the kind can give me. I have with much Content rec[eiv]ed many of Your Agreeable Letters this Last Summer, tho' one had Some Mixture of Concern wich Gave the Mellancholy Accou[n]t of good Mrs. Aaron Franks.[1] I was realy Sorry, for She Appeared to me to be a Senciable worthy woman. Her Young babes have the Greatest Loss, for the Afflictions of Death Soon pass away. The Spaniards have a Saying: dolor de' Codo Y: dolor de Esposo Devello mucho mas duro poco.[2] And in Scripture wee find these Words: "And Judah Lost his wife and was Comforted"[3] follows in the Same Line, Soe that I hope Your Uncle Aaron is or will Soon be Comforted. I have Shewn Your Father wath You Say Concerning drawing any more bills And reffer wath he Shall Say to You on that Subject to himself, for you know I am not Well Acquainted with theire Affairs. However, this I can Say, that your father does His Endeavours to Make all the remittance's he possiable can. Moses is Soe well Instructed in those Matters that he knows the buissness he is Imployed in requires ready money, and Unless he draws for it Att times, it cant be Dispatche'd. I wish from my Soul his Affairs was not Soe dependant,

1 This was Bilah Hart, daughter of Moses Hart, who married Aaron Franks on December 7, 1743. *Gentleman's Magazine* 13 (1743), 667.
2 A.F.'s Spanish needs some correction. *Devello* should be written *Duele* and *duro* written as *dura*. The phrase translates as "a pain in the elbow and the pain for a [lost] spouse hurts a great deal, but lasts a short time." Cf. Christy, comp., *Proverbs* 1:535, no. 22, "Sorrow for a husband is like a pain in the elbow, sharp and short."
3 See Genesis 38:12.

The Letters of Abigaill Levy Franks   155

for it gives me much Concern to See how Uneassy this finding of faults makes him. Mr. Lindseys death Att pres[en]t perplexes him, as it Leaves a Vessle Upon his hands, wich, however, he intends to dispose of as Soon as it Arrives. He Acquaints You with all the Perticulers of that Affair, Soe that I Shall Say noe more Abouth it, but enter into acc[oun]t of my Own triffles. I Send You Some things wich they Tell me is Called Ceader Cones. If they be the right Sort, pray Lett me know or Else instruct me better wath they are, and if they are to be had, I'll take Care and Send. I have Sent You Some Locus, red Ceader and Tullip trees. The dry wood You Are Soe Merry abouth that you rec[eiv]ed by Jeffereys, I did not bleive was of much worth, but Mrs. bayard[4] whoe Supplys me with all these things desire'ed I would send them. She is a Very Obligeing Neighbour And is Very ready to Serve me. Stephen bayard himself Went Yesterday, tho' it was bad blowing weather, Over to hoboak[5] And brought the Above

---

[4] This Mrs. Bayard could have been Frances Moore Bayard, who was the daughter of A.F.'s good friend. Commission of Forfeiture Papers, Office of the Clerk of Court of Appeals, Albany. In the latter reference, Frances Bayard, widow of Samuel Bayard of New York and Norwalk, Connecticut, renounces her position as executrix of her deceased husband's estate on November 5, 1787. See also Letter XVI, note 11. It may also have been Alide Vetch Bayard, who married another Samuel Bayard (1669–1745) on March 12, 1725. Mrs. Anson P. Atterbury, *The Bayard Family* (Baltimore, 1928), 16. The latter Samuel's son Stephen, born 1700 (seemingly of a prior marriage), was a merchant and mayor of New York from 1744 to 1747. This Stephen was possibly the one who fetched the trees and who was a business associate of Jacob Franks's during 1728–1730. Entry Books, Vol. 1, item 699, May 10, 1728 and item 1247, April 11, 1729; Vol. 2, item 1752, Nov. 12, 1730. He lived in the same ward as did the Frankses. NYAL, Dock Ward, Feb. 24, 1733.

[5] In October 1742, Samuel Bayard, father of Stephen, together with Francis Covenhoven, petitioned the Common Council for a license to operate a ferry to Weehawken, a small New Jersey community north of Hoboken. *MCC* 5: 67. The petition was not granted, but the Bayards' interest in the ferry may have continued. It may well have been a reason for Stephen's trip—to show the necessity and feasibility of such a conveyance even in "blowing weather." The first New York–New Jersey ferry license was granted in 1765 between New York and

trees himself. I beg You will Explain Your Self when You Send for anny of these things, for I am neither Gardener nor botanist & Consequently Understand Very Little of the Matter.[6] I am Sorry Moses is Soe Out of Temper with his New York Acquaintance, but if you Consider Rightly, he has not Soe Much reasson as he Imagines, for those people here that trade Largely have theire friends that they have Imployed a Great while, whoe have Discharge'd theire trust faithfully, Soe t[ha]t they cant well Leave them, and the Small traders its not worth while to have theire buissness, for they are Very triffleing, besides they require a good deall of Cr[edit]. I wonder he did not Speak to Sam: Stillwell,[7] for he went ovor on purpose to Settle a Corrispondence & intends to trade Largely. I Should be Well pleassed if Moses was once Settled in Some buissness, for it is allmost time. I dont wish him to come back again on no Accouts. You may Prehaps think it Unaturall not to wish my child[ren] with me, but Its quite ye reverse, for I Should think it my Greatest happy-ness, but As there is litle Appearance of any thing worth while to be don here and According to the Distination of Nature, I must Leave them. I had rather hear they doe well than in my Last Moments to have the mortification to See them dependant and Unable to be happyly Settled, for My Constant thought And wish is All Your Wellfare, wich, pray god, may be Accomplished to all your Own wishes, and Consequently, my Partiallity makes Me think they cant be but Equall to Your Deserts. I

Hoboken. George W. Edwards, *New York: An Eighteenth Century Municipality, 1731–1776* (New York, 1917), 185–187.

6 N.F.'s interest in science and botany was also probably used to advantage at Mortlake, Isaac Franks's and later N.F.'s home in England. See Letter XXXVI, Jan. 4, 1748, note 1.

7 Samuel Stillwell (d. 1767) was a New York merchant. Interestingly, Stillwell's will, proved on July 7, 1767, was torn into hundreds of pieces and then carefully sewn together. It seems that in 1764 Stillwell, who was a bachelor, became insane and ripped up all his papers, including his will. Francis Lewis to Gen. Horatio Gates, Dec. 10, 1764, Peter Warren Papers, NYHSL; Will no. 2054, HDC.

rejoyce to hear my dear Phila is Soe well. I hope her Anxiety is pritty well over on Account of child[ren]. Pray heaven preserve her to you to Lasting Joy. You Tell me in your Last you could not write for the Noise my brother Isaac made because you Said I was but two years older than he, but that was a mistake. He is not Quite Soe Old, tho' dont Lett him Impose Upon you that he is a Very youth (as his nonsence might Make you bleive). I Shall in a few days be fifty two & I am nine year And Eight months Older[8] than his worship. Tell him I Would Not Expose his Age as he is upon his Preferment, but doe it in revenge off his makeing Such a Jest of America and all things in it. I Spent the Summer Out of Town Very agreeable in a pleas[an]t Situation. Its the Last house in harlemtown Just Upon the river. I had my Views and prosspects &c &c[9] as you have at Mortlake, And If not with Such Embelishment of Art, Att Least More nature And Was as well Sattisfyed. Rodrick Random[10] pleassed Me Much, tho' I think Jo[seph] Andrews[11] Exceeds him. The Hermit[12] I was delighted with. The foundling[13] and the rest you Sent was Very Agree-

8 A.F. is correct in her account. She was born on November 26, 1696, and her brother's birthdate was July 19, 1706. Malcolm H. Stern, *Americans of Jewish Descent* (Cincinnati, 1960).

9 See Letter III, Oct. 7, 1733, note 3.

10 Tobias George Smollett (1721–1771), *The Adventures of Roderick Random* (London, 1748) in two volumes. See reference in the *Gentleman's Magazine* 18 (1748), 48.

11 Henry Fielding (1707–1754), *The History of the Adventures of Joseph Andrews and His Friend Mr. Abraham Adams* was published in London, 1742, in two volumes.

12 Peter Longueville (fl. 1727) was the author of *The Hermit: or, The unparalleled sufferings and surprising adventures of Philip Quarll, an Englishman: who was discovered by Mr. Dorrington, a Bristol Merchant, upon an uninhabited island in the South-Sea; where he lived about fifty years without human assistance,* which was published in London in 1746. This volume is also attributed to Philip Quarll as first published in 1727.

13 A.F. may refer to Sir Charles H. Williams (1708–1759), *The Foundling hospital for wit, intended for the reception and preservation of such feats of wit and humour, whose parents chuse to drop them,* which was published in five volumes in London

able, tho' I Own Littleton[14] on the death of a Wife Says too much. I Should have bleived his Griefe more Sincire had he Said Less, but Persons that have the happy Faculty of writting [to] please themseleves offtener then they doe theire readers. The Lady of the Gold watch[15] I Commited to the flames. I hate Such Impudent trash. I received your gratulations On the peace.[16] As You may Imagine, My Paciffic dispossition Should but wish for the honor of Brittian. Our Ennimies had bin a little more humble, but I am noe Pollition [Politician] and therefor am of the Number of Contents. And As My thought are now on the Cessation of arms, I will give you a Cessation of my Pen. With My blessing And prayers for your happyness, I Am, Dear Child,

Your Affectionate Mother,
Abigaill Franks

NF 2 Caggs Pickles

---

during the years 1743–1748, or to Edward Moore (1712–1757), *The Foundling*, a comedy of five acts which was produced at the Theatre Royal, Drury Lane, on February 13, 1748, and gave so much pleasure "that it has been exhibited ten nights and boxes taken for many more." *Gentleman's Magazine* 18 (1748), 51–54, 89, 96, and 114–115.

14 George Baron Lyttleton (1709–1773) wrote *To the Memory of a Lady* (Lucy Lyttleton), a comedy first published in London in 1747. A second edition was printed the following year.

15 A.F. probably refers to *The Fortunate Transport, or, the Secret History of the Life and Adventures of Polly Hayenk, alias Mrs. B——, the Lady of the Gold Watch*, written by a Creole and published in London in two volumes in 1748. *Gentleman's Magazine* 18 (1748), 96 and 144.

16 The articles of the Peace Treaty of Aix-la-Chapelle between England, France, Austria, and Spain which ended the War of the Austrian Succession were formally signed on October 18, 1748, but a tentative settlement had been reached in April of that year.

[Docket]

AF
Ans[were]d by Bryant
the 27 february 1748/9

[Address]

To
Mr. Napthaly Franks
London

(must take the Peaches from amongst
the peper and put fresh Vinegar to em
and Some Spice. *[fragment]*)

Bibliography

MANUSCRIPT SOURCES

CORRESPONDENCE AND PERSONAL PAPERS

Alexander Papers—NYHSL.
Alexander, James, Papers—NYHSL.
Alexander, Mary, Papers—NYHSL.
Alexander, William [Lord Stirling], Papers—NYHSL.
Bancker Family Papers—NYHSL.
Bayard Family Papers—NYHSL.
Bayard Genealogy and Bayard Family Notes [a typescript]—NYHSL.
Bayard, Hake, and Lynch Families—NYHSL.
Beekman Family Papers—NYHSL.
Beekman, Henry, Papers—NYHSL.
Boggs Collection—Rutgers University Library.
Brodhead, John R., Correspondence—Rutgers University Library.
Chalmers, George, Collection—NYPL.
Clarke, George, Papers-Home of Thomas Clarke, Springfield, New York.
Colden, Cadwallader, Letters—NYHSL.
Delancey Family Papers—NYHSL.
Delancey Papers—MCNY.
Delancey, Stephen and Oliver, Papers [bound volume]—NYHSL.
DeWitt, William, Daybook, 1739–1752—NYHSL.
Emmitt Collection—NYPL.
Etting Papers—HSP.
Evans, Peter, Papers—HSP.
Fielding Family, Receipt Book—NYHSL.
Gratz Papers—HSP.
Hendricks, Harmon, Collection—NYHSL.
Horsmanden, Daniel, Papers—NYHSL.

Jay, Peter, Day Book, 1722–1748—NYHSL.
Jay, Peter, Ledger, 1724–1768—NYHSL.
Johnson, William, Papers—Rutgers University Library.
Lyons, Jacques J., Collection—AJHSL.
Morris Family Papers—Rutgers University Library.
Morris, Lewis, Manuscripts—New Jersey Historical Society Library.
Morris, Robert Hunter, Papers—New Jersey Historical Society Library.
Morris, Robert Hunter, Papers—Rutgers University Library.
New York City Miscellaneous Manuscripts—NYHSL.
Norris, Capt. Matthew, Papers—NYHSL.
Oath of Allegiance dated April 27, 1741, signed by David, Daniel, and Mordecai Gomez, Samuel Myers Cohen, and twenty-five other Jews—NYHSL.
Oppenheim, Samuel, Collection—AJHSL.
Parker, James, Papers—Rutgers University Library.
Pennsylvania Miscellaneous Manuscripts, 1684–1772—HSP.
Richard, Paul, Manuscripts—NYHSL.
Riker, James, Collection—NYPL.
Sanders, Barent, Robert, and John, Invoice Book of Imported Goods, 1737–1749—NYHSL.
Schuyler, Elizabeth, Account Book, 1737–1769—NYHSL.
Simson, Nathan, Letter Books—Public Record Office, London, C104/13–14 [microfilm copy in American Jewish Archives, AJHSL, HDC, and Sleepy Hollow Restorations].
Van Rensselaer-Fort Papers—NYPL.
Warren, Peter, Papers—NYHSL.
Warren, Peter, Papers, in the Lord Gage Manuscript Collection,—Sussex Archaeological Society, Barbican House, Lewes, England [microfilm copy of part in HDC].
Watts Family Papers—NYHSL.
Watts, Robert, Papers—NYHSL.

CHURCH RECORDS

Christ Church, Philadelphia, Pa.
    Baptismal Record with Index, 1709–1786.
    Burial Record with Index, 1709–1785.
Congregation Shearith Israel, New York City.
    Vital Statistics.
Dutch Reformed Church of New York, John Street, New York City.

Trinity Church, Library of the Trinity Corporation, 32 Trinity Place, New York City.
    Register of Marriages, Vol. I, 1746–1816.
    Tombstone Inscriptions [a typescript].
    Trinity Vault Records [a typescript].
    Vital Statistics.

LEGAL RECORDS

New York
Chamberlain's Office, Journals, 1706–1736, 1736–1767—NYHSL.
Chamberlain's Office, Ledger 1700–1760—NYHSL.
Commission of Forfeiture Papers, Clerk's Office, Court of Appeals, Albany.
Conveyance Libers (to 1800).—Office of the Secretary of State, Albany; New York City Register's Office, 31 Chambers Street, New York City [microfilm copy at HDC].

Courts
Chancery Court
    Decrees before 1800—HDC.
    Minute Books, 1711–1770—NYCCO.
    Orders in Chancery, 1702–1800—HDC.
    Orders, Minutes, and Proceedings, 1740–1770—NYCCO.
Court of General Sessions
    Minutes, 1684–1800—NYCCO.
Mayor's Court
    Minutes, 1674–1800—NYCCO.
    Papers, 1664–1800. NYCCO [microfilm copy of papers relating to Jews at AJHSL].
Supreme Court of Judicature
    Minutes, 1691–1800—NYCCO.
    Parchment Rolls, Judgements—NYCCO.

Probate Records
Bonds of Administration, 1720–1800—Surrogate's Court Library, 31 Chambers Street, New York City.
Entry Books, 1728–1766—New York State Library, Albany.
Inventories of Estate
    Albany, 1665–1800—Clerk's Office of the Court of Appeals [now at HDC].
    New York, 1665–1800—Surrogate's Court Library [now at HDC].

Letters of Administration
  Albany, 1665–1800—Clerk's Office of the Court of Appeals [now at HDC].
  New York, 1665–1800—Surrogate's Court Library [now at HDC].
Wills
  Albany Originals and Libers, 1665–1800, Clerk's Office of the Court of Appeals. New York Originals and Libers, 1665–1800—Surrogate's Court Library [now at HDC].

Tax Rolls
New York Assessment Lists, 1699–1734 (Vol. 1709–1721 missing)—New York City Comptroller's Office, Rhinelander Building, 238 William Street, New York City [microfilm copy at HDC].

Pennsylvania
Conveyance Libers, 1730–1800—Department of Records, City Hall, Philadelphia.
Court of Common Pleas, 1706–1821—HSP.
Letters of Administration, 1730–1800—Registry's Office, City Hall, Philadelphia.
Wills, 1730–1800—Registry's Office, City Hall, Philadelphia.

South Carolina
Miscellaneous Volumes, 69A and 69B, 1736–1740—Probate Records, Charleston.

England
Letters of Administration and Wills, 1730–1800—PCC.
Naval Office Lists—Public Record Office, London, CO 5/1222–1229.
Parish Register, Mortlake, Surrey.
Proceedings in Chancery, 1730–1800—Public Record Office.

PRINTED SOURCES

Abstracts of Wills, New-York Historical Society Collections. 17 volumes. New York, 1892–1907.
Acts of Assembly Passed in the Province of New York from 1691 to 1718. London, 1719.
Acts of the Privy Council of England, Colonial Series. Volumes 3 and 4. London, 1910–1911.

Bibliography

Addison, Joseph. *Maxims, Observations, and Reflections, Moral, Political, and Divine.* London, 1719.

Apperson, George L. *English Proverbs and Proverbial Phrases.* London, 1929.

Arnold, Arthur P. "Anglo-Jewish Wills and Letters of Administration." *Anglo-Jewish Notabilities.* London, 1949.

Barnett, Lionel D., editor. *Bevis Marks Records: Being Contributions to the History of the Spanish and Portuguese Congregation of London.* Part I: *The Early History of the Congregation from the Beginning until 1800.* Oxford, 1940.

Boston News-Letter. 1704–1733.

Bridenbaugh, Carl, editor. *Gentleman's Progress: The Itinerarium of Dr. Alexander Hamilton, 1744.* Chapel Hill, 1948.

Brock, R. Alonzo, editor. "Journal of William Black, 1744." *Pennsylvania Magazine of History and Biography* 1 (1877), 117–132, 233–249, and 404–419.

Burghers and Freemen of New York, New-York Historical Society Collections. New York, 1885.

Calendar of State Papers, Colonial Series, America and West Indies. Volumes 42 and 43. London 1953, 1963.

Candler, Allen D., editor. *Colonial Records of the State of Georgia.* 26 volumes. Atlanta, 1904–1916.

Colden, Cadwallader. *Letters and Papers of Cadwallader Colden, 1711–1775 New-York Historical Society Collections.* 9 volumes. New York, 1918–1937.

Collections of the Huguenot Society of America. New York, 1886.

Colonial Laws of New York from the Year 1664 to the Revolution. 5 volumes. Albany, 1894–1896.

Complete Guide to All Persons Who Have Any Trade or Concern Within the City of London and Parts Adjacent. London, 1740.

Corwin Edward T, editor. *Ecclesiastical Records of the State of New York.* 7 volumes. Albany, 1910–1916.

Daily Advertiser (London). 1731–1748.

Defoe, Daniel [?]. "The Voyage of Don Manoel Gonzales (Late Merchant) of the City of Lisbon in Portugal to Great Britain . . . Translated from the Portuguese Manuscript." In *A Collection of Voyages and Travels.* Volume 7. London, 1752.

Defoe, Daniel. *A Tour Thro' London about 1725: Being Letter V and Letter VI of "A Tour thro' the Whole Island of Great Britain containing a Description of the City of London . . ." Reprinted from the Text of the Original Edition (1724–*

1726) by Daniel Defoe. Edited and annotated by Sir. Mayson M. Beeton and E. Beresford Chancellor. London, 1929.

Directory Containing an Alphabetical List of the Names and Places of Abode of the Directors of Companies, Persons in Public Business, Merchants and Other Eminent traders in the Cities of London, Westminster, and Borough of Southwark. London, 1736.

Dobree, Bonamy, editor. *The Letters of Philip Dormer Stanhope, Fourth Earl of Chesterfield.* 4 volumes. London, 1932.

Dykes, Oswald. *English Proverbs with Moral Reflexions.* 2 volumes. London, 1709.

Fernow, Berthold. *Calendar of Wills.* New York, 1896.

Gautier, John S., editor. "New York Marriage Licenses." *New York Genealogical and Biographical Records* 2 (1871), 25–28.

Gay, Joseph?. *The Lure of Venus; or a Harlot's Progress. An Heroic-comical Poem. Founded upon Mr. Hogarth's Six Paintings.* London, 1733.

Gay, Joseph?. *The Rake's Progress; or The Humors of Drury-Lane. A Poem in Eight Cantos. In Hudabrastick Verse.* London, 1735.

Gentlemen's Magazine: Or Monthly Intelligencer (London). 1731–1800.

Gomme, George Laurence. *The Gentleman's Magazine Library: Being A Classified Collection of the Chief Contents of the Gentleman's Magazine from 1731 to 1818.* 4 volumes. London, 1883–1885.

Hazard, Samuel, editor. *Pennsylvania Archives.* 2nd Series. Harrisburg, 1890.

Hershkowitz, Leo, editor. *Wills of Early New York Jews (1704–1799).* New York, 1967.

Intelligencer or Merchants Assistant. London, 1738.

Journal of the Legislative Council of the Colony of New York (1691–1775). 2 volumes. Albany, 1861.

Journal of the Votes and Proceedings of the General Assembly of the Colony of New York. 2 volumes. New York, 1764–1766.

Kalm, Peter. *Peter Kalm's Travels in North America.* 1772. Edited by Adolph B. Benson. 2 volumes. New York, 1966.

Korn, Harold, editor. "Receipt Book of Judah Hays." *PAJHS* 34 (1935), 117–122.

Laws of New York from 1691 to 1773. New York, 1774.

"Ledger of Daniel Gomez, 1739–1765." *PAJHS* 27 (1920), 279–317.

London Magazine: Or Gentleman's Monthly Intelligencer. London 1732–1748.

Marcus, Jacob R., editor. *American Jewry—Documents of the Eighteenth Century.* Cincinnati, 1959.

McAnear, Beverley, editor. "An American in London, 1735–1736." *Pennsylvania Magazine of History and Biography* 64 (1940), 164–217 and 356–406.

Miller, Francis T., editor. "Memoirs of an American Official in Service of the King." *Journal of American History* 4 (1910), 29–47.

"Minute Book of the Congregation Shearith Israel." *PAJHS* 21 (1913), 1–171.

Minutes of the Common Council of the City of New York 1675–1776. 8 volumes. New York, 1905.

Montesquieu, Louis de Secondat. *Persian Letters*. Translated by John Ozell. 3rd edition. London, 1736.

Morris, Richard B., editor. *Select Cases of the Mayor's Court of New York City, 1674–1784*. Washington, D.C., 1935.

A New and Compleat Survey of London in Ten Parts. 2 volumes. London, 1742.

New-York Evening Post. 1744–1753.

New-York Gazette. 1725–1744.

New-York Gazette, revived in the Weekly Post-Boy. 1747–1773.

New-York Gazette; or. Weekly Post-Boy. 1743–1747.

New-York Mercury. 1752–1768.

New-York Weekly Journal. 1733–1751.

O'Callaghan, Edmund B., editor. *Calendar of New York Colonial Commissions, 1680–1770*. New York, 1929.

———, editor. *Documentary History of the State of New York*. 4 volumes. Albany, 1850–1851.

———, editor. *New York Marriages (Names of Persons for Whom Marriage Licenses Were Issued by the Secretary of the Province of New York Previous to 1784)*. Albany, 1860.

O'Callaghan, Edmund B., and Berthold Fernow, editors *Documents Relative to the Colonial History of the State of New York*. 15 volumes. Albany, 1853–1887.

Oyster Bay Town Records 1653–1763. 7 volumes. New York, 1916–1931.

Pennsylvania Journal (Philadelphia). 1742–1748.

The Pennsylvania Gazette (Philadelphia). 1728–1748.

Pope, Alexander. *Mr. Pope's Literary Correspondence for Thirty Years; from 1704 to 1734. Being a Collection of Letters Which Passed between Him and Several Eminent Persons*. London, 1735.

Rapin de Thoyras, Paul. *The History of England*. Translated by N. Tindal. 4 volumes. London, 1732–1747.

Roth, Cecil. *Magna Bibliotheca Anglo-Judaica*. London, 1937.
———, editor. *Anglo-Jewish Letters, 1158–1917*. London, 1938.
Royal Society of London Philosophical Transactions, 1743–1750. Vol. 10. London, 1756.
Russell, Richard. *A Dissertation on the Use of Sea Water in the Diseases of the Glands . . . and Uses of All the Remarkable Mineral Waters of Great Britain*. 4th edition. London, 1760.
———. *A Treatise on the Nature, Properties and Medicinal Uses of Pyrmont, Spa and Seltzers . . . Being a Proper Supplement to Dr. Russel[l]'s Dissertation on the Uses of Sea Water, &c*. London, 1762.
Stern, Malcolm H. "The Sheftall Diaries, 1733–1808." *AJHQ* 54 (1965), 243–277.
Stillwell, John E., editor. *Historical and Genealogical Miscellany*. 5 volumes. New York, 1903–1932.
Street, Charles R., editor. *Huntington Town Records Including Babylon, Long Island, New York, 1653–1873*. 3 volumes. Huntington, 1887–1889.
Toland, John. *Reasons for Naturalizing the Jews in Great Britain and Ireland, on the Same Foot with All Nations. Containing also, a Defence of the Jews against All Vulgar Prejudices in All Countries*. London, 1714.
Universal Pocket Companion: A List of Merchants. London, 1741.

SECONDARY SOURCES

Abbott, Carl. "Neighborhoods of New York, 1760–1775." *New York History* 15 (1974), 35–54.
Abrahams, Dudley. "Jew Brokers of the City of London." *MJHSE* 3 (1937), 80–94.
Adler, Rachel. *Engendering Judaism*. Philadelphia, 1998.
———. "The Jew Who Wasn't There: Halakhah and the Jewish Woman." In Heschel, *On Being A Jewish Feminist*, 12–18.
Ahlstrom, Sydney E. *A Religious History of the American People*. New Haven, 1972.
Altmann, Alexander, editor. *Studies in Nineteenth-Century Jewish Intellectual History*. Cambridge, Mass., 1964.
Anderson, Howard, Philip B. Daghlian, and Irvin Ehrenpreis, editors. *The Familiar Letter in the Eighteenth Century*. Lawrence, Kans., 1966.
Archdeacon, Thomas J. *New York City, 1664–1710: Conquest and Change*. Ithaca, 1976.

Arnold, Arthur P. "A List of Jews and Their Households in London Extracted from the Census Lists of 1695." *MJHSE* 6 (1962), 73–141.

Ashton, Dianne. *Rebecca Gratz: Women and Judaism in Antebellum America.* Detroit, 1997.

Bailyn, Bernard. *The Peopling of British North America.* New York, 1986.

Balmer, Randall. *A Perfect Babel of Confusion: Dutch Religion and English Culture in the Middle Colonies.* New York, 1989.

Barnett, Richard D. "Anglo-Jewish History in the Eighteenth Century." In Lipman, *Three Centuries of Anglo-Jewish History,* 45–68.

———. "The Correspondence of Spanish and Portuguese Congregation of London during the Seventeenth and Eighteenth Centuries." *TJHSE* 20 (1964), 1–50.

———. "The Travels of Moses Cassuto." In John M. Shaftesley, editor, *Remember the Days: Essays on Anglo Jewish History presented to Cecil Roth by the Members of the Council of the Jewish Historical Society of England.* London, 1966, 74–121.

Baron, Salo W. "John Calvin and the Jews." In Lieberman and Schwarz, *Harry Austryn Wolfson Jubilee Volume,* 141–163.

Barquist, David L. *Myer Myers: Jewish Silversmith in Colonial New York.* New Haven, 2001.

Baskin, Judith R., editor. *Jewish Women in Historical Perspective.* Detroit, 1991.

Baum, Charlotte, Paula Hyman, and Michel Sonya. *The Jewish Woman in America.* New York, 1976.

Becker, Carl. *The History of Political Parties in the Province of New York, 1760–1776.* Madison, 1909.

Ben-Horin, Meir, Barnard D. Weinryb, and Soloman Zeitland, editors. *Studies and Essays in Honor of Abraham A. Neuman, President, Dropsie College for Hebrew and Cognate Learning.* Leiden, 1962.

Bentwich, Norman. "Anglo-Jewish Causes Célèbres: Leading Cases in English Courts from the Beginning of the Eighteenth Century." *TJHSE* 15 (1946), 93–120.

Bernardini, Paolo, and Norman Fiering, editors. *The Jews and the Expansion of Europe to the West, 1450 to 1800.* New York, 2001.

Black, Mary, and Jean Lipman. *American Folk Painting.* New York, 1987.

Blackmar, Elizabeth. *Manhattan for Rent, 1785–1850.* Ithaca, 1989.

Bodian, Miriam. *Hebrews of the Portuguese Nation: Conversos and Community in Early Modern Amsterdam.* Bloomington, 1997.

Bonomi, Patricia U. *A Factious People: Politics and Society in Colonial New York*. New York, 1971.

———. *The Lord Cornbury Scandal: The Politics of Reputation in British America*. Chapel Hill, 1998.

———. "New York: The Royal Colony." *New York History* 84 (Winter 2001), 5–24.

———. *Under the Cope of Heaven: Religion, Society, and Politics in Colonial America*. New York, 1986.

Bridenbaugh, Carl. *Cities in the Wilderness: The First Century of Urban Life in America, 1625–1742*. New York, 1955.

Brilliant, Richard. *Facing the New World: Jewish Portraits in Colonial and Federal America*. New York, 1997.

———. "Portraits as Silent Claimants: Jewish Class Aspirations and Representational Strategies in Colonial and Federal America." In Brilliant, *Facing the New World*, 1–8.

Burke, Ellin M. *The Jewish Community in Early New York, 1654–1800*. New York, 1979.

Burrows, Edwin, and Mike Wallace. *Gotham: A History of New York City to 1898*. New York, 1999.

Bushman, Richard L. *The Refinement of America: Persons, Houses, Cities*. New York, 1992.

Butler, Jon. *The Huguenots in America: A Refugee People in New World Society*. Cambridge, Mass., 1983.

Carlson, C. Lennart. *The First Magazine: A History of the Gentleman's Magazine*. Providence, R.I., 1938.

Chodorow, Nancy. *The Reproduction of Mothering: Psychoanalysis and the Sociology of Gender*. Berkeley, 1978.

Christy, Robert, compiler. *Proverbs, Maxims, and Phrases, Classified Subjectively and Arranged Alphabetically*, 2 volumes in 1. New York, 1903.

Chyet, Stanley F. *Lopez of Newport: Colonial American Merchant Prince*. Detroit, 1970.

Cohen, Robert. "Sampson and David Mears, Merchants." *AJHQ* 67 (1977–1978), 233–245.

Cohen, Steve M., and Paula Hyman, editors. *The Jewish Family: Myths and Reality*. New York, 1986.

Condon, Thomas J. *New York Beginnings: The Commercial Origins of New Netherlands*. New York, 1968.

Cott, Nancy F. *The Bonds of Womanhood: "Woman's Sphere" in New England, 1780–1835*. New Haven, 1977.

Countryman, Edward. *A People in Revolution: The American Revolution and Political Society in New York, 1760–1790*. Baltimore, 1981.

Crane, Elaine Forman, editor. *The Diary of Elizabeth Drinker: The Life Cycle of an Eighteenth-Century Woman*. 2 volumes. Boston, 1994.

Cundall, Frank. *The Governors of Jamaica in the First Half of the Eighteenth Century*. London, 1937.

Daiches-Dubens, Rachel. "Eighteenth-Century Anglo-Jewry in and around Richmond, Surrey." *TJHSE* 18 (1953–1954), 143–179.

Daniels, Doris Groshen. "Colonial Jewry: Religion, Domestic, and Social Relations." *AJHQ* 66 (1977), 375–400.

Davis, Thomas J. *A Rumor of Revolt: The Great "Negro Plot" in Colonial New York*. New York, 1985.

Dennis, Jessie McNab. "Lamerie Silver for the Franks Family." *Metropolitan Museum of Art Bulletin*, New Series 26 (Dec. 1967), 174–179.

Diner, Hasia R. *Hungering for America: Italian, Irish, and Jewish Foodways in the Age of Migration*. Cambridge, Mass., 2001.

———. *A Time for Gathering: The Second Migration, 1820–1880*. Baltimore, 1992.

Edwards, George W. *New York: An Eighteenth Century Municipality, 1731–1776*. New York, 1917.

Eisen, Arnold. *The Chosen People in America: A Study in Jewish Religious Ideology*. Bloomington, 1983.

Elzas, Barnett A. *The Jews of South Carolina*. Philadelphia, 1905.

Emmanuel, Isaac S. *Precious Stones of the Jews of Curaçao*. New York, 1957.

Endelman, Todd M. *The Jews of Georgian England, 1714–1830: Tradition and Change in a Liberal Society*. 2nd edition. Ann Arbor, 1999.

Ettinger, Amos A. *James Edward Oglethorpe*. Oxford, 1962.

Faber, Eli. *Jews, Slaves, and the Slave Trade: Setting the Record Straight*. New York, 1998.

———. *A Time for Planting: The First Migration, 1654–1820*. Baltimore, 1992.

Felsenstein, Frank, and Sharon Liberman Mintz. *The Jew as Other: A Century of English Caricature, 1730–1830*. New York, 1995.

Feurtado, Walter A. *Official and Other Personages of Jamaica from 1665 to 1790*. Kingston, Jamaica, 1896.

Finberg, Hilda F. "Jewish Residents in Eighteenth-Century Twickenham." *TJHSE* 16 (1945–1952), 129–136.

Fischel, Walter J. "From Cochin (India) to New York: Samuel Abraham, the Jewish Merchant of the 18th Century." In Lieberman and Schwarz, Harry Austryn *Wolfson Jubilee Volume*, 255–274.

———. "The Indian Archives: A Source for the History of the Jews of Asia (from the Sixteenth Century On)." In Neuman and Zeitlin, *The Seventy-Fifth Anniversary Volume*, 192–209.

Fisher, H. E. S. "Jews in England in the 18th-Century English Economy." *MJHSE* 12 (1978–1980), 156–165.

Foord, Archibald S. *His Majesty's Opposition, 1714–1830*. Oxford, 1964.

Foote, Thelma Willis. "Black Life in Colonial Manhattan, 1664–1786." Ph.D. dissertation, Harvard University, 1991.

Fortes, Meyer. *Kinship and the Social Order*. Chicago, 1969.

Fortune, Stephen Alexander. *Merchants and Jews: The Struggle for British West Indian Commerce, 1650–1750*. Gainesville, Fla., 1984.

Friedman, Lee M. "Jews in the Vice Admiralty Court of Rhode Island." *PAJHS* 37 (1947), 391–418.

———. "Wills of the Early Jewish Settlers in New York." *PAJHS* 23 (1915), 147–161.

Gardner, Albert Ten Eyck. "An Old New York Family." *Art in America* 51 (1963), 56–61.

Gelles, Edith B. *Abigail Adams: A Writing Life*. New York, 2002.

———. *Portia: The World of Abigail Adams*. Bloomington, 1992.

Gilligan, Carol. *In a Different Voice: Psychological Theory and Women's Development*. Cambridge, Mass., 1982.

Giuseppi, J. A. "Early Jewish Holders of Bank of England Stock (1694–1725)." *MJHSE* 6 (1962), 143–174.

———. "Sephardi Jews and the Early Years of the Bank of England." *TJHSE* 19 (1960), 53–63.

Glassman, Bernard. *Anti-Semitic Stereotypes without Jews: Images of the Jews in England, 1290–1700*. Detroit, 1975.

Goldman, Karla Ann. *Beyond the Gallery: The Place of Women in the Development of American Judaism*. Cambridge, Mass., 2000.

Goodfriend, Joyce D. *Before the Melting Pot: Society and Culture in Colonial New York City, 1664–1730*. Princeton, 1992.

Goody, Jack, editor. *The Character of Kinship*. Cambridge, Mass., 1973.

Gordon, Milton M. *Assimilation in American Life: The Role of Race, Religion, and National Origins*. New York, 1971.

Gottesman, Rita S. *Arts and Crafts in New York, 1726–1776*. New-York Historical Society Collections. New York, 1937.

Greenberg, Douglas. *Crime and Law Enforcement in the Colony of New York, 1691–1776*. Ithaca, 1974.

Greven, Philip. *Four Generations: Population, Land, and Family in Colonial Andover, Massachusetts*. Ithaca, 1970.

———. *The Protestant Temperament: Patterns of Child-Rearing, Religious Experience, and the Self in Early America*. New York, 1977.

Grinstein, Hyman B. *The Rise of the Jewish Community of New York, 1654–1860*. Philadelphia, 1945.

Harrington, Virginia D. *The New York Merchant on the Eve of the American Revolution*. New York, 1935.

Hazlitt, William C. *English Proverbs and Proverbial Phrases*. London, 1869.

Hershkowitz, Leo. "Another Abigail Franks Letter and a Genealogical Note." *AJHQ* 59 (Dec. 1969), 223–236.

———. "Asher Levy and the Inventories of Early New York Jews." *American Jewish History* 80 (Autumn 1990), 21–55.

———. "The Mill Street Synagogue Reconsidered." *AJHQ* 53 (1964), 404–410.

———. "New Amsterdam's Twenty-Three Jews: Myth or Reality." In Shalom Goldman, editor, *Hebrew and the Bible in America*. Hanover, N.H., 1993, 171–183.

———. "Some Aspects of the New York Jewish Merchant and Community, 1654–1820." *AJQ* 66 (1976–1977), 10–34.

Hershkowitz, Leo, and Isidore Meyer, editors. *Letters of the Franks Family (1733–1748)*. Waltham, Mass., 1968.

Hertzberg, Arthur. *The Jews in America*. New York, 1989.

Heschel, Susannah, editor. *On Being a Jewish Feminist*. New York, 1983.

Hirsh, Iyda R. "The Mears Family and Their Connections." *PAJHS* 33 (1934), 199–210.

Hirshler, Erica E. "The Levy-Franks Family Portraits." *The Magazine Antiques* (November 1990), 1020–1030.

———. *The Levy-Franks Family Portraits, Exhibition Brochure*. Boston, 1990.

Hodges, Graham Russell. *New York City Cartmen, 1667–1850*. New York, 1985.

———. *Root and Branch: African Americans in New York and East Jersey, 1613–1863*. Chapel Hill, 1999.

Hoffman, Ronald, and Peter J. Albert, editors. *Women in the Age of the American Revolution*. Charlottesville, Va., 1989.

Hoffman, Ronald, Mechal Sobel, and Fredrika J. Teute, editors. *Through a Glass Darkly: Reflections on Personal Identity in Early America.* Chapel Hill, 1997.

Hofstadter, Richard. *America at 1750: A Social Portrait.* New York, 1973.

Homberger, Eric. *The Historical Atlas of New York City: A Visual Celebration of Nearly 400 Years of New York City's History.* New York, 1994.

Huhner, Leon. "Daniel Gomez, a Pioneer Merchant of Early New York." In Karp, *The Jewish Experience in America*, 1: 175–193.

Hutchins, Catherine E., editor. *Shaping a National Culture: The Philadelphia Experience, 1750–1800.* Winterthur, Del., 1994.

Hyamson, Albert M. "Bibliography: List of Pamphlets Relating to the Jew Bill of 1753." *TJHSE* 6 (1912), 178–188.

———. "Items Relating to Congregation Shearith Israel." *PAJHS* 27 (1920), 1–125.

———. "The Jew Bill of 1753." *TJHSE* 6 (1912), 156–188.

———. "The Jewish Obituaries in the *Gentleman's Magazine*." *MJHSE* 4 (1942), 33–60.

———. "A Petition from Haslemere in 1753." *MJHSE* 1 (1925), 11–111.

Hyman, Paula E. *Gender and Assimilation in Modern Jewish History: Roles and Representations of Women.* Seattle, 1995.

———. "The Modern Jewish Family: Image and Reality." In Kraemer, *The Jewish Family*, 179–196.

Hyman, Paula E., and Deborah Dash Moore, editors. *Jewish Women in America: An Historical Encyclopedia.* 2 volumes. New York, 1997.

Jastrow, Morris. "Notes on the Jews of Philadelphia from Published Annals." *PAJHS* 1 (1893), 49–61.

Kammen, Michael. *Colonial New York: A History.* New York, 1975.

Kaplan, Marion A. *The Making of the Jewish Middle Class: Women, Family, and Identity in Imperial Germany.* New York, 1991.

Kaplan, Yosef. "The Jewish Profile of the Spanish-Portuguese Community of London during the Seventeenth Century." *Judaism* 41 (1992), 229–240.

Karp, Abraham J., editor. *The Jewish Experience in America: Selected Studies from the Publications of The American Jewish Historical Society.* Vol. 1: *The Colonial Period.* Waltham, Mass., 1969.

Katz, Jacob. *Emancipation and Assimilation: Studies in Modern Jewish History.* Westmead, Hants., 1972.

———. *Out of the Ghetto: The Social Background of Jewish Emancipation, 1770–1870.* Cambridge, Mass., 1973.

———. "The Term 'Jewish Emancipation,' Its Origin and Historical Impact," in Altmann, *Studies in Nineteenth-Century Jewish Intellectual History*, 1–26
Katz, Stanley Nider. *Newcastle's New York: Anglo-American Politics, 1732–1753*. Cambridge, Mass., 1968.
Kenney, Alice P. *Stubborn for Liberty: The Dutch in New York*. Syracuse, 1975.
Kerber, Linda K. *No Constitutional Right to Be Ladies: Women and Obligations of Citizenship*. New York, 1998.
Kierner, Cynthia A. *Traders and Gentlefolk: The Livingstons of New York, 1675–1790*. Ithaca, 1992.
Kim, Sung B. *Landlord and Tenant in Colonial New York Manorial Society, 1664–1775*. Chapel Hill, 1978.
Koehler, Lyle *A Search for Power: The "Weaker" Sex in Seventeenth-Century New England*. Urbana, 1980.
Kozol, Frank L. "Lee M. Friedman: A Biographical Profile (December 29, 1871-August 7, 1957)." *AJHQ* 56 (1967), 261–267.
Kraemer, David, editor. *The Jewish Family: Metaphor and Memory*. New York, 1989.
Lamb, Martha J., and Mrs. Burton Harrison. *History of the City of New York*. 3 volumes. New York, 1896.
Levy, Leonard W. "Did the Zenger Case Really Matter? Freedom of the Press in Colonial New York." *William and Mary Quarterly*, 3rd Series 18 (Jan. 1960), 35–50.
———. *The Emergence of a Free Press*. New York, 1985.
———. *Freedom of the Press from Zenger to Jefferson*. Durham, N.C., 1996.
Lieberman, Saul, and Leo Schwarz, editors. *Harry Austryn Wolfson Jubilee Volume on the Occasion of His Seventy-Fifth Birthday*. Volume I. Jerusalem, 1965.
Lillywhite, Bryant. *London Coffee Houses*. London, 1963.
Lipman, Vivian D. *Three Centuries of Anglo-Jewish History*. Cambridge, 1961.
Lockridge, Kenneth A. *Literacy in Colonial New England*. New York, 1974.
London, Hannah R. *Portraits of Jews by Gilbert Stuart and Other Early American Artists*. Rutland, Vt., 1969.
Macfarlane, Alan. *Marriage and Love in England: Modes of Reproduction, 1300–1840*. Oxford, 1986.
Marcus, Jacob R. "The Colonial American Jew." In Jonathan D. Sarna et al., eds. *Jews and the Founding of the Republic*. New York, 1985.
———. *The Colonial American Jew, 1492–1776*. 3 volumes. Detroit, 1970.

———. *Early American Jewry, 1649-1794*. 2 volumes. Philadelphia, 1951–1953), 2 vols.

———. "The Oldest Known Synagogue Record Book of Continental North America, 1720-1721." In Jacob R. Marcus, *Studies in American Jewish History: Studies and Addresses*. Cincinnati, 1969.

———. *To Count a People: American Jewish Population Data, 1585-1984*. Lanham, Md., 1990.

Mark, Irving. *Agrarian Conflicts in Colonial New York, 1711-1775*. New York, 1940.

Mather, Jacob R. *The Refugees of 1776 from Long Island to Connecticut*. Albany, 1813.

Matson, Cathy. *Merchants and Empire: Trading in Colonial New York*. Baltimore, 1998.

Meyer, Isidore S. "Lee Max Friedman." *PAJHS* 42 (1958), 211–215.

———. "Miscellaneous Items Relating to Jews in New York." *PAJHS* 27 (1920), 379–403.

Miles, Jack. *God: A Biography*. New York, 1995.

Molloy, J. Fitzgerald. *Court Life Below Stairs or London Under the First Georges, 1714-1760*. 2 volumes. London, 1882.

Morris, Richard B. "Civil Liberties and the Jewish Tradition in Early America." In Karp, *The Jewish Experience in America*, 1: 404–423.

Nadell, Pamela S., and Jonathan D. Sarna, editors. *Women and American Judaism: Historical Perspectives*. Boston, 2001.

Nash, Gary B. *The Urban Crucible: Social Change, Political Consciousness, and the Origins of the American Revolution*. Cambridge, Mass., 1979.

Neuman, Abraham A., and Solomon Zeitlin, editors. *The Seventy-Fifth Anniversary Volume of The Jewish Quarterly Review*. Philadelphia, 1967.

Newman, Aubrey. "Anglo-Jewry in the 18th Century: A Presidential Address." *TJHSE* 27 (1982), 1–9.

Nichols, John. *The Rise and Progress of the Gentleman's Magazine with Anecdotes of the Projector and His Early Associates, Being a Prefatory Introduction to the General Index to That Work from 1787 to 1818*. London, 1821.

Noddings, Nel. *Caring: A Feminine Approach to Ethics and Moral Education*. Berkeley, 1984.

Nooter, Eric, and Patricia U. Bonomi, editors. *Colonial Dutch Studies: An Interdisciplinary Approach*. New York, 1988.

Norden, Margaret K. "A Bibliography of the Writings of Lee Max Friedman." *AJHQ* 51 (1961), 30–48.

Norton, Mary Beth. *Founding Mothers & Fathers: Gendered Power and the Forming of American Society.* New York, 1996.

———. *Liberty's Daughters: The Revolutionary Experience of American Women, 1750–1800.* Boston, 1980.

Oliver, Vere L. *History of the Island of Antigua* 3 vols. London, 1896.

Oppenheim, Samuel. "Genealogical Notes on Jacob Franks." *PAJHS* 25 (1917), 75–80.

Oppenheim, Samuel. "Supplemental Notes on the Jacob Franks Genealogy." *PAJHS* 26 (1918), 260–266.

Pares, Richard. *War and Trade in the West Indies, 1739–1763.* London, 1963.

Pateman, Carole. *The Sexual Contract.* Stanford, 1988.

Perry, Thomas W. *Public Opinion, Propaganda and Politics in Eighteenth-Century England: A Study of the Jew Bill of 1753.* Cambridge, Mass., 1962.

Phillips, N. Taylor "The Levy and Seixas Families of Newport and New York." *PAJHS* 4 (1896), 189–214.

Picciotto, James. *Sketches of Anglo-Jewish History.* London, 1875.

Plaskow, Judith. *Standing Again at Sinai: Judaism from a Feminist Perspective.* San Francisco, 1990.

Pool, David de Sola. "The Earliest Extant Minute Book of the Spanish and Portuguese Congregation Shearith Israel in New York, 1728–1786." *PAJHS.* 21 (1913), 1–171.

———. "Gershom Mendes Seixas' Letters, 1813–1815, to His Daughter Sarah (Seixas) Kursheedt and His Son-in-Law Israel Baer Kursheedt." *PAJHS* 35 (1939), 189–205.

———. *The Mill Street Synagogue (1730–1787) of the Congregation Shearith Israel.* New York, 1930.

———. *Portraits Etched in Stone: Early Jewish Settlers, 1682–1831.* New York, 1952.

Pool, David de Sola, and Tamara de Sola Pool. *An Old Faith in a New World: Portrait of Shearith Israel, 1654–1954.* New York, 1955.

Price, Lucien. *Dialogues with Alfred North Whitehead, as Recorded by Lucien Price.* Boston, 1954.

Pye, Michael. *The Drowning Room.* New York, 1995.

Rich, Adrienne. *Of Woman Born: Motherhood as Experience and Institution.* New York, 1986.

Richardson, A. E. *Georgian England.* London, 1931.

Rink, Oliver A. *Holland on the Hudson: An Economic and Social History of Dutch New York.* Ithaca, 1986.

———. "The People of New Netherlands: Notes on the English Migration to New York in the Seventeenth Century." *New York History* 62 (1981), 5–42.

Rischin, Moses. *The Promised City: New York's Jews, 1870–1914.* Cambridge, Mass., 1962.

Ritchie, Robert C. *The Duke's Province: A Study of New York Politics and Society, 1644–1691.* Chapel Hill, 1977.

Roscoe, Edward S. *The English Scene in the Eighteenth Century.* London, 1960.

Rosenbaum, Jeanette W. *Myer Myers, Goldsmith, 1723–1795.* Philadelphia, 1954.

Rosenbloom, Joseph R. *A Biographical Dictionary of Early American Jews.* Lexington, Ky., 1960.

Rosendale, Simon W. "A Document Concerning the Franks Family." *PAJHS* 1 (1893), 103–104.

Rosenwaike, Ira. "An Estimate and Analysis of the Jewish Population of the United States in 1790." In Karp, *The Jewish Experience in America*, 1: 391–413.

———. *Population History of New York City.* Syracuse, 1972.

Roth, Cecil. *Essays and Portraits in Anglo-Jewish History.* Philadelphia, 1962.

———. *The Great Synagogue, London, 1690–1940.* London, 1950.

———. "The Portsmouth Community and its Historical Background." *TJHSE.* 13 (1936), 157–187.

———. *The Rise of Provincial Jewry.* London, 1950.

———. "Some Jewish Loyalists in the War of American Independence." In Karp, *The Jewish Experience in America*, 1: 292–318.

Roth, Cecil, editor. *Jewish Art: An Illustrated History.* New York, 1961.

Rothschild, Nan A. *New York City Neighborhoods: The 18th Century.* New York, 1990.

Rubens, Alfred. *Anglo-Jewish Portraits.* London, 1935.

Ruddick, Sara. "Maternal Thinking." In Thorne and Yalom, *Rethinking the Family*, 76–94.

Salaman, Redcliffe N. "The Jewish Fellows of the Royal Society." *MJHSE* 5 (1948), 146–175.

Salomon, Herman P. "K.K. Shearith Israel's First Language: Portuguese." *Tradition* (Fall 1995), 74–84.

Samuel, Edgar R. "Dr. Meyer Schomberg's Attack on the Jews of London, 1746." *TJHSE* 20 (1964), 83–111.

Sarna, Jonathan D. *American Judaism*. New Haven, 2004.
———. "Colonial Judaism." In Barquist, *Myer Myers*, 8–23.
———. *Jacksonian Jew: The Two Worlds of Mordecai Noah*. New York, 1981.
———. "The Jews in British America." In Paolo Bernardini and Norman Fiering, editors. *The Jews and the Expansion of Europe to the West, 1450–1800*. New York, 2001.
Sarna, Jonathan D., editor. *Jews and the Founding of the Republic*. New York, 1985.
Schlesinger, Arthur M., Sr. *The Colonial Merchants and the American Revolution, 1763–1766*. New York, 1939.
Seixas, Peter, Peter Sterns, and Sam Wineburg. "History, Memory, Research, and the Schools." *American Historical Association Perspectives* 37 (Mar. 1999), 1 ff.
Shields, David S. *Civil Tongues and Polite Letters in British America*. Chapel Hill, 1997.
Shulvass, Moses A. *From East to West: The Westward Migration of Jews from Eastern Europe during the Seventeenth and Eighteenth Centuries*. Detroit, 1971.
Smith, Ellen. "Portraits of a Community: The Image and Experience of Early American Jews." In Brilliant, *Facing the New World*, 9–21.
Snyder, Holly. "A Sense of Place: Jews, Identity, and Social Status in Colonial British America, 1654–1831." Ph.D. dissertation, Brandeis University, 2000.
Solomons, Israel. "David Niero and Some of His Contemporaries" *TJHSE* 12 (1931), 1–102.
Spiegel, David. "Mothering, Fathering, and Mental Illness." In Thorne and Yalom, *Rethinking the Family*, 95–110.
Stern, Malcolm H. *Americans of Jewish Descent*. Cincinnati, 1960.
———. "Asher Levy—A New Look at Our Jewish Founding Father." *American Jewish Archives* 26 (1974), 66–77.
———. *First American Jewish Families: 600 Genealogies, 1654–1988*. 3rd revised edition. Baltimore, 1991.
Stern, Malcolm H., and Marc D. Angel. *New York's Early Jews: Some Myths and Misconceptions*. New York, 1976.
Stokes, I. N. P. *Iconography of Manhattan Island*. 6 volumes. New York, 1895–1928.
Stone, Lawrence. *The Family, Sex, and Marriage in England, 1500–1800*. New York, 1977.

Story, D. A. *The Delanceys.* Canada, 1931.
Sutherland, Lucy S. *A London Merchant, 1695–1774.* New York, 1962.
Thorne, Barrie, with Marilyn Yalom, editors. *Rethinking the Family: Some Feminist Questions.* New York, 1982.
Turberville, A. S. *English Men and Manners in the Eighteenth Century.* Oxford, 1926.
Ulrich, Laurel Thatcher. *Good Wives: Image and Reality in the Lives of Women in Northern New England, 1650–1750.* New York, 1983.
———. *A Midwife's Tale: The Life of Martha Ballard, Based on Her Diary, 1785–1812.* New York, 1990.
Van Der Zee, Henri, and Barbara Van Der Zee. *A Sweet and Alien Land: The Story of Dutch New York.* New York, 1978.
Weissler, Chava. "Prayers in Yiddish and the Religious World of Ashkenazic Women." In Baskin, *Jewish Women in Historical Perspective,* 159–181.
Wiener, Max. "John Toland and Judaism." *Hebrew Union College Annual* 16 (1941), 215–242.
Wilkenfeld, Bruce M. "New York City Neighborhoods, 1730." *New York History* 17 (1976), 165–82.
———. *The Social and Economic Structure of the City of New York, 1695–1796.* New York, 1975.
Wiznitzer, Arnold. "The Exodus from Brazil and Arrival in New Amsterdam of the Jewish Pilgrim Fathers, 1654." In Karp, *The Jewish Experience in America,* 1: 19–36.
Wolf, Edwin, 2nd. "Torah, Trade, and Kinship." In Hutchins, *Shaping a National Culture,* 169–180.
Wolf, Edwin, 2nd, and Maxwell Whiteman. *The History of the Jews of Philadelphia from Colonial Times to the Age of Jackson.* Philadelphia, 1957.
Woody, Thomas. *A History of Women's Education in the United States.* 2 volumes. New York, 1929.
Woolf, Maurice. "Eighteenth-Century London Jewish Shipowners." *MJHSE* 9 (1970–1973), 198–204.
———. "Foreign Trade of London Jews in the Seventeenth Century." *TJHSE* 24 (1970–1973), 38–58.
Yerushalmi, Yosef Hayim. *Zakhor: Jewish History and Jewish Memory.* Seattle, 1982.
Zipperstein, Steven J. *Imagining Russian Jewry: Memory, History, Identity.* Seattle, 1999.

Index

Addison, Joseph, xxxi, 5, 113n, 145
Aesops Fables, 113n
AJHS, xiii, xv, xxx
Alexander, James, xxvii, 43n, 46n
Amsterdam, xxxi, 131, 138
Antigua, 8
antisemitism, 5n
Ashkenazim, xx, xxxi, xxxiii–iv, xlix, 68, 130n, 138n

Barasshind, 121n
Bath, 55, 58n, 60, 61, 152
Bayard, Fanny (Frances) Moore, 155
Bayard, Samuel, 76, 100n, 127n, 155n
Bayard, Stephen, 126n, 155
Beckford, Mollie, 27, 28n, 31, 43, 52, 75, 109
Beekman, Henry, 124
Bevis Marks, 138
Bickley, Elizabeth, 159
Billeter Square, London, 151
Bloomingdale, 125n, 128n
Bowling Green, xvii, 25
Bradford, William, 37n, 46n
Brazil snuff. *See* snuff
Brinckerhoff, George, 24
British-America, xi, xv, xxii, xxxix
British Jews, xlviii, 206
Brooklyn. *See* Flatbush
Brownell, George, xxii, 4, 12
Bryant, Capt. William, 43, 55, 82, 93

Burgis, William, xlv n, 105
Burling Slip, 5n
Burr, Esther Edwards, xvii
Business: Franks, x, xvi, xxi, xxxviii, xlvi n, 120, 126n; Grace Hays, 48n

Caesar (slave), 92n, 150n
Calvin, John, xxxii, 124
Caribbean, 73, 109n
Cartagena expedition, 92
Carts, xxiv
catalogue of books, 14
Catholics, xlvi n, xlviii n, 92n
Ceaser (slave) 92n, 150n
Charleston, 107n
Chesterfield, Philip Dormer Stanhope, Fourth Earl of, 52, 100n
child rearing, xxxix, 142; and Judaism, xl, xli
Christians, xvi, xxxvi–vii, xlvi n, 5, 126
churches, xxiii
citizens, Jews as, xxv, xxvi, xlvi n
Clarke, George, 43, 46, 47, 57n, 109n
Clarke, Molly (m. George), 28, 43, 52
Coenties: market, 80n; slip, 89n, 127n
Cohen, Samuel Myers, 17n, 29n, 71n, 79n, 92n, 95, 126n
Colly. *See* Salomons, Coleman
companionate marriage, xxxv
Compton, Elizabeth, xxii, 72, 75, 86, 131

181

congregation, 31, 48, 62. *See also* Shearith Israel
Cornhill, 9n
Cosby, Elizabeth. *See* Fitzroy, Elizabeth
Cosby, Grace (m. William) 26, 28
Cosby, Grace. (m. Thomas) *See* Freeman, Grace
Cosby, Henry (son of William), 39n
Cosby, Gov. William, xxvi, xxix, 16n, 21n, 22n, 34n, 37, 46, 57n
Cosby-Morris Dispute, xxix, 19n, 23n, 36–37
Costas, Mrs., 26, 28

Delancey (Delancy), James, xxvii
Delancey, Oliver, xxxv, xxxvii, xl, xli n, 27n, 31n, 85n; marriage to Phila Franks, xxxv, 124, 133–34, 140n
Delancey, Phila Franks, xxxiii–viii, 4, 12, 18, 31, 50, 61n, 85; marriage, 121, 123–28, 134–35, 140n
Delancey, Stephen, 27n, 124
Delancey, Susanna. *See* Warren, Susanna
Dock Ward, xxiv, 17n, 72n, 89n, 124n, 126–27n
Dryden, John, xxxi, 30
Duke Street, xxxi, 24n, 89n, 126n
Dutch, xxii–iii, xxxv, 24
Duyckinck, Gerardus, xxix, xlvii n, 24n, 29n, 42n, 79n

education, Franks children, xxi, xxxii. *See also* school
epidemics, 123n, 146n
Evans, Margaret, xxxviii, 5n, 124n, 140n, 142n
ez hayyim, 137

femes couvert, xxxiii, xlviii
fiction, xvii

Fielding, Henry, xxxi, 116n, 157n; *A History of the Adventures of Joseph Andrews,* 126n
Fitzroy, Lord Augustus, 22n
Fitzroy, Elizabeth Cosby (m. Augustus), 22n
Flatbush, 123
flute, 56–57
Fonseca, Moses Lopez da, 12n, 13n
Franks, Aaron (son of AF and JF), xxi, xxxv, 64n
Franks, Aaron (brother of JF), xx, xxliii, 6n, 7, 52, 57, 59, 60, 61n, 80, 120, 126, 128, 134, 135n, 139, 144n, 154
Franks, Abigaill Levy (m. Jacob): advice to NF, 7, 26, 33, 40, 45, 62, 66, 70, 83; food, 27, 50, 53, 56, 61, 85, 93, 100, 102, 128, 146, 150, 152, 158–59; A good conscience, 5, 113; children, xxi, 50, 64, 68, 156; child rearing, xxi, xxxii, xxxvi, xxxix–xli, 67, 98, 117; depression, xxxvi, 126, 131; education: AF, xix; Franks children, xxi, xxxii; fears, 45, 47, 79n, 98, 120, 124n; flitch of bacon, 115; griefs, xviii, xxxvi–vii, 45n, 140; health, xxxviii, 90, 91, 98, 115; irreverence, xvi, xxv, 105, 123, 141; letters, 39, 62; literature, xvii, xxx, xxxi, xxxii; malapropism, 33, 115; opinions, 25, 44, 46, 50, 61, 69, 76, 78, 84, 90, 105; passions, xviii, xx, 21, 87; religion, xvi, xxxiii, xxxvii, xxxix, xli, 7, 68, 82, 96n; Sabbath, xx, xxx, xxxii, xxxvii, 131n; snuff, 62, 80, 93, 95, 103, 110, 166
Franks, Abraham, (brother of JF), xx, 6n, 50, 61, 102, 128
Franks, David, xxi, xxxi, xlix n, 4, 5n, 50, 57, 71n, 128; in business, 74, 87, 144n, 91, 107, 108n, 112, 113, 136; let-

Index

ters from, 119–22; marriage, xxxviii, xl, 140, 142
Franks, Isaac (brother of JF), xix, xx, xxxii, xxxiv, xxxvii, 3n, 6n, 7, 8, 10n, 33n, 50n, 55; death of, 58; will of, 59n, 61n, 124n, 134n, 151, 212n
Franks, Jacob (m. Abigaill), xix, xxv, xxxi, xxxviii, xliii, 5n; on Phila's marriage, xxxvii, 133–35; quarrel with Mears, 27; to NF, 132–38; AF's description of, 55, 58, 67,73, 86, 91, 140–41
Franks, Moses (son of AF), xxi, xl, xliii, 11, 12n, 32, 41n, 42, 49, 56, 57, 63, 66, 71n, 75–76, 79, 85, 92n, 142, 151, 152, 156; business, 93n, 99, 108, 144, 150, 154
Franks, Moses (brother of JF) 4n, 11n
Franks, Naphtali, marriage, 114; birth of child, 143
Franks, Phila (m. Naphtali), xxxiv, xliin, 3n, 4n, 67n, 102, 104, 123, 128, 147, 157
Franks, Phila (m. Moses), 144n
Franks Phila: *See* Delancey
Franks, Poyer (daugher of AF and JF), xxi, xl, 39, 67, 101, 126, 153
Franks, Rebecca "Becky" (daughter of AF and JF), xxi, xl, l, 67, 123n, 209
Franks, Richa (daughter of AF and JF), xxi, xl, xlviii n, l, 8, 41, 42, 49, 67, 74, 110, 143; and England, 135, 198; and Phila, 128, suitor, xxxiv, 117
Franks, Sara (daughter of AF and JF), xxi, xxxv
Freeman, Grace Cosby (m. Thomas Freeman), 22n
Friedman, Lee Max, x-xi

Gentleman's Magazine, xxxi, 3n, 116, 145n
Georgia, 109n, 111, 135–37

glasses. *See* spectacles
Gomez, David, xxxiv, xxxix, 117
Gomez, Lewis, 92n
Gomez, Mordecai, 128, 146n
Gomez, Moses, xxxi, 79
gossip, xxii, xxv
Greenwich Village, 94n, 121n, 124n, 146n
Griffith, Capt. John, 123n, 133, 195

Hamilton, Alexander, 18n, 47n, 124n, 140n
Harlem (Harlemtown), xxiv, xlii, 10n, 123n, 146n, 157
harpsicord, 41
Hart, Moses, 69n, 88n, 129n, 150n, 154n
Hart, Rachel, 125, 145
Hart, Solomon, 69, 75, 129, 130
Hays, David (m. Grace), 42, 75, 83n, 84n
Hays, Grace Mears Levy, xviii, 42, 48, 60, 75; as businesswoman 48n; death of, 84
Hays, Judah, 21n, 29, 92
hazzan, 12n, 13n
health, 5, 169. *See also* AF
Hebrew, xix, xxii, 12, 13n, 18n, 145n, 146n
Hershkowitz, Leo, x, xii
High Holidays, xxxii, xxxvii, 96
Holland, 43; cloth, 50
Horsmenden, Daniel, 8n, 153
Hudson: River, xxiii, 61n; Valley xxvii
Huntington, Long Island, 28, 30, 71n

Immigrants, xvi, xxiv, xli, xlviii n
India, 120, 130n, 131n
Indians (Native Americans), xvi, xxi, xxv, 146
Indies (East), 11; (West), 78, 79n, 87, 111
intermarriage, xliii, 124n

Jamaica, 87n, 99n, 100n, 109n, 134n

Kalm, Peter, 61n, 149n
kashroot. *See* kosher
Kearny, Sarah Morris, xxii, xlvi n, 16n
kosher, xxi, xxxii, 7

Levy, Asher (brother of AF), xix, 6n, 7, 29, 38, 56, 58, 60, 65, 75, 82, 112–13
Levy, Isaac (brother of AF), xix, xlii, 6n, 13n, 30, 34n, 49, 60, 78, 82–83, 91, 96, 98–99, 108n, 121, 127, 152, 157
Levy, Grace. *See* Grace Hays
Levy, Joseph, 13n, 107n, 112n
Levy, Michael (brother of AF), xix, 99, 112
Levy, Moses (father of AF), xviii, xix, xxii–xxiii, xlii n, 27, 48n, 60n, 84n
Levy, Nathan, xix, 6n, 17, 48n, 56, 60n, 82n, 96, 102, 107, 108n, 112, 113, 120, 129
Levy, Richa Asher (mother of AF), xviii
Levy, Samuel, 70–71, 79n, 87, 100n, 107, 111, 126
Levy, Simson, 57, 75–76, 87n, 89, 99–100, 103, 105, 106n
Livingston family, xxxii, xlvi, lii
Livingston, Peter, 10n, 42n
Livingston, Robert, 98n, 126n
Lopez, Moses. *See* Fonseca
lottery, 87, 88n, 129
loyalists, xl, xlix
Lucena, Abraham de, 31n, 150n
Lucena, Esther, 31n
Lucena, Rebecca, 184
Lucena (slave), 150n
Luther, Martin, xxxii, 68
Lyttleton, George, 158

Macbeth, 45
Machado, David Mendez, 13
Madras, 130n, 131n
Malcolm, Alexander, 11, 12n, 13n, 41n, 42
Manhattan, 22n, 125n
markets, xxi, xxiii, 24n, 92n
Mears, Grace. *See* Hays, Grace
Mears, Jochebed (Josey) Michaels, 31n, 27n, 30
Mears, Judah, 21n, 27, 30, 84, 98n, 125n
memory, collective, xli
merchants, xviii, xix, xxiii, xxv, xxxvii, xlvi, 5n, 11n, 85, 130n, 144
Merlin, British (almanac), 120
Michaels, Jochebed. *See* Mears, Jochebed
Michaels, Rachel, 17n, 20n, 105n
Michaels, Rebecca, 21n, 29n
Mill Street Synagogue. *See* Shearith Israel
Montague, Lady Mary Wortley, ix
Montesquieu, Baron Charles, xxxi, 51n
Moore, Frances (Fanny) Lambert, (m. Col. John), xxii, 5
Moore, Col. John, 10, 25, 37n, 46n
Moravian, xxiii
Mordecai (slave), 92n
Morris, Col. Robert, 23, 28, 34, 36, 41, 46n, 47, 54, 89n
Morris-Cosby Dispute, xxvii–xxix, 23, 37n, 43n
Morrisiana, xxii, 31
Mortlake, Surrey, 10n, 156n
motherhood, xvi, xx, xxxvi, xxxviii, xxxix; blame, xl

navy: Franks as suppliers, 155n, 99n, 191n
Needham, Henry, 99–100, 103
Negro Plot (Revolt), 92n, 93n, 150n

Index

neighborhoods, xxiv, xlv n
neighbors, Franks family, xxiv, xlvii, xlvi n, 121n, 126n, 155
New Jersey, 75n, 83
newspapers, xxxviii, 51n, 54n, 92n, 124n, 127n; *New York Gazette* (pro-Cosby), 37n, 46n; *Weekly Journal* (Zenger's), xxvii, 23, 37n, 46n; New York City: early eighteenth century, xxxii–xxxv; politics, xv–xxix; Jews in, xxxi–xxxiii, xl. *See also* Negro Plot; Morris-Cosby Dispute
Norris, Euphemia Morris (m. Capt. Matthew), 13n, 34, 47n
Norris, Capt. Matthew, 37, 41

Ogelthorpe, James, 111n, 137
opinions. *See* Abigaill Franks
outmarriages, xviii, xxxvi, xxxix
Oyster Bay, Long Island, 28n, 29n

Pachebell, Charles Theodore, 41n
Pacheco, Rodrigo, 15, 51, 68, 77, 78, 85, 88, 113, 130n
parnas, (synagogue president), xx, xxxi, 70n
Pearse, Mary (m. Morris), xxii, 88, 89n, 91, 100, 102
Persian Letters (Montesquieu), xxxi, 51
Philipse, Frederick, xxvi, xlvi, 17
Phillips, Teresa Constantia, 160n
Poland, History of, xxxi, 62
Pope, Alexander, 51, 63
Population: of NYC, xxii–xxiii; xliv n; Jews in NYC, xxii
portraits: of AF, xxix–xxx, xlvii n, xlviii; of Moses, 29
Portuguese, xlix n, 78
Presbyterians, xxiii, xlv, xlvi
president. *See* parnas
press, freedom of, xxvii
prison, xxxvi, 126

QDG ("Whom God Protect"), 9
Quakers, xxiii, xlvi n, xlviii

Rapin-Thoyras, Paul de, xxxi, 18, 43
religious freedom, xlv n, xlvi n
residence, Franks, 24n, 48n, 81n, 123n, 126n, 127n, 151n
Richard, Mrs. Paul, 25, 46n
Richard, Paul, 117n
Riggs, Fanny (m. John), 31, 35, 38, 49
Riggs, John, 10, 131
rimonim (Torah ornaments), 194
ritual, xxx, xxxii, xxxvii, xli
Roberts, Alexander, 99n, 100n, 136

Salomons (Solomons), Abigail (JF's sister), 21, 29, 64, 70, 85, 102
Salomons, Coleman (Colly), xx, 6, 15, 19, 27, 34, 43, 53, 64, 69, 76, 80
Salomons, Moses, xx, 71, 80, 87, 107, 107n, 111, 113, 116, 117n, 130n, 132n, 139
Samson (slave), 92n, 120
school, xxii, xxv, xxxii, 11n, 12n
Schuyler, Myndert, 13n, 24n, 182n
Seixas, Isaac Mendes, xxxiv, 68n, 75, 78, 83–84
Seixas, Rachel Levy, xxxiv, 75, 78, 83
sephardim, xxxi, xxxiv, xlviii, xlix, 68n, 130n
Shakespeare, 48n, 59n
Shearith Israel, xxii xxxi–xxxiv, xlviii n, 12n, 17n, 126n
shohet (ritual slaughterer), xxi, 17n, 69n, 129n
Simson, Joseph, 29, 79n
slaves, xxi, xxii, xliv n, 60n, 92n, 140. *See also,* Caesar, Lucena, Mordecai, Samson, Negro Plot
Smith, William, xxvii, 5n, 23, 43n
Smith-Murray Debate, 19
snuff, 62, 80, 93, 95, 103, 110, 120, 166

South Carolina, 71n, 80n, 87n, 111n, 126, 132n, 136
Spain, war with, 73n, 78n, 109n, 111, 148n, 158n
Spaniards, 95–96, 138n, 154
Spanish language, xxii, 9n, 12, 13
spectacles, 15, 30, 53, 100
squirrels, 104
Stanhope. See Chesterfield
Stepmother. See Grace Mears, Levy, Hays
synagogue, xxi, xxxi, xxxiii, lxviii n, 11n, 12n, 138n, 146; ladies at, 105

teacher, xxii, 3, 13, 41, 49n, 84n
temper, xx, 15, 75, 21, 68, 74, 84, 126, 128, 149
Thoyras. See Rapin
Tudesco, xlviii, 68n, 78

Van Dam, xxvii, 23, 46, 47n, 57
victuallers, 87n, 135n

Villareal, Catherine, 15
violin, 12n

Walk in Kensington Gardens, 121
Walpole, Sir Robert, 23n, 78n, 109n
Warren, Peter, 31n, 94–95, 113, 124, 125n, 142
Warren, Susanna Delancey (m. Peter), 31n. 94n, 124n
weather, cold, 61, 155
WGP ("Whom God Protect"), 9n. See QDG
Williams, Mr., 38, 47, 50
women, xv, xix, xxviii, xxix, xxxii, lx, 25, 48, 100n
worship, xxiii, xxiv, xlv

Yiddish, xix, xx, xxxiii, xlviii n
Yom Kippur, 96n

Zenger, John Peter, xxvi, 23, 24n, 37n, 46n, 47n